The Big Book
of
Great Teaching Ideas

SHIRLEY BARISH

The Big Book
of
Great Teaching Ideas

For Jewish Schools, Youth Groups, Camps, and Retreats

Illustrated by Ann D. Koffsky

UAHC Press
New York, New York

Library of Congress Cataloging-in-Publication Data

Barish, Shirley.
    The big book of great teaching ideas / Shirley Barish.
        p.   cm.
    Includes bibliographical references.
    ISBN 0-8074-0555-8 (pbk. : alk. paper)
    1. Judaism—Study and teaching. 2. Jewish religious education of children. 3.
    Jewish religious education of teenagers. I. Title.
BM103.B36 1996
296.6'8—dc20
                                                                        96-43410
                                                                          CIP

CONTENTS

HELPFUL HINTS

PREFACE

In August 1983, I retired after twenty-five years of teaching and became the educational consultant for the Southwest Council of the Union of American Hebrew Congregations. In this position, my goal was to reach out to teachers, the educators who work in the classrooms, not the people in the front offices. As a result of this goal, for the past twelve years I have been writing a newsletter, *V'Shinantam*, which is sent directly to teachers in the Southwest Council. It provides them with teaching ideas, reviews of new materials, and ways to improve their teaching ability.

This book is a compilation of teaching ideas culled from the twelve years of the newsletter's publication. It has been divided into different age- and grade-appropriate activities, but this doesn't mean that an activity found in the intermediate section should not be used with primary school students or junior and senior high school students. Most of the activities can be easily adapted to any age group, and I encourage you to do so. I have tried to separate the activities and designate the subject areas in which each can be used, but most of the activities are flexible. Many of them can be applied to a variety of subjects. Just use your imagination!

Where do all these teaching ideas come from? Most of them come from programs and materials I have developed during my twenty-five years of teaching. A good number were inspired by materials created for secular schools. I find that much of the secular material is easily adapted to the Jewish religious school classroom. Unless otherwise indicated, most of the activity ideas are mine.

Finally, and to keep this short and sweet, I must say that over the years there have been many people who have touched my heart! I am not going to name them all, for fear of leaving someone out. I must thank one person, though, who has been a major force in my life. Without his support and encouragement, all this never would have happened. Thank you, Marvin!

KINDERGARTEN–PRIMARY GRADES

Children in kindergarten and the primary grades are a delight to teach. They are usually eager and willing to experience new things as long as they are in a safe setting. The religious school is where they will learn that the synagogue is another home, a safe haven, a place where they not only learn about who they are as Jews, but have some fun. It is the teacher who provides the right atmosphere, positive support, and encouragement.

Even for the youngest children, variety is the "spice" of the classroom. The more variety, the more eager the child is to see what is going to happen next and "what I am going to learn today." A myriad of appropriate activities is provided in this chapter. Some focus on specifically Jewish matters, while others are more general and can be used for any Jewish holiday or subject matter. Almost all of the activities can be easily adapted for use by children of any age within this group.

OPENING DAY ACTIVITIES

Here are a variety of opening day activities to get your class off to a good start:

Before School Begins

This activity is good for children coming to religious school for the first time, the young ones who will be consecrated during Simchat Torah. You have an opportunity to begin their first school year in a very special way.

Obtain your class list from the school. Find a picture of yourself and make enough copies for everyone in the class. Write a letter introducing yourself, things you like to do, your hobbies, the names of your children, your pets, what special events will take place in your class, and how you are looking forward to meeting the class. Send the letter and your picture to each child a week before school begins. On the opening day, welcome the children, take a Polaroid picture of each of them, and work with them to create a collage bulletin board that tells who each child is, what each likes to do, and the things that make each of them unique.

NEAT AND SIMPLE

Getting to Know You

For this activity you will need a box of tissues. Pass it around and ask the children to take as many as they wish. Most of them will take a few, but some will take a good number. Once they all have some tissues, explain that for each tissue they have in their hands, they must tell the class something about themselves.

Name Tags

Let the children create their own individual, collage-type name tags—whatever size and shape they want. Provide boxes of supplies: markers, pens, scissors, glue, scraps of cloth, foil, wrapping paper, pipe cleaners, wire, string, yarn, glitter, sequins, magazines and old workbooks with pictures, etc. Tell the children to create name tags that include not only their names, but their likes and dislikes, their favorite Jewish holiday, what they do well, and what they hope to learn in religious school this year. When the name tags are completed, have the children share their name tags with one another before posting them around the room.

"We Are the Stars" Bulletin Board

Before school begins, prepare your bulletin board with a colorful background and head it "We Are the Stars." Cut out large Jewish stars from colored paper, making one star for each child in the class. Cut out some smaller stars and scatter them around the bulletin board. You might even place some cotton balls on the board to give the effect of clouds.

On the first day give out stars and ask the children to draw self-portraits on them, or take Polaroid pictures of the children and place the photos in the center of the stars. Have the children hold up their stars and introduce themselves. When they are done, put their portraits on the bulletin board.

We Are One

You will need a large ball of string or yarn for this activity. Have everyone stand up. Hand the ball of string or yarn on from child to child, with the children, in succession, wrapping it around their wrists and introducing themselves as it comes to them; if you prefer, carry the string around the room instead of passing it from child to child.

Begin by giving the ball of string to a child and tying one end of the string around the child's wrist. After saying, "My name is _____," the first child passes the ball of string to the next child, who does the same thing, and so on. Continue until all the children are "tied up" and have introduced themselves.

Point out that there are X number of children in the class and each of them is a unique individual. Then add that they all have something in common, *they are all Jews!* Next, unwind the string, beginning with the last child, who again says, "My name is _____," but also introduces and unties the next child. The second child introduces the next child and unties the string. Continue in this manner until each child has introduced the next child and everyone is untied. The last child can introduce the teacher.

Welcome Puzzles

Children enjoy puzzles, so greet your pupils on the first day of school with a "welcome" puzzle. Prepare decorative welcome puzzles by writing "welcome" or "welcome to school" in Hebrew and English (*baruch haba levet sefer*) on colored paper or tagboard. Decorate as desired with Jewish symbols, smiles, etc. Cut into puzzle pieces—small pieces for older children, large pieces for the younger children. Place one puzzle in an envelope for each child with the child's name on the outside. Hand out the envelopes as the children arrive. They will have fun putting the puzzles together.

Polaroid Pictures on Opening Day

You will need a Jewish star for each child. It should be large enough for a Polaroid picture to be placed in the center and either a small picture or some writing in each of the six corners.

Take Polaroid pictures of your pupils as they arrive on the first day. Give them their pictures and a Jewish star each. Have the children glue their pictures in the center of the stars and print their names under the pictures (omit this if they don't know how to write). In each corner of the star, have the children provide some information about themselves, either in words or by drawing an appropriate picture. For example, you might ask them to indicate:

1. Birthdate.
2. Favorite Jewish holiday.
3. Public school attended.
4. Favorite Jewish song.
5. Favorite activity.
6. Hobby.
7. Favorite Jewish food.
8. Pet.

The children can wear their stars as name tags. When they complete their stars, have them go around the room and read everyone else's tags.

The stars can also be a means of taking attendance. Place the stars on your desk. As the children arrive, have them pick up their stars and hang them either on a line in a corner of the room or in a designated place on the bulletin board. The stars remaining on your desk belong to anyone who is absent that day.

Holiday Match-Up

This is a good opening day activity. You will need 3 x 5 index cards. Collect pictures covering all aspects of a Jewish holiday. Mount a picture on each card; laminate it or cover it with clear contact paper. Cut the cards into two puzzle pieces. As the children enter the room, distribute the puzzle pieces, one to each child. When all the children have arrived, ask them to find the partner with the matching piece. When they have identified their partners, they are to introduce themselves to each other. They are also to get to know each other better by asking such questions as:

Do you have any brothers or sisters?

What is your favorite Jewish holiday?

What game do you like best?

What is your favorite color?

Once the partners are acquainted, have them introduce each other to the whole class and tell about each other.

A Class Tree

Make a class tree—a tree of learning or knowledge. Begin this activity on opening day and continue it throughout the year. Have the children cut out leaf designs from red, orange, yellow, and green construction paper. Take a Polaroid picture of each child, or have the children bring pictures of themselves from home. Have the children glue their pictures in the center of one of the leaves. On a large piece of butcher paper, draw a large tree with many branches but no leaves. Mount each child's picture leaf on a different branch of the tree—one branch to a child. Whenever a child learns something new or accomplishes something major, have the child decorate a leaf with a symbol or drawing representing the new achievement. Add the leaf to the child's personal branch.

NEAT AND SIMPLE

Scent Patches and Stickers

Place a scratch-and-sniff sticker on each child's clothing as the children arrive. Make sure there are only two children for each scent. After the class has settled in, have the children find their matching scents. Have the matching pairs of children go aside and learn everything they can about each other. Then have them introduce each other to the class.

Place Cards

Marking each child's place with a simple name card will make the children feel at home in the classroom. Place cards can be made from 6 x 8 index cards or oaktag cut to the same size. Fold in four parts to make a triangle that can stand alone. Paste the ends together. Get some smile stickers or make your own stickers out of contact paper. If you make your own, decorate them with Jewish symbols. Cut out the stickers and paste them on pieces of oaktag of the same size. Glue to the top of the place card. Print the child's name on bright-colored glow paper and glue it onto the place card. Put the finished product on the desk or chair where you want each child to sit on opening day.

Celebrate Summer Birthdays

Welcome the children back to religious school with a celebration. Before school begins, find out who had birthdays during the summer. Make "Happy Birthday" banners marked with their names for those who had summer birthdays. Hang the banners prominently in the room. Have a surprise party for the birthday children. Let them take their banners home at the end of the day.

Name Mobile

For this activity you will need long strips of colored yarn, colored markers, a hole puncher (unless you punch the holes in advance), colored construction paper, and hangers. Cut out a variety of Jewish symbols. Make enough for each child to have three or four different symbols. Tell the children to print their names on one symbol and use the others to describe things they like (e.g., Jewish songs, holidays, hobbies, pets). Children who do not know how to write can draw pictures representing what they want to tell the class about themselves. Punch holes in the symbols, thread the yarn through them, and hang each set of symbols on a hanger as the children introduce themselves to their classmates.

JEWISH HOLIDAYS
Shabbat

CREATING A SHABBAT TABLE

Use a large piece of white butcher paper or an old white sheet as a tablecloth. Tell the children how we celebrate the Sabbath and make it a very special day. Ask them how they prepare for the Sabbath at home. Are there any special foods? How is the table set? Lead into how they can prepare and decorate their own Shabbat tables. First they will have to decide what to put on the table. Help them make a list of appropriate items (e.g., Kiddush cup, candlesticks, challah plate). Have them "gather" the items by drawing or making them. In addition, they can decorate the table with crepe paper streamers, pre-glued colored paper in different shapes, and tissue paper flowers. Once the table is prepared, lead the class through the rituals of Friday evening Shabbat dinner.

SHABBAT CANDLES

By giving each child a pair of candles to go with a pair of candlesticks made in class, you may be able to stimulate the families of some of the children in your class to light Shabbat candles on Friday nights. With the candles, include the candle blessings in English, Hebrew, and transliteration, but only do this after studying Shabbat with the class and making sure that everyone has learned the blessings. If you send candles home every week for a month, the children and their families just might get in the habit of celebrating the Sabbath.

High Holy Days: Yom Kippur

This lesson was created by a young man, Paul D. Keeper, whom I have known since he was a child. Now an attorney, he teaches first and second grade in religious school. The three exercises in this lesson can be done in a class period of an hour and a half.

EXERCISE 1

Without explaining the purpose, I told the children to go to the farthest reaches of the room, spacing themselves at equal distances from each other, and facing the wall. I told them to make a circle in which everyone was to hold hands, emphasizing that they were to do this without turning around. (There was much giggling and stumbling.)

After they did this, we talked about:

How hard was that to do?

What made it hard to do?

Isn't living much like trying to make the circle, not knowing what is coming next, bumping into things, getting bruises, getting into trouble? Wouldn't it be helpful to see where we are going?

EXERCISE 2

Without offering any explanation, I took two kids and put them in the middle of the class with everyone looking on. I told the two kids to look at each other carefully for about a minute. Then I told them to stand back to back. I picked one to tell me about the other: hair style, hair color, eye color, clothing, shoes, glasses, etc. Then the other kid got to do the same. The mistakes came very quickly, and the class had a hoot laughing. When they finished, we talked about:

Why was this hard to do?

Didn't the kids see the person they were describing?

How could they have made so many obvious mistakes so quickly?

Do we stay as aware as we would like in living our lives?

Why not? What gets in the way?

How can we be helpful to others, to our friends, if we don't, or can't, notice them?

EXERCISE 3

I put a small table at the front of the class. On the table I put a small chair. I asked for a volunteer (a kid named Jake, whose mother is another religious school teacher) and had him sit on the table. All the while, I was using my best *adult* voice to talk about Yom Kippur in the most vapid way I knew how: "We all know, boys and girls, that Yom Kippur is one of the most important days of the Jewish year. That is because Yom Kippur is a solemn day...etc."

I then draped a towel around Jake's neck. Still talking about Yom Kippur, I took a half-gallon pitcher full of water that I had hidden up to this point and, without stopping my lecture (to which no one was listening), I made it clear that something outrageous was about to happen in Sunday school. (Disbelief, smiles, laughter were taking place now.) Without ceasing the drone of my "what Yom Kippur should mean to you" speech, I slowly poured most of the contents of the pitcher on Jake's head. (Absolute hilarity, kids were lying on the floor roaring with laughter, and

Jake took it in stride.)

I then chastised Jake for not looking presentable for class. I handed him a comb and asked him to comb his hair. Of course, he made a mess of the job without a mirror. I asked him what he needed, and he told me that a mirror would be nice. I asked him what use he intended to make of the mirror, and he told me that a mirror would help him see what he was doing. I gave him a mirror and a chance to prove its value. When he finished, I gave him a towel to dry off and helped him off the table. Then the whole class talked about:

What was funny about the water on Jake's head?

Why did Jake need a comb?

How did a mirror help?

How often does life unexpectedly pour water on our heads?

How often would a mirror be helpful?

Would it help if we had a mirror in our lives so that we could see how well, or how poorly, we were doing?

What is the function of Yom Kippur, if not to give us a chance to do exactly that?

Why are people so somber about all this?

Would it help if we could laugh more at ourselves and less at others?

At this point we launched more into the substance of Yom Kippur. I tried to pose questions instead of lecturing. These are some of the kinds of questions that could be asked:

Who in the class fasts? Why?

Who stays home from school? Why?

Why do we stay with our families on Yom Kippur?

Who in the class attends worship services? Why?

Where do you break the fast?

I concluded the lesson by telling the children the story "If Not Higher" by the Yiddish writer I. L. Peretz. It is the story of a rabbi who disappears every Yom Kippur. The congregation suspects the rabbi of consorting with devils, and a member hides under the rabbi's bed and follows him on Yom Kippur. The member discovers that the rabbi disguises himself as a wood cutter and gives wood to the poor.

After the story, we talked about:

Rabbis—who they are and what they do. (By the way, my school has no rabbi.)

The importance of helping the poor.

The danger of telling untrue stories about others (an introduction to leshon hara).

How Yom Kippur means different things to different people.

We ended the class session with the children sharing their answers to the question "What does Yom Kippur mean to me?"

Sukot and Simchat Torah

ISRAELI FLAGS FOR SIMCHAT TORAH

You will need crayon cloth cut to the size you wish to use, dowels, and crayons. Provide the class with designs for the flag. Have the children in the class color the designs with crayon, using different colors. The colors can be made permanent by covering the cloth with a piece of wax paper, covering the wax paper with newspaper, and pressing with a lukewarm iron. Then attach the flags to the dowels.

FELT FLAGS

Use scraps of felt for the designs and a felt square or rectangle for the flag. Glue felt scraps as desired on the felt square or rectangle and attach to a dowel.

BURLAP FLAGS

Cut burlap pieces in the desired size and pull some threads around the outside of each piece to make fringes. Have the children draw designs on their flags, or provide them with a template of a design. Show them how to embroider the design on the burlap. When the flags are completed, attach them to dowels.

AN ADDED DIMENSION TO THE SUKAH

If you are building a *sukah*, have the children bring in pictures of the members of their families, including pets, cut out the faces, paste them onto popsicle sticks, and place the figures in the *sukah*. Or have them draw figures (without heads) on the inside walls of the *sukah* and put the faces on each of the figures.

Chanukah

NEAT AND SIMPLE

WHO OR WHAT AM I?

This is an oldie, but the kids have fun with it. Put the names of people, symbols, or items related to the holiday on cards. If the children in the class do not know how to read, use pictures. Put a card on each child's back. Taking turns, and going one at a time, each child tries to guess what is on the card by asking questions of the other children.

THE FOODS WE EAT

Divide the class into two teams. Present pictures of foods that are eaten on holidays (e.g., *latkes* for Chanukah, *matzot* for Passover). Taking turns, the teams identify the holiday on which each food is eaten.

PUBLIC RELATIONS

Tell the children to pretend they are working for an advertising agency. A new client, who is a descendant of the Maccabees, has hired them to advertise the miracle of the oil and the fight for religious freedom. Their assignment is to provide the best possible ad for the client. To do the job well, they will need to understand and be able to explain the following:

1. What was the miracle of the oil, and what events led up to it?

2. What were the ancestors of your new client like?

3. What customs do your client and modern Jews practice in relation to the miracle and the fight for religious freedom?

Once the children have all the necessary information, help them to plan an advertising campaign that includes some of the following: slogans, jingles, radio and TV commercials.

AN EDIBLE CHANUKIAH

You will need nine peppermint sticks and nine candy kisses per child.

To make the *chanukiah*, insert the nine peppermint sticks into a narrow length of styrofoam. Put some canned cake frosting on top of each candle to provide a sticky base, and then add a wrapped candy kiss as the "flame." When all the candles are "lit," the *chanukiah* can be eaten in celebration of the holiday.

A CHANUKAH GIFT

To make a nice picture frame as a gift for parents or grandparents, you will need a small snapshot of each child (if the children cannot bring these from home, take Polaroid pictures in class), pinking shears, one wooden shower curtain ring for each child, small round-headed wood screws, felt in a variety of colors, glue, bric-a-brac, and lengths of narrow ribbon or yarn.

1. Cut the felt with pinking shears to fit the wooden curtain rings.

2. Glue the felt pieces to the back of the wooden rings, cut pictures to fit inside, and glue to the felt.

3. Glue bric-a-brac around the picture frame if desired.

4. Either pre-make tiny bows for each child or help the children to make tiny bows; glue the bows to the top of the rings.

5. Screw a wood screw into the back of each finished frame.

Depending on the age and ability of your class, you may have to do some of the above in advance (e.g, pre-cut the felt, make the tiny bows, place the screws in the wooden rings). Then the children simply put everything together.

Tu Bishvat

HOW PLANTS GROW

A simple, inexpensive method that shows children how plants grow is to place carrot tops in a saucer of water. The children will enjoy checking the amount of growth each week. Another good plant is parsley. Distribute paper or plastic cups filled with earth or potting soil to each child. Have the children plant a few seeds in their cups. Over the weeks that follow they can keep track of the parsley's growth and water it when necessary; with luck, it will be ready to harvest for Pesach, and then they can use their own home-grown parsley for the seder.

MAKE A TREE

Save those jelly jars! Set a tree branch into a jar filled with sand or colored marbles to hold it in place. Have the children make flowers and cut leaves out of construction paper. They can decorate the tree branch with the flowers and leaves, or even with fruit to show what kind of tree it is.

A SIMPLE GAME

Cut out pictures of items that are made from trees or grow on trees (e.g., pencils, furniture, houses, rulers, paper, fruits). Also cut out pictures of items that are not made from trees (e.g., a dress, pants, glasses, dishes, pots and pans). Mount each picture on a small index card and laminate or cover with clear contact paper. Design a simple game board with a beginning and an end. Make a space on the game board for the cards and put them face down in this space. You will need a game marker for each student and a pair of dice. Use poker chips or the tops of colored marking pens (after they are used up, of course) for the game markers; even buttons make good game pieces. Each player chooses a card. If the card is an item made from or grown on a tree, the player throws the dice and moves forward that number of spaces. If the item is not made from a tree, the player stays in the same place. Continue playing until someone reaches the end of the game.

THE GIVING TREE

Read Shel Silverstein's *The Giving Tree*. With the class, make a list of all the things we get from trees and how trees benefit us and the animals in the forest (e.g., food, pencils, furniture, paper, oxygen, shade, protection from wind, homes for birds and small animals). Prepare a large piece of butcher paper with a drawing of a large tree with branches but no leaves. Draw a number of leaves on a sheet of paper and copy, then cut out the leaves and distribute several to each child. Ask the children to draw on the leaves whatever they like best about what we get from trees. Fasten their finished drawings to the branches of the tree and title it "Our Giving Tree."

Purim

MAKING GRAGGERS

There are many ways to make graggers. Here are a few.

Take two plastic tops of the same size, like the ones that come off spray cans. Put any kind of dry, uncooked beans, peas, etc., in the tops. Fasten the two tops together with glue and let dry. Then tape them together securely with colorful tape. Have the children decorate them as they desire.

A drink mix container also makes a good gragger. Just seal the top with tape after you have filled the container with dried beans or peas for noisemaking. Cover the container with colorful contact paper or construction paper. Decorate as desired.

Instead of putting dried beans or peas in the graggers, have the children bring some coins from home. Put these in the containers. Use them during Purim, then let the children choose a charity to which they can donate their gragger coins.

This one is a little different: you will need a small paper plate, dried beans, stapler, tongue depressors or popsicle sticks, and crayons or colored markers. To make: fold the paper plate in half. Put some dried beans inside and staple the plate shut. Staple or glue the stick to the plate to make a handle, then let the children decorate as they desire.

For this one you will need a glass baby food jar with a lid for each child in the class, along with dried beans, newspaper, wallpaper paste, paint, and shellac. Fill the jars halfway with dried beans. Make sure the lids are secure, then wrap the jars with 3-inch strips of newspaper which have been dipped in the wallpaper paste. Let dry. For a handle, tightly roll one sheet of newspaper, dip it in wallpaper paste, and attach it to the top end of the covered jar. Allow to dry. Paint and decorate, then cover with shellac.

One more gragger: you will need two paper or styrofoam cups per child, dried beans, masking tape, colored markers, bits of colored paper, used gift-wrapping paper cut into small pieces, glue, and any other decorating materials you have handy. Take the two cups and add a handful of dried beans to one of them. Tape the tops of the two cups together. Using the materials you have available, let the children glue, cut, and paste to their heart's desire to decorate their graggers.

A CLASS MEGILLAH

Tell the story of Esther and Purim as found in the Megillah. Divide the class into small groups. Give each group a different scene to illustrate. Either unroll a large roll of butcher paper or art paper on the floor and assign each group a space in the proper order, or give each group a large piece of butcher paper or art paper on which to draw the illustrations, then collect the finished pages and tape together in the proper order. Fasten them to a dowel and roll up to make a large class Megillah.

Mask-Making with a Purpose

Children enjoy acting out the story of Purim. Assign the different characters in the story to children in the class. Have them make masks of the characters they will play, using construction paper, cotton for eyebrows or beards, wool string for hair, and a stick for holding the mask. Once the masks are made the children can act out the story of Purim. Another option: instead of assigning roles, let the children choose their own; after they make the masks, the class has to identify which character they are impersonating.

NEAT AND SIMPLE

Missing Faces

Make photocopies of scenes from the Purim story, but blank out the facial expressions of the characters. Let the children fill in the faces. When they are finished, tape the scenes together in the proper sequence. Ask the children to explain their choice of facial expressions (as best they can), then roll up to make a class Megillah scroll.

Pesach (Passover)

Matzah Magnet

You will need a tea cracker matzah, fabric, a button, white glue, eyes, red felt, and magnet tape for each child. To make: Coat the tea cracker thickly with glue. Let dry. Glue on little eyes—the kind that move—a button nose, and a red felt mouth. Make a hat and a collar from the fabric if you desire. All these items can be pre-cut to make it easier for the children. Glue these to the matzah. Finally, place the magnet on the back.

Time to Rise

The Israelites had to leave Egypt before their bread had a chance to rise. The children may find it difficult to understand the concept of dough rising. Here is a simple experiment that will help them.

Fill two glasses half-full of warm water. Stir a tablespoon of flour into one glass. In the other, mix half a package of yeast with the water. Add a tablespoon of flour with a little sugar, and mix. Put both glasses in a warm place for 20 to 30 minutes (if you use fast-rising yeast it will not take this long). This experiment will provide a very visual dramatic explanation!

Pesach Sort Game

Collect pictures of the different symbols and foods related to Pesach. Also have a selection of pictures that have nothing to do with Pesach, but pertain to another Jewish holiday. Mount the pictures on index cards and laminate or cover with clear contact paper. Fasten two pockets large enough for the index cards onto a posterboard. Label one *Pesach* and the other *Jewish Holidays*. Title the posterboard, *Pesach Sort*. Shuffle the pictures thoroughly and have the children identify the ones which are for

Pesach; these go into the Pesach pocket. When they encounter a picture that doesn't belong to Pesach, see if they know what holiday it belongs to, then place it in the other pocket.

RACING BOARD PESACH GAME

A simple game board can be created by using pictures of items related to Pesach and large colored adhesive dots (found in any office supply store). Collect pictures of Pesach symbols, as small as possible. Reduce them on a copying machine if necessary. Use the round dots to make the game board, placing the Pesach pictures after every few spaces. Indicate the beginning point and the ending point on the game board.

To play, you will need markers and dice. Each player throws the dice and moves forward the number of spaces indicated. A player who lands on a Pesach picture must identify the object, maybe even telling what it is used for if this applies. If the picture is identified correctly, the player stays on that space; if it is not identified correctly, the player goes back to the place where the turn began. Continue until everyone has gone around the entire game board.

BECOME A STORYTELLER

Tell some stories about Elijah. To prepare, read about Elijah in the Bible (see I Kings 17–19, Malachi 3:23–24) or the *Encyclopaedia Judaica* and the *Jewish Encyclopedia*. Write out a synopsis of each story, then tell it verbally. After the stories, tell the children how Elijah is represented at the seder table. The children can then make something to be used during the seder. For example:

1. Placemats for the Cup of Elijah. Use construction paper, oak-tag, wall paper, flannel-backed oil cloth, etc. To make them special, cut out the size you desire with pinking shears. Let the children decorate them by drawing symbols; if necessary, provide stencils of Pesach symbols. Colored plastic or cloth tape makes nice decorations along with the usual glitter, bric-a-brac, etc. Laminate each placemat, or cover with clear contact paper.

2. Cups for Elijah's wine. Use clear plastic cups. Provide glue, glitter, colored sticky dots, colored stones (from old costume jewelry), heavy-duty foil cut into different Pesach symbols, and anything else that might be useful for decorating. Let the children use their own creativity in making the special wine cups.

GETTING READY FOR PESACH: FIND THE CHAMETZ!

Chametz is the forbidden food of Pesach. It is any food or drink made from even the smallest quantity of wheat, barley, rye, oats, or any food that is fermented or causes fermentation.

To search for chametz you will need bread crumbs, feathers, flashlights (in place of candles), paper dustpans, and a plastic bag.

Before class begins, save or purchase some bread crumbs. Spread the

14

crumbs around the room so that they are "hidden" but still visible. Gather together some feathers, or take an old feather duster and cut the feathers off. Provide one feather for each child. Have ready, in the center of the room, a garbage can or wastebasket with a plastic liner. You can use oaktag or ordinary paper for the paper dustpans.

When the children arrive, tell them how the family usually prepares the home for Pesach. The house is cleaned from top to bottom; in some homes, dishes, pots and pans, and silverware are changed, and special dishes which are used only during Pesach are brought out. Most importantly, though, the chametz is cleaned out of every corner and crevice of the home. Be sure to explain what chametz is.

Traditionally, the hunt for chametz is done with a candle and a feather, but the children will use flashlights instead of a candle for safety reasons.

Give each child a feather and a paper dustpan. Point out the wastebasket in the center of the room where they are to deposit their findings. Divide the class into groups of two or three, give out the flashlights, and have them search the room to gather up the crumbs in their paper dustpans. As they gather the crumbs, they are to dump them into the plastic bag and then go back for more. After they have cleared the room of chametz, praise them for a job well done. Now the "home" is ready for Pesach.

FIND THE MATZAH

Time this activity to take place close to snacktime. Either use real matzah, which is best, or prepare one cardboard matzah for each child. Before the children arrive, hide the matzah around the room.

Begin the activity by telling the children, briefly, the story of how the Israelites were slaves in Egypt, how Moses kept going to the Pharaoh asking him to let his people go, and finally, when the Pharaoh told Moses his people could leave, how they had to do so quickly. Explain that the Israelites had just begun to prepare their bread, but because they had to leave Egypt in such a hurry the bread did not have time to rise. The bread baked in the sun as they rushed out of Egypt, and this became the unleavened bread—matzah—we eat on Passover. Now tell the children that there is matzah hidden around the room, one piece for each of them, and they have to find it. After they have found their pieces of matzah, have some jelly ready along with a drink. Help them prepare their matzah, and let them enjoy!

RECOGNIZING PESACH RITUAL SYMBOLS

The old standby is to prepare a sheet with pictures of the ritual symbols of Passover. Include a few pictures which do not belong. Distribute the sheets. Have the children circle and color the items that are part of the Pesach rituals.

Another approach would be to mount individual pictures on tagboard. Make sure the pictures are large enough to be seen whether the children are sitting on the floor or in their chairs. Place the pictures around the room in any order. Ask the children to take turns identifying them with something like this:

Who can show us—

A family at the seder table.

The Egyptian and the Israelite.

A slave.

Matzah.

The four cups of wine.

The Haggadah

Charoset.

An item that doesn't belong.

As each picture is identified, tell how it is part of the seder.

CREATING A SEDER PLATE

Before the children begin to make their own seder plates, show them a real seder plate and the items which are placed on it. Show the items one at a time. See if the children know what each item is, then tell them what it represents as you place it on the real seder plate. After you have explained each item, help them to make their own seder plates.

There are several ways to create seder plates. Here are some options:

1. Hard paper plate: Draw six large circles on the center of the plate. Prepare pictures of the items to fit in the circles. Have the children color the pictures, cut them out, and paste them in the circles.

2. Use brightly colored 8.5 x 11 or 9 x 12 tagboard or oaktag. Draw six large circles around the paper. Continue as in no. 1.

3. Use 10-inch cardboard cake boards (obtainable from any bakery or from Maid of Scandinavia–Sweet Celebrations, 7009 Washington Avenue South, Edina, MN 55439). Cover with brightly colored contact paper or paint them with watercolors. Use contact paper to make six large circles for each seder plate. Put these on after it has been painted or covered. Then continue as in no. 1.

4. Use a large paper plate. You will also need six muffin cups per plate. Prepare small pictures of the items to be placed on the seder plate. Copy these and let children color them, cut them out, and glue them around the outside rim of the paper plate. Next to each picture, glue a small muffin cup.

WHAT THE SEDER PLATE ITEMS REPRESENT

Zeroa, the roasted shankbone, symbolizes the paschal offering that was brought to the Temple. It also represents the animal whose blood was put on the doorposts so that the Angel of Death would recognize the Israelites' homes and "pass over" them during the final plague.

Karpas is a green vegetable, usually parsley, but lettuce and celery tops are also used. It symbolizes the green of spring and the spirit and hope for the future. It also recalls the meager food the Israelites had as slaves in Egypt.

Maror literally means "bitters" and is usually horseradish root. It symbolizes the bitterness of slavery.

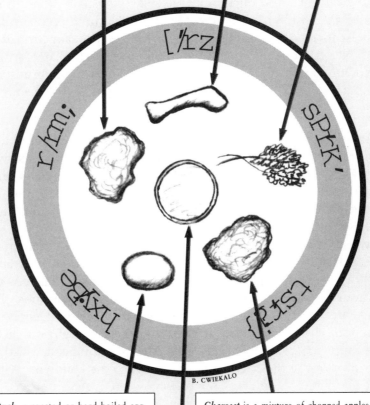

B. CWIEKALO

Betzah, a roasted or hard-boiled egg, symbolizes new life and reflects the spring theme of rebirth. Because of its roundness, having no beginning or end, it also represents eternal life. It is also said to represent the festival offerings made at the Temple in Jerusalem. Another source says it symbolizes the Jewish people. Most foods, when cooked, get soft, but not the egg. Similarly, the more the Jewish people are oppressed by the nations of the world, the harder they become in their determination not to yield and to remain faithful to the Covenant.

Charoset is a mixture of chopped apples and nuts, cinnamon, and grape juice or sweet red wine. It symbolizes the mortar used by the Israelites to lay the bricks for Pharaoh's building projects. Note: make enough charoset for the children to have a Hillel sandwich as a snack.

Chazeret is a bitter herb. It can be a cucumber, watercress, radish, or any other vegetable which tends to be bitter. We have two bitter herbs on the seder plate because in Numbers 9:11 it says, "With unleavened bread and bitter herbs." Bitter herbs is in the plural, so it is used along with the maror.

KORECH—THE HILLEL SANDWICH

For a snack prepare enough charoset for the children to eat after they have made their seder plates. The tradition of eating a Hillel sandwich comes from the story that the ancient sage Hillel, in the era when the Temple still stood, used to combine matzah and maror and eat them together, in accordance with the biblical verse, "They shall eat it with matzah and bitter herbs" (Numbers 9:11). Mixing maror with charoset dulls the sharpness of the bitter herbs. This is symbolic of God's loving-kindness, which dulled the bitterness of slavery.

DIPPING THE PARSLEY AND EGG IN SALT WATER

Try this with just the parsley, but a word of warning: the kids probably won't like the taste. The dipping at the seder is usually done to get the attention of the children. Traditionally, though, the dipping in the salt water represents the dipping of bunches of hyssop (a bushy aromatic herb with small blue flowers) into the blood of the first paschal lamb at the time of the Exodus, so that the blood could be daubed on the doorposts of the Israelite homes as a sign to the Angel of Death to "pass over" them.

THE FOUR QUESTIONS

Traditionally, the youngest son was the one who asked the Four Questions. In ancient times the questions were spontaneous, but if the child was not alert enough to ask questions on his own, he was prepared in advance. Today, the text of the questions is given in the Haggadah, and except among the Orthodox, they are usually asked by the youngest child, whether a boy or a girl.

The words Mah Nishtanah, literally meaning "what is different about," begin the Arba Kushiyot, or Four Questions. They have been extended to read, "Why is this night different from all other nights?" There is no reason why even the youngest child cannot learn the Four Questions. Prepare four pages, one question to a page. On each page have the Hebrew text, a transliteration, and the English. Most important, though, on each page also have a nice-size picture that represents the question being asked.

Begin by showing the pages, one at a time, to the children. With each page, ask the children to identify the picture and tell what it means. At the beginning, help them as needed. Read in Hebrew and English the question that goes with each picture. Do this for a few minutes every day. Gradually, begin having the children repeat the Hebrew after you. Through this repetition the children will learn the Four Questions. Right before the first seder, prepare the Four Questions sheets as little booklets to be taken home. The children can use them during the seder when it comes time to ask the Four Questions. The pictures on each page will be a good reminder for them of what question is to be asked.

THE STORY OF THE EXODUS

Before telling the story, make some preparations for the children to act out the Exodus. Using pinking shears, cut holes in some large old towels for the head to slip through when the towel is folded in half; old sheets and tablecloths will also work as costumes. Help the children to make a rod for Moses, shields for the Egyptian soldiers, trays of matzah, and any other items the Israelites will be taking with them when they leave Egypt. List the different roles the kids can take (e.g., Israelites, Moses, Miriam, Aaron, Pharaoh, Egyptians).

Plan an Exodus route using the different areas of your facility. At the place where you decide to locate the Reed Sea, place chairs two or three high on either side, and cover them with blue cloth or paper to look somewhat like water. Place two chairs side by side to block the Israelites' path until Moses raises his arms and rod. Take the two chairs away when it is time for the children to cross over on dry land. Then return them to their places to prevent the Egyptians from crossing over.

When everything is ready, have the children dress up in their costumes and assemble to hear the story of the Exodus. Have them act out the story as you tell it. Include some Passover songs that tie in with the different parts of the story. (Several tape cassettes are available which include some very good songs for this purpose. Cindy Paley, *Celebrate with Cindy*, vol. 2; *Shalom Sesame*; and Fran Avni's *Mostly Matzah* are good resources.) When the children get close to the Reed Sea, have the Egyptians begin coming after them, but be sure that the Reed Sea opens up before the Egyptians get there. End the Exodus on the other side of the Reed Sea with all the children singing Dayenu.

FINDING THE AFIKOMAN

The afikoman is the "dessert" of the seder. It is usually hidden by a parent; sometimes the children take it and hold it for ransom, since the seder cannot be completed until the afikoman is redeemed. The afikoman is shared with everyone, and since it is the "dessert," nothing else is eaten afterwards. Here are a few activities you can do:

1. Prepare pictures of rooms in a home and hide a piece of matzah in the room. Have the children study the pictures and circle the afikoman when they find it.

2. Create a maze which the children are to follow until they can reach the hidden afikoman.

3. Divide the class into two teams. Give each team a chance to hide the afikoman. While one team is hiding its afikoman, the other team goes out of the room. Once it is hidden, the team returns and begins to hunt for it. The children can sing loudly when the team is close to finding it, or sing softly if the team is far away. After the afikoman is found, the team that hid it goes out of the room, and the team that found it gets a chance to hide it.

NUTS TO THE KIDS!

Traditionally, in Eastern Europe, families would give nuts to the children on the seder night to arouse their interest and curiosity. The reason nuts were used for this purpose may have been that the numerical value of the Hebrew word for "nuts," *egoz*, is the same as that of the Hebrew word for "good," *tov*. Several games can be played with the nuts.

1. Nut Toss. Place a large plastic bowl at an appropriate distance. Give each player three to five nuts. The children take turns trying to toss their nuts into the bowl. Whoever gets the most nuts into the bowl wins. The winner chooses the next story to be told, the next song to be sung, the next game to be played, etc.

2. Nut Relay. Divide the class into two teams, and provide a 12-inch ruler and five nuts for each team. Place the nuts on a ruler. The first player on one team's line takes the ruler with the nuts, walks carefully to a designated place, and returns to the team's line. The next player takes the ruler and does the same thing, and so on. One catch, though: if a nut falls off the ruler, the player has to go back to the line and begin again. The team that finishes first is declared the winner.

3. Right or Left. Holding both hands out of sight of the other children, the first player takes a nut in one hand. With clenched fists, so as to hide the nut, the player extends both hands frontwards. The next player has to guess which hand the nut is in. If the guess is correct, the second player gets the nut, and so on.

PESACH SONGS: CHAD GADYA

Several traditional Passover songs lend themselves well to "active" singing that keeps the children moving around. Chad Gadya is actually an allegory describing the history of Israel.

The kid is Israel	Stick: Persia
The two zuzim are the two tablets of the Law.	Fire: Greece
	Water: Rome
(The rest are the oppressors of Israel.)	Ox: Saracens
	Butcher: The Crusaders
Cat: Assyria	Angel of Death: Ottoman Turks
Dog: Babylonia	

The song ends on the hope that when the Holy One (God) slays the Angel of Death, the Jewish people will be blessed with peace and life.

Using brightly colored tagboard, prepare some fairly large cutouts of the different things mentioned in the song. Make two of each, since they will be glued together—as many pairs as needed so that each child has one set. Have popsicle or craft sticks for each pair of cutouts. Have the children decorate the cutouts as they desire, then glue the sticks in between the two cutouts at the bottom.

As they sing the song, the children wave the appropriate item when it is mentioned.

PESACH SONGS: WHO KNOWS ONE?

This is a fun song, and virtually the same thing can be done with it, using cutouts of the numbers and symbols mentioned. Or you can number the children one through thirteen, and whenever their number is said they have to jump up, then sit down. You can even have one child for one, two children for two, three children for three, and so on.

THE STORY OF PASSOVER

The story of Pesach can be developed into a puppet show or play with the children playing the different parts. Use the basic story as the beginning; then develop it into a play, making sure to include episodes that provide enough parts for everyone in the class. Some of the episodes could be:

Finding Moses in the basket as a baby.

Moses grown and slaying the Egyptian slavemaster.

Moses and the burning bush.

Moses and Aaron encountering Pharaoh with the Ten Plagues.

Encourage the children to use their imaginations in creating impressions of the Ten Plagues. Be sure to include some fun songs in different parts of the production. The play would make a great family program for Pesach.

Activities for Any Jewish Holiday

WHAT DOESN'T BELONG?

This is an old one, but good enough to repeat. Arrange some ritual objects related to a specific Jewish holiday on a table. Help the children to identify each object: how it is used during the holiday, what it represents, etc. Then place the objects in a bag. Without the children seeing you, add another ritual object that is not part of the holiday. Shake the items up. Then ask a child to feel the items in the bag to identify the one that does not belong. Pull out that item. Talk with the children about the new item: What is it? What is it used for? When is it used? Have other items ready to place in the bag so you can continue the activity and introduce new ritual objects.

HOLIDAY CHARTS

Prepare strips of colored paper, each with the name of a Jewish holiday. Limit the number of holidays to four or five so as not to cause confusion. Mount large sheets of white paper on the wall, one for each holiday. Divide the class into small groups, one for each holiday. Give each group one of the holiday strips. Have magazines and old workbooks, or copy sheets of pictures of rituals, symbols, and foods for the different holidays. The children cut out the correct pictures, color them, and place them on the appropriate holiday strip. Monitor the groups, giving clues as necessary, to help the children as they work. Upon completion, each group presents its work and discusses its holiday, then places its strips on the appropriate holiday sheet on the wall.

HOLIDAY MATCH-UP

Prepare a good number of cards with pictures of holiday symbols and ritual objects. Limit the number of holidays so as not to confuse the children. Include pictures of items that do not belong to the holidays you are covering. Spread the picture cards out on a table. Have the children choose partners. One pair at a time, the partners are to choose at least three picture cards that go together. They show their pictures and tell what holiday they represent and why they go together. Continue until everyone in the class has had a turn.

HOLIDAYS AND ANIMAL STORIES

Most kids like animals, and many have pets of their own, so this will be fun for them. Collect pictures of animals—all kinds, even frogs, turtles, and fish—and let each child choose two favorites. Ask the children to pretend that their animals can talk to each other. Let them create a conversation between the two animals about how their owners celebrate a certain holiday—telling what they do, what food they eat, and who comes over to help with the celebration. For children who can print, the conversation could be in the form of a comic strip. To do this, more copies of the animal pictures will be needed so that the kids can create a comic strip with talk balloons over the heads of the animals. The children can then share their Jewish holiday comic strip with their classmates.

HOLIDAY CARDS: PERFORM A MITZVAH

Making cards is an old favorite for younger children. They usually make High Holy Day cards and maybe Mother's Day and Father's Day cards. Why not perform a mitzvah? Have them make holiday cards for the residents of a home for the aged. If there is no Jewish home in your area, make generic cards for any home for the aged. For the Jewish homes, don't forget holidays like Purim and Pesach, as well as the others. Purim cards can include a favorite Jewish joke or story in addition to decorations. Pesach can have the theme of freedom or of spring and renewal. The residents of the homes will enjoy receiving messages from young children, and your class will have performed a mitzvah.

HOLIDAY T-SHIRTS

Have the children bring white or light-colored T-shirts from home on which they can draw. Then have them choose their favorite Jewish holidays and discuss possible ideas for designs to be used on the T-shirts. Have them draw the designs on paper, which allows for making corrections, additions, and sizing changes. When the children are satisfied with their designs, have them draw the final versions directly on the shirts with colorful dye sticks or fabric paints.

WHAT'S THE DIFFERENCE?

Display two holiday ritual objects which are similar yet different (e.g., Shabbat candlesticks/Havdalah candleholder, menorah/chanukiot, round challah/oblong twisted challah). If the real thing is not available, use pictures. Divide the class into small groups. Each group is to examine the items and identify them, explaining how they are similar and how they are different, and when each is used. With your assistance each group then shares its discoveries with the class.

PACK A SUITCASE

Fill a suitcase with ritual objects or pictures of ritual objects related to the holiday you are studying. Include a few unrelated items. Bring the suitcase to class.

Tell the students: "We are going on a trip to Grandma's house for _____ (the holiday), and in our suitcase we will pack _____." Show the pictures or ritual objects to the class and let the kids call out which of them will be needed and therefore should be put in the suitcase. What about the items not packed?

See if the children know what they are and when they are used.

Alternatively, gather the children around the suitcase and have all the items readily available. They are to tell you which objects are needed for the holiday; as each is identified, put it in the suitcase. Or, "Grandma is coming to visit us for the holiday and she is packing her suitcase—what will she put in it?"

KEEPING A RECORD

Before each holiday, mount a large sheet of white paper on the wall. At the top, write the name of the approaching holiday. With the children, brainstorm about what we do to celebrate the holiday. Be sure to include the appropriate rituals and symbols. Write the children's responses on the holiday sheet and keep it posted. When the next holiday approaches, do the same thing. Continue throughout the school year. As the end of the year approaches, have the class compare the lists. What was similar and what was different? By the time the year is over the children will have become familiar with most of the Jewish holidays, how they are celebrated, and the differences and similarities in the celebrations.

FROM DOT TO DOT

Provide colored adhesive dots, construction paper, and crayons or markers for each child. Ask the class to imagine a picture that has something to do with the holiday. Give each child seven or eight dots, construction paper, and crayons or markers. Ask the children to place their dots on the paper, then draw a picture tying the dots together into a picture which tells something about the Jewish holiday. Let the children share their dot-to-dot pictures with their classmates and explain what their picture tells about the holiday.

PRETENDING TO BE A JEWISH SYMBOL

Collect pictures and drawings of symbols and rituals related to the Jewish holiday you wish to study. Mount the pictures on tagboard and laminate. Note: If the pictures are small, as found in most workbooks, enlarge them to fill at least an 8.5 x 11 sheet of paper.

Display the pictures. Take one at a time and talk with the class about what it is, what it means, how it is used during the holiday, and what purpose it serves. Then have each child, in turn, choose a picture and describe it. When the description is completed, ask the child to pretend to be the object described. Hold the picture in front of the child's face and have the child say a sentence that the object would say if it could speak. Consider recording the session so you can play it back.

HOLIDAY CONCENTRATION

For this game you will need two pieces of fiberboard, the kind used for posters or displays. Prepare at least 24 matching pairs of small pictures of things related to the holiday being studied. Cut out circles the size of a checker from one piece of fiberboard. You will need one circle for each picture.

Mark the other fiberboard in the same exact places you have cut out the circles. Glue the pictures in the marked spaces on this fiberboard, making sure they match the cutout circles. This becomes the picture board. Now take the other fiberboard, match the open circles to the pictures, then glue or tape the two fiberboards together. Place checkers or chips in the open circles to cover the pictures.

To play: This game is for two or more players. Each player has a turn and takes off two chips showing the pictures underneath. If the pictures do not match, the player replaces the chips; but remind the players to try and remember the location of the pictures. If the pictures match, the player can remove the chips and keep them. The object of the game, of course, is to match up the pictures and collect the most chips.

HOLIDAY SORT

Children can become more familiar with the symbols and ritual objects of different holidays by sorting them into appropriate categories. Bring in pictures of symbols and ritual objects for the Jewish holidays. Make up a sheet or two of these pictures and copy them for each child. Prepare a set of envelopes for each holiday, one set per child. If you have a large class, divide it into small groups and prepare a set of envelopes for each group. Tell the children to color the pictures, label them, then cut out each picture and place it in the appropriate envelope. Have the children exchange envelopes when they are finished to check each other's categories. If they think any of the symbols or ritual objects has been placed incorrectly, they are to show the picture to you, or to the class, for verification.

WHAT DO YOU SEE?

Collect pictures of families celebrating a Jewish holiday or participating in related activities. Try to choose pictures which show a number of details. Mount the pictures on tagboard and laminate. One at a time, show a picture to the class and tell the children to look closely at it and try to remember the details. After a few seconds, turn the picture face down. Ask the children to tell what they saw, making notes of their responses on the board. Show the picture again, asking, "Did you see _____?" Be specific to elicit details from them. When they have seen everything in one picture, go on to another. After a few more, let them draw a picture of their own family celebrating the same holiday. Then have the children share their pictures with their classmates, explaining what they and their families are doing.

THE CLASS WRITES A STORY

Use the same kinds of pictures as in the preceding exercise, but this time let the children select one they would like to write a story about. Make sure they look at the pictures carefully before choosing. Ask them for story ideas, titles, etc. Next have the class choose a title, guiding the children into giving reasons for their choice. Help them to compose a class story for the picture. As they develop the story, write it on the blackboard or on a large piece of lined paper posted on the wall. Encourage everyone to participate in adding to the story or revising it. Then help the class read the story. Later, make copies of the class story for the children to take home.

CREATIVE DRAMA IN THE CLASSROOM

Divide the class into small groups. Place on a table one ritual object which is part of the holiday to be studied (for Shabbat it could be a pair of candlesticks; for Pesach, a seder plate; for Purim, a Megillah or gragger).

Each group is to create a dramatization, no more than 3–5 minutes long, involving the ritual object. Give enough time for the group members to discuss ideas for the play. They can use the ritual object any way they wish in the drama. After all the groups have made their presentations, talk about how they arrived at their way of using the ritual object.

IDENTIFYING RITUAL OBJECTS AND HOLIDAY SYMBOLS

You will need a set of small white index cards. On each card put a word and a picture of a ritual object or symbol for the Jewish holiday. Around the classroom, place real ritual objects and pictures of symbols. If ritual objects are not available, use large pictures. With the children, read the word, then ask a child to take the card to the object it describes. Continue until all the objects have been identified.

SHOEBOX HOLIDAY SORT

Decorate three or four shoeboxes with contact or construction paper. Cut slits in the box lids large enough for a 3 x 5 index card to slip through. Place the lid on top, but do not seal. Label each box with the name of a Jewish holiday. Collect pictures related to each of the Jewish holidays for which shoeboxes have been made. Mount the pictures on 3 x 5 index cards and laminate if you want to be able to use them time and time again. Make enough cards for each child to have a complete set. The object is to place the appropriate holiday card in the corresponding holiday box.

TRANSPARENT HOLIDAY WINDOW PICTURES

Draw an outline of a holiday symbol or ritual object design with very black ink or marker on drawing paper. Make enough copies for the whole class and distribute. Have the children color the outline any way they wish; they can even leave some white space if they prefer. When they have finished coloring, turn the picture over and lay it on newspaper. Rub cooking oil over the back of the picture to make it transparent. When the pictures are dry, fasten them in the windows of the classroom.

HOLIDAY STAMPS

Dry sponges are the best material for making holiday stamps. Take some new sponges, cut out different Jewish symbols and ritual objects, and glue to a wooden block or empty spool of thread, which will serve as a handle. Use stamp pads with different-color inks or shallow pie pans filled with different colors of tempera paint. The kids can make cards and stationery with the stamps, and can use them for decorations of just about any kind.

NEAT AND SIMPLE

EASY MOSAICS

Bags of small bits of pre-glued colored paper cut in different shapes and sizes are available at any arts and crafts store. These can be used to make colorful mosaics of Jewish symbols. Draw a simple design for a holiday symbol or ritual object. Copy it on colored paper. Show the children how to use the bits of paper, then let them create their own colorful mosaics.

FILL THE HOLIDAY BOX

Draw two boxes large enough and with enough open space for cutouts of holiday items to be pasted inside them. Label one box *Food* and the other *Symbols and Ritual Objects*. Then copy for the children.

Prepare a sheet of paper with a variety of pictures of symbols, foods, and ritual objects related to the holiday. Slip in a few pictures which do not belong to the holiday and see if the children catch them. The pictures must be small enough to fit inside the boxes, but large enough for the children to be able to color and cut them out. Copy on white paper if they are to color them, or on bright colored paper if they are just to cut them out and paste them in the boxes. Give the sheets to the children and tell them to cut out the pictures and paste them in the appropriate boxes.

ANOTHER HOLIDAY SORT

Bring in a good number of pictures from old Jewish textbooks, workbooks, magazines, etc. Copy the pictures, then cut out. Paste each picture on a 4 x 6 index card and laminate or cover with clear contact paper so it can be used again and again. Ask the children to sort the pictures according to your directions, which could be something like this:

Find all the pictures that have Shabbat symbols.

Find all the pictures that have to do with Pesach.

Find all the pictures for Rosh Hashanah and Yom Kippur.

And so on.

NAPKIN RINGS MAKE A NICE HOLIDAY GIFT

Cut pieces of felt of various colors into 6 x 1 strips. It would be best for the children to make napkin rings for everyone in their immediate families, but if this is not possible, make sure there is enough material for them to at least make one each. From additional felt, in different colors, cut out small Jewish symbols appropriate for the holiday. Have glue ready.

Show the children how to make a circle with each strip by overlapping about 1 inch and gluing together. Give each child one symbol for each napkin ring. The symbol is to be glued on to the overlapped material to hide this part of the napkin ring. When the glue dries the children can add any other decorations they wish in order to make the rings even more attractive. When finished, they can take the napkin rings home for use during their family's holiday dinner.

THE HOLIDAY WORM

Draw the head of a large worm—oblong, but slightly round. Draw big eyes, a nose, and smiling mouth on the head, cut out and then laminate. If you wish, add a few oblong circles to the head for the beginning of the body—laminate these as well. Place the Holiday Worm on the bulletin board along with the name of the holiday.

Prepare numerous body sections, in oblong shapes, out of construction paper. The children can either draw pictures of how the holiday is celebrated on the worm shapes, or cut pictures out and paste them on. As the children complete their pictures, put the body parts on the board and see how long a Holiday Worm they can create.

HOLIDAY PUZZLES

Use 6 x 8 index cards or tagboard cut to the same size. Gather pictures of symbols, ritual objects, and foods for the holiday. Glue one picture to each card. Laminate or cover with clear contact paper. Cut each card into two puzzle pieces. Talk about the holiday and pass out a puzzle piece to each child. Have the children match up their puzzle pieces. Let them tell what their puzzles represent and how they are part of the holiday. If they do not know, help them to identify the symbol or ritual and what it is.

HOLIDAY MAIL

Children can deliver the mail. Make a letter-carrier's hat—something simple and a size to fit the average three- to five-year-old. You can even use a baseball cap with a label saying *mail* attached to it.

Draw an outline of a house; again keep it simple. Trace it six to ten times, or copy it on tagboard, so that you have the makings of a nice "neighborhood." On each house print the name of the holiday. In addition, place a picture of a major symbol of the holiday on each house. Laminate the houses and then cut out.

Put the same holiday symbols on some playing or index cards. Laminate or cover with clear contact paper. Note: if the pictures are in black and white, it might be a good idea to color them. If you do so, color before laminating.

The task for the child is to put on the mail hat, take the mail in hand, and deliver it to the right house by matching the symbols.

HOLIDAY FOODS

Prepare a large picture of a stove. Be sure that the front of the stove—the oven is best—is open so that the children can put cutout pictures in this space. Talk about the holiday and ask the children to think about what foods they eat on this occasion. Ask them to draw or cut out pictures of the foods they eat and place them in the stove.

PERFECT TRIANGLES FOR THE STAR OF DAVID

Can't find just the right size Jewish star for your class project, holiday cards, etc.? Make your own! All you need are two perfect triangles. All three sides of the triangle must be the same length. Using a ruler on graph paper, draw several separate triangles. Use these as your stencil. Then copy on tagboard. Cut out as many triangles as you need for the class. Two are necessary for each star. Show the class how to put two triangles together to make a Star of David. The children are now ready to make whatever it is you need for your project.

HOLIDAY QUICK THINK: A GAME

Divide the class into two teams. You will need a bean bag or small ball that can be tossed from one team to the other.

A member of one team tosses the bean bag to a member of the other team, calls out loud the name of a holiday, and immediately begins counting to ten. Before the first player reaches ten, the player on the other team must call out loud the name of a symbol, ritual object, food, book, song, etc., that has to do with the holiday. If the player fails to name an object before the thrower counts to ten, the thrower's team wins a point. A point is also scored if anyone on the other team names an object that has already been named. Continue playing, going back and forth from one team to the other. Of course, the team with the most points wins. In addition, you have found out how much the children know about the different holidays.

HOLIDAYS OUT OF PLACE

Gather together a variety of pictures of symbols, ritual objects, foods, etc., pertaining to different Jewish holidays. Make up sheets of pictures for each holiday, but include several pictures that do not belong to it. Copy the sheets, pass them out, and ask the children to color only the pictures that have to do with that sheet's particular holiday. Let the children share the results.

KEEPING PARENTS INFORMED

The children will be learning about the holidays, but how much do the parents know? Prepare a simple two-page background information sheet about each holiday covered in class, using 8.5 x 14 sheets. Include the history of the festival, the customs, how it is celebrated in synagogue and home, and any blessings associated with it, in Hebrew, transliteration, and English. In addition, put in an activity or two for families to do together, and even a recipe or two of typical holiday foods. Send the sheets home with the children a week or so before the holiday.

YE OLD SWIMMING HOLE

This one is an oldie, but it is good for young children. You will need an old plastic swimming pool, one foil pie pan per holiday, construction paper, a homemade fishing pole with a magnet on the end, a large posterboard, paperclips, and glue.

Label each pie pan with a holiday name. Glue the holiday pans onto the posterboard and place it next to the "swimming hole." Draw and color a variety of Jewish symbols for all the holidays, making them at least 2 inches in size. Cut them out after you have laminated the sheets or covered them with clear contact paper. Glue a paperclip to the back of each symbol. Fill your swimming hole with all the holiday symbols. Each child takes a turn with the fishing pole, trying to catch a symbol and place it in the correct holiday pan.

WHAT'S MISSING? COMPLETE A PICTURE!

Collect large pictures, or enlarge small ones, of Jewish activities and celebrations. Cut out one item from each picture (e.g., from a Shabbat family dinner scene, cut out the challah). Do this with all the pictures. Mount the cutouts on small index cards and put them in a box.

Show the pictures one at a time. Ask the children to look carefully, describing the activity that is taking place in the picture. Ask, "What is missing?" Let them find the missing piece in the box and put it in to complete the picture.

SYMBOLS, RITUALS, AND CONCEPTS

The Artifact Bag

This is a variation of an old activity. Make a bag large enough to hold several objects (e.g., candles, candlesticks, Kiddush cup, Yahrzeit candle, etrog, Chanukah candles). Use a dark-colored fabric so that the objects in the bag cannot be seen. A shoestring or cord can used for a drawstring at the top. Place in the bag a number of small Jewish objects, plus a few objects which are not necessarily Jewish. Attach a blindfold to the bag. Have a child put on the blindfold, insert a hand into the bag to feel one object, and tell the class five things about the object touched and felt. The class then tries to guess what the object is.

A Child's Jewish Senses

Make a sheet with pictures of the five senses as a heading: eyes, nose, ears, mouth, and hands. Leave space below each picture for the children to add pictures of their own. Copy for the students. Have on hand lots of magazines, old workbooks or sheets of pictures of Jewish activities, symbols, ritual objects, foods, etc. Scissors and glue will also be needed. The children are to cut out pictures of Jewish things they do and place them in the area pertaining to that sense. A spice box, for instance, would be placed under *nose*; challah under *mouth*. When the children finish, have them share their Jewish Sense Sheets with their classmates.

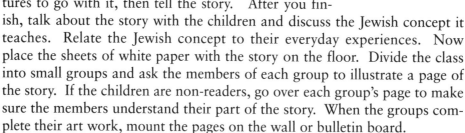

Illustrating a Story

Choose a story the children will like. Make sure is it one that teaches a Jewish concept. Prepare the story, a few sentences at a time, on large sheets of white paper. Before telling the story, ask the children to listen carefully because you are going to ask them to draw pictures to go with it, then tell the story. After you finish, talk about the story with the children and discuss the Jewish concept it teaches. Relate the Jewish concept to their everyday experiences. Now place the sheets of white paper with the story on the floor. Divide the class into small groups and ask the members of each group to illustrate a page of the story. If the children are non-readers, go over each group's page to make sure the members understand their part of the story. When the groups complete their art work, mount the pages on the wall or bulletin board.

ALTERNATIVE

Prepare the story, a few sentences for each page, on several sheets of plain white 8.5 x 11 paper. Make copies for each child. After the discussion, ask the children to illustrate them. When they finish, they will have storybooks to take home.

A Perfect Gift

Save those flower catalogues—they can be used for this one. Cut two 8.5-inch squares out of colored construction paper, using two different colors, for each child. Cut 1 x 8.5 inch strips for the handles for each child. Give the children two squares each, one of each color. Show the class how to fold and cut doily designs into one of the squares. Fold the uncut square first to form an X, then unfold and refold it into a + shape. Unfold and glue the doily cutout to the paper that was folded. Unfold the "basket" and glue on the handle. Now have the children go through the flower catalogues and cut out flowers to glue into their baskets. As a special added feature, have them place an extra "gift" in the basket—for example, a slip of paper on which is written "I will wash the dinner dishes" or "I will take out the trash," which can be redeemed by the parents.

Kashrut

Go over the different identifying marks for kosher items found in the grocery store. Once the children are familiar with the symbols, ask them to make lists of foodstuffs found in their own homes that are kosher. They can share their findings with the whole class when they return to school. Go over the different foods mentioned in the Bible that are considered kosher and those that are not. Then ask the parents to take their children to the grocery store and list the items in the store which are kosher. Also ask the children to list kosher items their parents purchase on a regular basis. Have the children share their lists, talking about the items their parents purchase on a regular basis. What is their reaction on learning that many items their parents purchase are kosher (especially if they do not actually keep kosher)? Interestingly, more and more people are buying kosher these days because they know that foods from kosher food manufacturers have to pass stringent cleanliness regulations.

The Jewish Calendar

Even young children can become familiar with the Jewish calendar year. You will need a paper about 60 inches long and 10 inches wide. It can be bigger if you have the wall space to display it. Divide the sheet in half, 5 inches on the top and 5 inches on the bottom. Across the long part, divide into twelve sections. (If it happens to be a Jewish leap year with two months of Adar, you can still use twelve sections; just divide the Adar section in half.) Across the top half, label each section with the names of the secular months. Across the bottom half, label each section with the names of the Jewish months.

Collect a selection of small pictures representing the Jewish holidays. Laminate and cut out. During each class period, take a few minutes to talk about what Jewish holiday, if any, occurred during the past week. Let the children pick out the pictures that fit the holiday and place them in the section for the appropriate Jewish month. You can even recognize children's birthdays by placing their names in the Jewish and secular months in which they were born. As the children add to the calendar each class period, they will be able to see how the Jewish calendar corresponds to the secular year.

A Calendar Alternative

The fall is a good time for the children to become familiar with the Jewish calendar in relation to the secular calendar. Prepare two or three months of the Jewish calendar with the corresponding secular months, using colored 9 x 12 construction paper, divided in half. On each page, write the name of each month, both Jewish and secular, with one on top and the other on the bottom. Post on the bulletin board. On different-colored paper strips write the names of special Jewish events or mount pictures of Jewish symbols which correspond to the Jewish events (holidays). Have the children place the strips around the Jewish and secular months. With yarn, connect one end to the strips and the other end to the day when the holiday takes place.

Protecting the Environment—with Emphasis on Littering

Litter, litter everywhere, and you're the one who puts it there. This activity is a takeoff on musical chairs, played with musical paper litter. Before class begins, scatter pieces of scrap paper around the room, one less then the number of children in your class. Play music and have the children pick up the litter. The child who doesn't pick up a piece of litter is eliminated. Play the game again, always taking up a piece of litter so there is one less than the number of children. Continue playing until all the litter is eliminated. Talk about the Jewish concept of tikun olam and the effect littering has on our environment. Have the children suggest ways to avoid littering.

Jewish Symbol Placemats

The placemats made in this activity can be used in the classroom or sent home; the choice is yours. Placemats are very inexpensive to make, just use colored construction paper the size you desire. Have the children draw a design representing a Jewish holiday, ritual, or concept on the construction paper. Or they can draw designs on different-colored paper, then cut out and glue on to the piece of paper that is going to be the placemat. Cover with clear contact paper or laminate. The children now have a placemat to do their art work on at school or to use at home.

ALTERNATIVE

Prepare different Jewish symbols, making sure there are enough for all the children to have several to put on their placemats. They can cut them out, then glue the symbols to make their own designs on the placemats. They can add whatever drawings or decorations they desire around each symbol. Then cover with clear contact paper or laminate.

Synagogue Symbols

You will need pictures of the different objects found in the synagogue (e.g., menorah, ner tamid, bimah, ark, Torah crown, Torah breastplate, yad, Torah scroll, siddur). Mount these pictures on a sheet of paper and make enough copies for each child to have a Synagogue Symbol Sheet.

Take the children into the sanctuary. Have them look at the different objects found there and find them on their Symbol Sheets. Return to the classroom and have them color the pictures in the same colors as the objects they saw in the sanctuary. Then ask them to cut out the pictures and paste them to a posterboard and write the name of each object under its picture. Or, paste pictures on index cards and have the children name each object.

Another Synagogue Activity

Take the class into the sanctuary. With you have a large note pad and pencil. Let the children look around the sanctuary. Invite them to choose an object that they would want to write a story about. Once their choice is made, help them develop a story about the object they have selected. In the story they can include the name of the object, how it is used, when it is used, how old it is, where it is located, etc. Back in the classroom, copy their story on large chart paper, leaving room between the lines. Read the story to the class, and invite the children to make additions, changes, and revisions until they like what they have created. Before the next class, type the story, a few sentences to a page, and make a copy for each child. Have the children draw pictures on each page to illustrate the story. They can share their creative work with the whole class.

Symbol Games

Using construction paper, draw or trace Jewish symbols that represent holidays or events. Laminate. Cut out each symbol and be sure you have enough to give each child a complete set. Use a large plastic tablecloth to make a Twister gameboard. Place the gameboard on the floor. Tell the children to place a Rosh Hashanah symbol on the board and hold it there with their hands. Then tell them to place a Shabbat symbol on the gameboard and hold it there with one of their feet. You can continue until they are all twisted up in the new game.

ALTERNATIVE

Another use for the symbols would be to pass out one for each holiday to each child. Then play Simon Says. "Simon Says: Sukot, stand up. Simon says: Shabbat, raise your hand." And so on, using all the different symbols.

Tzedakah: Helping Others

Prepare several cutout silhouettes of people, making one fairly large. Make the others smaller but large enough for pictures to either be drawn or pasted on them. Make one for each child and one for you. Talk with the class about how there are different kinds of people who help others. Ask them to name someone who often helps other people. Take one of the silhouettes and place it on the bulletin board. Write the person's name on the silhouette. Ask the children what this person does to help other people, then ask them to cut out pictures from magazines that illustrate some of the things this person does. Glue the pictures on the silhouette.

Now give each child a silhouette. Ask the children what they do to help other people. Try to elicit responses other than giving money to charity. The answers can be as simple as taking the garbage out for mother, setting the table, hanging up their clothes, etc. Make a list of all the different things the children do to help others. Ask them to cut pictures out of the magazines which represent things they do to help others. Upon completion, place their silhouettes around the larger one to create a Helping Others bulletin board.

Tzedakah: More Than Money

Instead of collecting money, why not ask the children to bring to school one toy, in good condition that they do not use any more. Toys collected can be given to a children's shelter.

ALTERNATIVE

Have a clothing drive. Ask the children, with their parents, to go through their closets, choose some articles of clothing in good condition that they no longer wear, and bring them to school. Maybe you can get parents to help with the project, even delivering the clothes to a shelter.

ANOTHER ALTERNATIVE

Encourage the children, when buying a birthday present for a friend, to buy an extra one and give it to a shelter.

Tzedakah Box: A Simple Creation

Get the children, as well as their parents and friends, to save used postage stamps and juice containers with their lids. You will also need glue, varnish, and brushes for this project. Begin by showing the class a finished tzedakah box. Then give each child an assortment of stamps, glue, and a juice container. The children can glue the stamps in any design they wish, even letting them overlap on the container. Let the glue dry. Once it is dry, have them apply the varnish, then let that dry. Cut a slit in the lid and place on top. Besides making an attractive tzedakah box, this could also become a nice gift of a pencil holder for parents. As a tzedakah box, though, it gives you a chance to talk about tzedakah and the different ways we help others.

Thank You, God!

You will need brightly colored construction paper cut into 1 x 6 inch strips, colored yarn, a stapler, glue, a hole puncher, magazines, and scissors.

Staple or glue the ends of one strip to make a ring. The children pull another strip through this ring and glue or staple. They continue until they have a long chain of rings. Using a hole puncher, place a small hole in every third or fourth ring. Thread a piece of yarn through the holes. The children then look through magazines and cut out pictures of those things for which they would like to thank God. Glue a picture at the end of each piece of yarn. Make more than one chain. When the chains are completed, your room can be decorated with them. Then talk with the children about the choices they made.

The Jewish Family

Talk with the children about things their family does during holidays, special Jewish events, the Sabbath, etc.—how they celebrate, what special things they do, etc. Guide them to focus on family traditions. The children can either draw pictures or bring in pictures of their families taken during these special celebrations; copy these, enlarging as you do so. If they make their own drawings, ask them to color any that are copied from pictures from home.

Ask the children to show their pictures and tell about the celebrations. Help them print the stories underneath their pictures to make a Family Jewish Celebrations booklet. When each booklet is complete, laminate the pages or cover with clear contact paper. Ask the children to design covers for their booklets. Laminate, then bind each booklet together. This makes a nice gift for the family, and you have emphasized Jewish family life.

THE BIBLE AND JEWISH HISTORY

Making Jewish History

History doesn't have much meaning for very young children, but here is a way to introduce Jewish history and prepare them for their future studies.

Keep a record of the school year with a scrapbook of pictures. Take pictures of the children doing different activities during the school year. Mount the pictures, one to a page, and have the children write captions for the pictures. If they cannot write, have them dictate the action shown in the picture, and you put it in writing. Get the parents involved too. Ask them to take pictures when celebrating Jewish holidays or events, and include these in the scrapbook. Make arrangements with the librarian to place the scrapbook in the library. Just imagine, years from now, the children coming back and looking through "their" Jewish history!

Noah's Ark

From colored paper, cut out shapes of the different animals that went into Noah's Ark. Help the children create short stories about each animal's life on the Ark during the Flood. When they have completed their stories, they can put the animals in the Ark, which you have mounted on the bulletin board.

Take the stories the children have written and combine into a booklet. Make enough copies for the children to take home and share with their parents. Put one copy on the bulletin board with Noah's Ark.

COAT OF MANY COLORS

Joseph's coat lends itself well to arts and crafts, but there is a larger dimension to creating a coat of many colors. When telling the story of Joseph and the sibling rivalry between the brothers, talk about how the brothers became angry when Jacob gave Joseph this special coat. Talk about why the brothers were angry, asking the children whether they have ever been angry, what makes them angry, how they control their anger, what it means to control anger, etc. Emphasize the idea of controlling one's anger.

This activity is an opportunity for some creative activity. Here's one to try: when creating a coat of many colors, show the children how to make a coat hanger out of a pipe cleaner. Then give out pipe cleaners and have them make hangers. Then show them how to make a coat of many colors. Cut white construction paper to fit on the hanger. Cut a hole in the top of the "coat" so that it will fit over the top of the hanger. Let the children design and color their coats of many colors, then hang them on the hangers. Display their creations for all to see.

NEAT AND SIMPLE

A Puzzle for Reviewing a Bible Portion

This is a good way to review a unit of study, whether in Bible or Jewish history. Make a puzzle out of posterboard using pictures related to your unit of study. Develop a series of multiple-choice questions on the subject matter. Whoever answers a question correctly gets to put a piece of the puzzle in place. Continue the review with the class until the puzzle is completed.

The Story of Creation

This will make your lesson interactive with the class. Prepare seven blank pieces of posterboard or make a felt board with seven blank spaces. Number each space.

For a posterboard: Cut out a number of pictures which correspond to each day of the Creation. As you tell the story, the children can place the correct pictures on the appropriately numbered board.

For a felt board: Cut your pictures out of pieces of felt. Follow the procedure above.

CREATION BOOK

Prepare a series of pictures representing each day of the Creation. As you tell the story, let the children color the page for that day. When the story is completed, they can compile a colored picture book of the story.

Identify the Pictures

This activity can be used either for Jewish history or for Bible. It makes a good review lesson or a closure to a lesson. Gather together pictures and objects related to your unit of study. After your lesson, display the pictures and objects. Have the class identify each item and explain where it can be found, how it can be used, its relationship to the topic, etc. If there is a picture or object they cannot identify, discuss with them what it is, where it is from, and how it is used.

Jewish Concepts in the Bible

This is another lesson developed by my friend Paul D. Keeper. The goal of the lesson is to explore the concepts of mercy, good and bad, good and evil, things we should and should not do, things that are and are not good for us, and things we are told are or are not good for us.

EXERCISE 1

Place the following items all together on a table, then tell the class to arrange them into two groups, good and bad:

Candy (an assortment).

Drugs (some over-the-counter, and words on index cards).

Pain (write the word on an index card).

Sleeping late (write on an index card).

Fruit (an assortment).

Jogging (write on an index card).

Allow time for the class to perform this task. Then say: "Assume that you are an old person and are on a strict diet. You have to take certain medicines every day by injection. You have been told to get plenty of rest and not to over-exert yourself. Arrange the same items into good and bad." Allow time for the class to perform this task.

Now, talk about:

How can we tell if something is good or bad?

What are the characteristics of something that is good?

Of something that is bad?

When we talk about good, does it have a dimension of time, place, manner?

How about bad?

When can something bad become something good?

Are there degrees of good? Of bad?

What is evil?

Give some examples of evil.

If evil is the worst form of bad, what is the best form of good? Do we have a word for it?

What is tzedakah? (Here talk about the different forms which tzedakah can take.)

Tell this story to the class:

> You are standing on a bridge with your family, watching the sun set over a swiftly flowing river. Suddenly, an airplane comes in low overhead and crashes in the water. The doors of the airplane open and people start jumping out. You barely know how to swim, and no one else in your family knows how to swim. You tell your family that you are going to jump in the water to try and save some of the people from the plane. Your parents beg you not to jump in. They tell you: "It's too dangerous, the passengers will drown anyway, you can't swim well enough to help them, and we fear for your life."

To the class: What do you do?

Allow a few minutes for responses, then talk about:

If you decide to jump in and risk your life, have you done a good thing or a bad thing?

If you save someone's life but you drown, have you done a good thing or a bad thing?

If you save ten people's lives but you drown, have you done a good thing or a bad thing?

If you save ten people's lives and don't drown, have you done a good thing or a bad thing? (Remember, your parents told you not to jump in.)

How important is it to do what other people tell us?

Why do other people think it is important to tell us to do or not do certain things?

What is the value of their experience for us?

What would have happened if your parents had said, "We won't let you jump in the river," and you jumped anyway? Would that have been more bad, more good, evil?

Tell this story to the children:

> Your parents and you go to Australia for a vacation. When the vacation is over, your parents put you on an airplane home, but they stay behind for a few more weeks. The airplane is full of other kids who are also being sent home. You are the oldest kid on the plane. The pilot has a heart attack and dies. The plane crashes on an island. All of the kids survive. They come to and are frightened. You decide that your job is to keep them safe until a rescue plane comes to find you. You decide that the first thing you need to do is to put together a list of rules.

For this exercise, the children must make up a list of rules and a list of punishments for kids who break the rules. Remember, these are little kids. (As the children call out rules and punishments, write them on the board.)

At this point, tell the class the story of Abraham and the three visitors. Start with God telling Abraham that Sodom and Gomorrah will be destroyed, and Abraham asking God to spare the cities if good people can be found in them. Go through the story until Lot and his family are taken out and Lot's wife looks back and is turned into a pillar of salt. After the story, stimulate a discussion by asking questions from the list that follows, or use your own questions along the same lines.

Why did God decide to destroy Sodom and Gomorrah?

What rules had the citizens broken?

Had the citizens agreed to abide by these rules?

What bothered Abraham about God's decision to destroy the cities?

Was Abraham concerned only about his nephew Lot being destroyed?

Why did Lot live in the city of Sodom, anyway?

Why did Abraham bargain with God from 50 to 40 to 10 righteous men?

What gave Abraham the right to bargain with God?

What special relationship did Abraham have with God?

Who were the mysterious servants of God?

How many appeared to Abraham? How many appeared to Lot? What happened to the third?

Why was Lot sitting in the gate of the city? Didn't he have a job?

Why was he willing to believe the strangers?

Why were his sons-in-law so unwilling to believe Lot when he told them that the city was going to be destroyed?

Why did Lot linger in the city before it was destroyed? What would have made Lot want to linger?

Why did God not want the escapees to look back? Was God embarrassed by what was being done to the cities? What other reasons did God have for not wanting them to look back?

Why did Lot's wife look back?

Did she know that the punishment for looking was so severe?

Why salt?

Why was it OK for Lot to look back the next morning and see the smoke, but it was forbidden for his wife to look back and see the fire?

Who knows the definition of "mercy"?

When Abraham negotiated with God about saving the city if it had a certain number of righteous men in it, was he asking for mercy for himself?

For his brother?

For whom?

Have we ever been like Lot, staying in a situation that we knew was bad, and not trying to change it?

How hard is it to change our ways?

When Lot knew the city was to be destroyed, he decided to change his ways and get out. Is it necessary to know that something bad will happen to us if we don't change in order for us to change our ways?

Sometimes bad things happen to people without any warning. Did Lot's wife have a warning? Did she know what the punishment would be for breaking the rule? If she had known, would she have looked back?

When you were the leader of the island, was it hard for you to think of a way to punish the breaking of any particular rule? Which one?

Do people get punished for every bad thing they do?

Do some people get punished in ways they don't expect?

Do some people get punished for things they didn't do?

Do some people get punished for simply being in the wrong place at the wrong time?

What can we do to avoid the pain of punishment?

Is every pain a punishment for something we have done wrong?

ISRAEL

Israel Bulletin Board

Collect pictures of places in Israel and scenes of Israeli life. Note: Travel brochures on Israel have some great pictures. El Al Airlines is also a good source. Some travel brochures provide pictures of other countries and locations. Ask travel agencies to save their old brochures for you, otherwise they usually toss them.

Mix in with the pictures of Israel some that have nothing to do with Israel. Place each picture on a large index card or tagboard, and laminate. There are several ways to use these pictures.

1. Make three pockets in which the pictures will fit. Label the pockets *person, place,* and *thing.* Have the children put the pictures in the appropriate pocket.

2. Make up pairs of the pictures—things that go together (e.g., Jerusalem/Western

Wall, Haifa/Mount Carmel; Safed/Lake Kinneret). Shuffle the cards, then pass them out. Have the children match up the pairs.

3. Create a bulletin board on the State of Israel. As the children identify the pictures, let them put the picture on the bulletin board.

JEWISH IDENTITY

Building a Sense of Jewish Community: Kelal Yisrael

You will need a ball of colored yarn. Sit the children in a circle. Explain that they are about to share something special about themselves, something they do well. If this is a new group, have them begin by introducing themselves.

Give the ball of yarn to the first child, who begins, "My name is Sam, and I'm good at singing Jewish songs." While holding on to the end of the yarn, he rolls the yarn to the person across from him. Continue this process until all the children in the circle have shared something about themselves. Be sure they pass the ball of yarn back and forth each time until everyone is holding part of the yarn. Then talk about:

What does the "spider web" of yarn look like? (Note any symbolism, design, community involvement.)

What helps to build community when people get involved?

What activities bring Jewish people closer together?

Listen to the responses and ask additional questions based on them. Emphasize the concept of Kelal Yisrael.

How Do You Feel?

Begin by making facial-expression puppets. You will need three tongue depressors or popsicle sticks per child, six colored tagboard circles per child, glue, and colored markers or crayons.

Have the children draw faces on three of their circles which express a feeling (e.g., a smile, a frown/sadness, surprise). Glue tongue depressors on the back of the faces and glue the second circle on the back to cover the tongue depressor.

When the puppets are completed, compile a list of statements that elicit feelings. These statements can be on the holidays, Bible, Jewish history, etc. This is to give the children a chance to express how they feel about a celebration or a historical event. It is also a safe way to deal with positive self-esteem and how the actions of their peers make them feel.

Read the statements, one at a time. The children show the puppet which reveals their feelings about that statement. Discuss, each time, how they reacted and the reasons for their reactions.

Jewish Traits Bulletin Board

The children can use magazines to find pictures which reflect who they are as Jews. They are each to make a collage from the pictures they find: what they like as Jews, what they do as Jews, etc. When the collages are completed, ask the children to share the results. Then have them place the collages on the bulletin board in an attractive design.

Building Blocks

Prepare a sheet with "building blocks" standing one on top of the other like a brick wall. Make the blocks large enough for the children to either draw a Jewish symbol or glue a picture on them. You will need only five or six blocks. Copy and distribute.

Ask the children to think about who they are as Jews: which holidays are their favorites and why, special family Jewish celebrations, etc. Tell them they can either draw a symbol, write a word, or cut out or draw some pictures in each block which represent who they are as Jews. Have some magazines available, as well as crayons and markers for drawing, and let them get to work. When finished, they can share their building blocks with their classmates and talk about the reasons for their choices.

Children's Time-Line

Have the children bring in at least five pictures of themselves at different ages. It would be great if these show them doing some Jewish activity, but the pictures can include parents and siblings, other relatives, pets, and friends.

Give each child six large index cards. Help the children string the cards on colorful yarn, vertically. Then they are to paste one picture to a card in chronological order, leaving the top card blank and with space enough next to each picture for them to draw a small design of a Jewish activity they participated in at that age (e.g., Shabbat, Chanukah, Pesach, Consecration). The top card becomes the title card, which each child designs and entitles something like "The Jewish Me."

Their Jewish Home

Have the children draw maps of their Jewish homes, including the rooms where they eat, sleep, and play. Decorate the rooms with appropriate Jewish items (e.g., Shabbat candlesticks in the dining room, Bible on the bookshelf in the bedroom, mezuzot on the doorposts, pictures wherever desired, etc.).

A POTPOURRI OF USEFUL IDEAS

Bleach Painting

A word of caution on this activity: bleach fumes can be dangerous—either open the windows of the classroom or do the activity outside. Have all the children wear aprons or old shirts from home. You will need bleach, paint cups or small glass jars, cotton swabs, crayons, and dark-colored construction paper—the kind you never really use when you purchase a package of assorted colors.

1. Give each child a small amount of bleach, a cotton swab, and crayons.

2. Tell the children to draw a simple picture on the dark construction paper.

3. After they complete their drawings, have them dip their cotton swabs in the bleach and "paint" along the lines of their pictures.

4. Leave the "paintings" to dry either outside or in a well-ventilated indoor area.

Note: The change doesn't take place immediately, but slowly the bleach will take out the color, leaving the drawing lines highlighted in gray or off-white.

A Class Movie

This is a year-long project, but makes a good closure for the school year. Does your school have a video camera? Or can you borrow one? At the beginning of school, start the year with an opening-day video event. Tell the children you will be taking videos of their activities throughout the year, in order to keep a record of what they do in school. Talk about the different things you will be doing and let the children get excited by offering their suggestions. During the school year make videos of special events and activities. Be sure to include every child in the class. As the end of the school year approaches, go over the video with the children. Help them to develop a narration for use when it is shown. You can even include songs they have learned. When all is ready, have a family program to show the video of the school year and the program prepared by the children.

Simple Puppets and a Show

You will need one and a half large white paper plates for each child, a stapler, crayons or colored markers, yarn, and construction paper.

To make a simple puppet, staple the half-plate to the front of the whole plate to form a hand pocket which will allow the children to insert a hand to maneuver the puppets. Tell the children to design appropriate faces on their paper-plate puppets. The puppets they make should be related to your unit of study. Suggest which characters are needed.

On the board, write a list of suggested activities to go with your unit of study. Divide the class into small groups, assigning a topic to each group. Give the children time to develop their puppet characters and puppet shows. When all is ready—on with the shows!

Make Your Own Puzzles

There are blank puzzles on the market which come in a variety of sizes and with a various number of pieces per puzzle. You can write, draw, or glue pictures on the puzzle to make it suitable for use with any Jewish subject. Here are a few ideas:

QUIZ GAME

Create a list of questions, one for each puzzle piece. Place a picture related to your unit of study on a puzzle. Laminate, then cut out. If you have a large class and will need to work in two groups, make two puzzles. Divide the class into two groups. Each child who answers a question correctly receives a piece to add to the puzzle. The group that completes a puzzle first will have a picture that will also provide another learning experience. You can then talk about the picture and what it means.

GETTING ACQUAINTED

This is a good opening-day activity. Put a quotation or picture on a puzzle. Be sure you have at least one puzzle piece per child. Laminate and then cut out. As the children enter the classroom, give each of them one or two pieces of the puzzle. When all the children have arrived, have them put the puzzle together. While engaged in putting the puzzle together they will also be getting acquainted.

A MISSING PIECE

Create a puzzle using a quotation, Jewish symbol, logo, or picture. Hand out all the pieces except one. Have the children put the puzzle together, then talk about the missing piece and what it represents. Depending on your unit of study, it could represent Jews who are still not free to be Jewish, the six million lost in the Holocaust, etc.

Puzzle Story

Divide the class into two small groups. Prepare in advance a puzzle for each group. Use pictures which have something to do with your unit of study. Laminate. Cut into pieces corresponding to the number of children in each group. Put all the puzzle pieces together in a box and have each child take one.

The children are then to circulate to find others with matching puzzle pieces. They must do this without talking! Once their puzzle is completed, they may talk. The members of each group are to make up a story relating to the picture they have formed with their puzzle. One member of each group is to be the storyteller and tell the story to the whole class.

Puzzle Folder

Put three pockets on the left side of a manila file folder. Put the instructions on the right inside. If the children cannot read, tell them how and what to do. Cover the folder with clear contact paper and slit the pocket openings. Make simple three-part puzzles using oaktag. For example: You want to reinforce the Sabbath, using some of the symbols. The three puzzles you make might be: challah, candlesticks and candles, Kiddush cup and wine. Cut out the pictures to be used, glue to card stock, cover with clear contact paper or laminate. Cut each picture into three small puzzle pieces that fit into the pockets you made in the folder. Mix the pieces up and place them in the folder pockets. Instruct the children to remove the puzzle pieces and match them. Remember, only the correct answers will fit together.

Jewish Parenting Ideas

Several years ago, I attended a meeting in New York of UAHC consultants. One of the activities at the meeting was to make a list of ideas and activities for infants and toddlers to provide new and stimulating ideas for Jewish parenting groups. Here is the list we compiled. Take a good look at it and you will find ways to involve the children in your class.

Write a naming ceremony.

Encourage the creation of family rituals.

Establish daily Jewish routines.

Associate the Jewish year with the cycle of nature.

Create Jewish rituals for the child's birthday.

Get together with other families for Shabbat and sing zemirot.

Develop a set of rituals: highlight the tzedakah box, candle lighting, Kiddush.

Have the child hold the challah when the Motzi is recited.

Bathing: select Jewish bath toys.

Sing Hebrew songs and point to the child's body parts in Hebrew.

Sing the Shema with the child at bedtime.

Rock the child, singing Jewish lullabies.

Read Jewish stories and poems at bedtime.

Play Jewish musical tapes at playtime.

Adapt nursery rhymes to include a Jewish theme.

Create Jewish sound effects equivalent to "what does a cow say?"

Color plastic tablecloths for Shabbat.

Hang Jewish pictures on the child's bedroom wall.

Create building blocks with Jewish symbols or Hebrew letters.

Fill a pail with Jewish items to take out and put back in.

Use Jewish-symbol molds for sandbox play (cookie cutters).

Make stuffed Hebrew letters, ritual objects, and symbols, and other Jewish soft toys.

DRAMA AND STORYTELLING

A Picture Story

Display a picture, based on your unit of study, that tells a story and includes several different people and objects. With the children, discuss the objects and the role or roles they play in the picture. Lead the children into developing the story that the picture is telling them. Make notes as they develop the story. When you have elicited as much as you can from the children, tell the real story of the picture, then let them compare your story with the one they developed.

Reading Pictures

Provide a number of pictures based on your unit of study. Let each child choose a picture to talk about. Ask the children to tell what they see or "read" in the picture. What story is the picture telling? Help them as necessary to make sure that they learn your lesson for the day.

Provide a sentence strip for each child. Help the children to write sentences about their pictures. Let them "read" their sentences, then post the pictures with their sentences around the room.

Acting Out a Story

Take a story the children have heard and like. Encourage them to create a play from their favorite story. Talk about what they need to do: how they can begin, what costumes and props will be needed, etc. Give clues or ask questions that provide some direction. Help them to create or obtain any needed props. Give them time for rehearsals, then decide on a date and time for their presentation. Invite parents to attend. Before the production, have the class make a large banner to announce the production. You might even ask a parent to make a video of the play.

ALTERNATIVE

Acting out stories is fun. After a story is told, ask for volunteers from the class to act it out. Give them parts, all verbal, and an opportunity to practice, then put on their play.

Box of Stories

On large index cards prepare sets of three or four pictures which the children can use to tell a story. The pictures should be related to your unit of study, with people, symbols, ritual objects, trees, flowers, etc. Mount each picture on a card, and put each set of three or four pictures in a box or an envelope. Divide the class into small groups. Give a different set of pictures to each group. Encourage the group members to use their creative imaginations to develop a story based on the pictures you have given them. Allow some time for creative work, then have each group make its presentation.

What Do You See?

Talk to the children about how, when we hear a story, we often imagine or "see" pictures in our mind of what is taking place. Ask the children to close their eyes, listen carefully, and "see" what they can see as the story is told. Then read a short story. After the reading, have the children describe what they "saw" with as much detail as possible. Ask them to draw pictures of what they "saw." Read the story again while the children share their drawings.

Action Stories

Remember how the children shake their graggers whenever Haman's name is said during the reading of the Purim story? Well, the same method can be used with just about any story. Once, for instance, while relating the story of Chanukah, I told the children that I needed their help. I asked that whenever I said the word *Maccabee*, they were to clap and cry "yeh" as loud as they could. When I said the word *Syrians*, they were to stamp their feet and yell "boo" as loud as they could. They really got into the story and had a good time as I told it, and they added the sound effects just as I had asked.

So any story will do; but before you begin, go over the noises, motions, etc., that you want the children to make and when they are to make them.

Ways to Use Pictures for Storytelling

Did you ever listen to the little ones playing? They may be playing house or school, but they are really telling stories. They love to tell stories, and with a little encouragement from the teacher they can tell stories in class. To make visual "story starters," you will need to cut out or copy pictures from magazines and workbooks. Use pictures related to your unit of study. Glue them to card stock of an appropriate size. Laminate if you want to use them over and over again. Here are a few things you can do with story starters:

1. Take one card and show it to the children, then tell a short story based on what is in the picture. This will give the kids an idea of what is expected of them. Distribute cards to all of the children and invite them to tell the stories they see in the pictures. Make sure that everyone who wants to participate is given a chance.

2. Divide the class into small groups. Select several picture cards and put them in a plastic sandwich bag. They can be grouped by theme or subjects which you have discussed with the children. Give the group members time to create their stories, talking together about what they are going to say. Have each group tell its story. You might consider recording the stories so they can be played back for parents at a later date.

Brainteasers—Riddles

Have a few minutes left? Don't waste them. Here is an idea which can be used for any subject matter. Just prepare some riddles in advance and have them ready to use anytime you need to fill a "space." Make up at least 15 or 20 short teasers or riddles like this:

It hops, skips and jumps,
It's damp and full of lumps,
It filled the land of Egypt
With awful groans and grumps.
What was it?

Children have fun with these, and you can even let them create their own riddles to stump their classmates.

NEAT AND SIMPLE

Charades

Prepare large index cards with pictures related to your unit of study. Divide the class into two teams. The players select a picture card from a face-down pile, then take turns acting out what the picture is "saying" for the opposing team to guess.

Simple Hebrew Words

Help the children learn some simple Hebrew words. Instead of using English for everyday things, sprinkle your vocabulary with a few words of Hebrew. This way, the children will become familiar with some Hebrew words and you are helping to build their Hebrew vocabularies.

When you use a Hebrew word, say it in Hebrew and then define it in English, to make sure the children understand what it means. Introduce just one or two words during a lesson and repeat them often so that they become familiar. Before you know it, the class will feel very comfortable using these words. Some appropriate words include:

shalom—peace.

tov me'od—very good.

shalom bayit—peaceful home.

kol hakavod—I'm proud of you.

tov—good.

Am Yisrael—the people of Israel.

Hebrew Train

Make railroad engines out of construction paper for everyone in the class. Write the children's names on the engines and mount them on the bulletin board. Prepare a good number of train cars out of construction paper, using many different colors. Whenever a child learns a Hebrew word, write it on a train car and add the car to the child's engine. Keep the trains posted during the year, and at the end of the year let the children take them home.

Research Projects

With a little direction, especially for the younger ones, our children can become life-long inquirers. Divide the class into small groups, distribute a list of topics based on your unit of study, and let each group choose its own topic. Allowing choice is important, because the children are more likely to follow through on a project if they are working on something they are interested in. Arrange for the class to have some time in the library, and ask the librarian to suggest a list of books the children can use for their research.

After the children have gathered as much information as they can on their topics, each group is to create a book for the whole class to read. The books are to identify the most important facts the group members have discovered. Have them write this information on plain white paper, two or three sentences to a page. Encourage the children to enhance the material by illustrating the pages. Each group is also to design a cover and a title page, listing the names of the authors, for its book. Once the groups have compiled their books, they are to share their work with the whole class.

Streamers of Knowledge

Streamers of Knowledge can be hung from a wire or string which has been extended across a wall of the classroom. The streamers can be made of extra-wide paper ribbon on which you have placed a laminated picture of a child and the child's name. You will need streamers for every child in the class (laminated because they have to last the entire year). Whenever a child achieves a specific goal or learns a new Jewish skill, a symbol representing that goal or skill can be cut out and glued to the streamer. When parents bring their children to school, they can quickly see what their child has mastered. At the end of the year, the children can take their Streamers of Knowledge home.

Matching Pairs: A Bulletin Board

Place a colorful background on your bulletin board. If you don't have a bulletin board in your classroom, use a large fiber board of the type that older students use for projects and create your own bulletin board space.

1. Cut out Jewish stars, shofars, or any Jewish symbols large enough to either write on or mount pictures on.
2. On each pair of symbols write the names of corresponding words, or mount pictures that correspond or relate to your unit of study. For Shabbat use pairs (e.g., candles/candlesticks, Kiddush/cup, challah/challah cover, Havdalah/candle, spices/ruach).
3. Scatter the symbols around on the board.
4. Have the children match the pairs and put the correct symbols, words, or pictures together. As they put them together, they can tell how they are used, what they are for, and even say a blessing if it applies.
5. Then ask the children to think of other pairs or find pictures of other pairs to make their own matching pairs. Scatter these on the board, and have their classmates place them together.

Mystery Picture

Use pictures from old holiday greeting cards, workbooks, Jewish magazines, etc., that go with your unit of study. It is easier to use larger pictures for this activity, so enlarge your pictures if necessary. Mount pictures on tagboard and cut construction paper the size of the picture. Cut 1-inch squares out of the construction paper in various areas of the picture. Using paperclips, fasten the construction paper, with the cutouts, over the picture. Prepare a number of Mystery Pictures and place them around the room. Ask the children to study what they can see of the picture, then try to guess what the picture is about. Give them some clues if you wish. When they guess right, take the construction paper off the picture. If there is a picture they cannot guess, enlarge one square at a time to give them more clues.

End of the School Year: A Mural of the Year's Activities

The children can summarize their year of study with a giant mural. To begin, brainstorm with them, making a list of all the activities, special events, projects, and subject matter they covered each month.

Take a large piece of white butcher or art paper and place it on the floor. Divide the paper into nine or ten sections (the number of months your class met during the year). Divide the class into small groups. Assign each group a month and ask the members to draw pictures of what the class covered during that month. You may have to give some groups two months to cover, which is okay because you do not have to finish this mural in one day. Hang the completed mural in the classroom or school hallway so that everyone can admire the children's work.

INTERMEDIATE GRADES

Youngsters in the intermediate age group begin to be a challenge! They are still eager to learn, but the teacher has to be more creative and diversified in developing lessons and activities.

This chapter provides a variety of lesson possibilities in a myriad of subject areas. Some are for specific subject matter, while others are generic and can be used for just about any topic. Almost all of the teaching ideas can be easily adapted to children of any age within this group.

OPENING DAY ACTIVITIES

Before School Begins

Send everyone in the class a letter of welcome. Introduce yourself, and tell about your hobbies, pets, family, etc. Give a brief overview of the course and indicate the room in which the class will be meeting. Include a lunch bag with the recipient's name on it. Ask the students to fill the bag with items that describe their Jewish selves, including photos and artifacts of their Jewish life of any kind that will fit in the bag. They are to bring the bags to class on opening day. The first day of school, they will introduce themselves to their classmates and explain the significance of the objects in their bags.

Getting Acquainted

Prepare "Getting to Know You" sheets for everyone in the class. The sheets could look something like this:

Find someone who likes the Sabbath.

Name _____

Find someone who appreciates good music.

Name _____

Find someone who likes religious school.

Name _____

Find someone who likes Chanukah.

Name _____

Put as many statements on the list as there are pupils in the class. The youngsters are to mingle with one other, introduce themselves to anyone who looks likely to fill one of the slots, and then write the person's name down, continuing in this manner until the list is completed.

Who Am I?

Have the students draw self-portraits on 9 x 12 drawing paper. Then, with construction paper, they are to create disguises (e.g., moustaches, beards, thick eyebrows) and glue them atop their portraits. Next tell them to print nouns that begin with each letter of their name randomly around the paper, as well as at least three more words that are not nouns. Collect the papers and redistribute them, making sure the recipients do not get their own papers. Everyone must now identify the disguised student on the paper just received; this can be done by crossing off the words that are not nouns and, using the first letters of the nouns, constructing the name.

Write a Riddle

Have the students write riddles about themselves. The riddles should include clues about their physical characteristics, hobbies, etc. They are to draw illustrations around the riddle and sign their names on the back of the paper. Collect the riddles and redistribute them, making sure the recipients do not get their own riddles back. Each student, in turn, reads a riddle aloud, and the class tries to identify the person to whom it pertains.

Numbers of the Stars

Draw a large Jewish star on the board, or make a large star out of poster-board and laminate. Pick a number that has meaning for you, such as the number of years you have been teaching, the number of members in your family, the number of children you have, your birthdate, etc. Write it in the center of the star. The students are to try to discover the significance of the number by asking questions like: Does it represent distance? Is it related to your family?

When the class has the answer, ask whether your number has any personal significance for anyone else. Allow time for responses. Then give the students an opportunity to do the same thing. Continue until everyone has had a chance to place a number in the star.

A Getting-Acquainted Puzzle

On posterboard, draw a picture or write a quotation that has something to do with your unit of study. Use a black marker to section off pieces for a puzzle, then cut up the puzzle on the black lines. You will need one puzzle piece for each student and one for yourself. Give the students their puzzle pieces as they arrive for class. Ask them to work together to complete the puzzle. Put your piece in last. Once the puzzle is assembled, make sure everyone knows everyone else's name, then discuss the picture or quotation you used for the puzzle.

Options for Opening Day Activities

Here are some activities to be done in class on opening day:

Draw a picture of something Jewish you did this summer.

Write a poem about a Jewish summer activity in which you took part.

Write a story about a new Jewish person you met this summer.

Make a collage that tells about some of your Jewish summer activities.

If any students say they did nothing Jewish this summer, ask them to write about or draw a Jewish activity they would have liked to have done.

Name Sheets

There are plenty of name games, but this one is a little different. Prepare a name sheet with outlines of different Jewish symbols (e.g., Star of David, shofar, lulav/etrog, menorah, chanukiot). For each Jewish symbol give the students different instructions. For example:

Star of David: Write the names of those who have blond hair (in the class).

Shofar: Write the names of those with brown hair.

Menorah: Write the names of those with blue eyes.

Lulav/etrog: Write the names of those with brown eyes.

Chanukiot: Write the names of the girls on four branches, the names of the boys on four branches.

This can go on and on, using many different ways to write the names of everyone in the class.

Interviews

You will need 3 x 5 index cards, a box, and an interview form for everyone in the class. Have the students write their names on the index cards and decorate them with their favorite Jewish symbols. Place all the cards in a box.

Prepare an interview form including such things as name, a new friend's name, siblings' names and ages, pets, favorite Jewish holiday, Jewish books you have read, what you do well, hobbies, favorite Jewish song, etc.

Each student picks a name card from the box. Those who draw their own names are to put them back and draw another one. Using the interview form, the students interview the classmates whose cards they drew. When the interviews are complete, have the students introduce and tell about their new friends.

Letter of Introduction

Having youngsters write letters of introduction to someone they do not know is a good way to get them to describe themselves thoroughly. Ask them to tell all about themselves, so that the recipient will know "the real you." Remind them to include physical descriptions, hobbies, family, school and activities, sports they like, pets, favorite Jewish holidays and events, and anything else that is important to them. Upon completion, have the students exchange letters several times till they know more about one other. Or collect the letters and read them aloud, without giving the writers' names. The class is to guess whom each letter is describing.

Billboard Ad

Use this one for an opening day activity when you have a group whose members don't know each other very well. You will need colored markers, construction paper, magazines, scissors, and glue.

Explain to the youngsters that they are to create billboard ads advertising who they are, what they do well, and what their many talents and abilities are. Ask them to think of jingles, slogans, and commercial ads for the billboards. They can either draw pictures or cut pictures out of magazines for their ads.

Upon completion, have your students share their personal ads. Post them on the bulletin board or on a large sheet of butcher paper mounted on the wall. You can use the ads as a border, then add class events and achievements as you go through the school year.

Polaroid Pictures

Here are a few ways to use a Polaroid camera on opening day:

1. Take closeup pictures of the pupils as they arrive. Have them glue the pictures in the center of a sheet of paper. Around the picture, they are to draw the members of their family; yes, they can include pets. When they have completed the work, make a bulletin board of all the pictures, headed: "This Is Our Great Class!"

2. Prepare a large map of the community and put it on the bulletin board. Take pictures of the pupils as they arrive. One at a time, have them locate their homes on the map and fasten their pictures there. They are to introduce themselves as they place their pictures near their home sites.

3. Prepare a Jewish symbol large enough to hold a picture in the center. Fasten a string or piece of yarn across a portion of the wall or on the bulletin board. Have the youngsters introduce themselves, then hang their pictures on the string with a clothes pin or paperclip. The pictures can be used for roll call: when the youngsters arrive they take their pictures off the line and place them on your desk.

NEAT AND SIMPLE

"My Name Is…" Bulletin Board

Mount a large piece of butcher paper or colored art paper on the wall or bulletin board. Sign in with the name you want the students to use and draw a picture of something Jewish you like to do. As the students arrive, they are to do the same thing on a section of the paper.

"The Jewish Me" Bulletin Board

Cover the bulletin board with bright paper. Make an attractive sign saying "The Jewish Me" and place it at the top. Prepare sheets of paper with large talk balloons of the sort found in comic strips. Copy and give one to each student. Tell the students to place their names somewhere in the balloons, then think of one thing that describes "The Jewish Me." On their balloons, they are to write a short sentence which describes who they are as a Jew. Let the students introduce themselves, one at a time, then place their balloons on the bulletin board.

License Plates Bulletin Board

Bring in several old license plates, from different states if possible. Show these to the class so that everyone can see what designs and information the license plates contain (name of state, county indicator, a picture/slogan/logo, numbers, etc.). Give each student a piece of tagboard cut to the size of a license plate. Ask the students to design license plates that will represent them as Jewish students. They can write, draw, cut out pictures, even make their plates three-dimensional. Have the students place their personal license plates on their desks with two-way carpet tape or hang them on a license plate bulletin board after introducing themselves.

A Self-Collage

Have the students describe themselves in collages made on sheets of 9 x 12 colored construction paper, using words, logos, and pictures. Suggest that they include such things as favorite Jewish holiday, last Jewish celebration, and Hebrew name. They can cut pictures from magazines or draw their own, write poems, create logos, etc. Upon completion, combine all the collages to make a bulletin board.

JEWISH HOLIDAYS
Shabbat

ELEMENTS OF SABBATH

After learning about the three different elements of the Sabbath—menuchah, oneg, and kedushah—ask the students to choose the one they like the best, the one which is their favorite. Have lots of magazines, scissors, glue, and construction paper ready. Ask them to make collages explaining why the chosen element is special. Share the collages with the class, then post around the room.

BLESSINGS

Parents traditionally bless their children before Friday night dinner. Go over the blessing with the class. Ask the students to write a text with which they can bless their parents on Friday nights after their parents have blessed them.

SHABBAT IS SPECIAL

Tell the students they have been hired by a Jewish publishing firm to run an advertising campaign promoting Shabbat observance. They are to create ads for this purpose, using logos, slogans, jingles, songs, fliers, posters, bumper stickers, and the like to convey their message. They can also use a radio or TV format. You can even make arrangements to let them do their "sell" throughout the congregation.

JEWISH SABBATH AND CHRISTIAN SABBATH

After the class has researched the differences between the Jewish and Christian Sabbaths, ask the students to write letters to the editor of the local newspaper describing the differences between the two Sabbaths: how each is celebrated, when and where, symbols, related food, prayers, etc.

SHABBAT KITS

Here is a project in which the students will not only learn about the Sabbath, but will be performing a mitzvah. It will take more than one session to complete, but is worth the time. Provide one shoebox for everyone in the class. Have the students cover their boxes with contact or construction paper and decorate them with Jewish symbols.

Next each student is to make the following:

Candlesticks (made from hardened and painted clay or from small glasses into which they glue candleholders bought at a candle shop and then decorated as desired).

Challah cover (use a large white handkerchief decorated as desired).

Kiddush cup (decorate a small plastic glass as desired).

Do some brainstorming with the class to make a list of what information families need in order to celebrate the Sabbath. Divide the class into small groups and assign each a specific area for which to write instructions on how to celebrate the Sabbath. Include all the blessings, in Hebrew, transliteration, and English; maybe even a recipe or two. The group members are to compile this information attractively and make it into a little "Shabbat manual." Have them wrap the different articles for the Shabbat Kit in white tissue paper and place in the decorated Shabbat box, along with the booklet and a letter to parents about the project. The Shabbat Kits can be taken home or can be given to new "Jews by Choice" as a gift at the time of their conversion.

A Shabbat Experience

You will need an 8-foot-long table, or two tables if you have a large class. Cover the table with white butcher paper. Have crayons or colored markers for everyone. The students will be setting a Shabbat table with them.

First have the students draw their own place settings. Next assign each youngster one aspect of the Sabbath table to draw (e.g., candles, challot, Kiddush cup, flowers, special foods). Interrupt the drawing activity from time to time for the class to sing a Shabbat song, learn the blessings, discuss Shabbat values, or listen to a Shabbat story. When the table is completed, have the students welcome Shabbat by reciting the appropriate blessings over the candles, wine, challah, and a special blessing for the welfare of the class, the Jewish people, and those less fortunate.

In addition, consider inviting parents to join in the experience. If any of the students are part of a "blended" family or have one non-Jewish parent, this would provide a nonthreatening educational experience for all the family members.

As a closure, offer a tasty food with sweet fragrances to symbolize what we can experience on the Sabbath.

High Holy Days

Rosh Hashanah and Yom Kippur: The "Good" and "Evil" Times

You will need a lot of current newspapers, blank paper, scissors, and glue. Divide the class into small groups. Have the youngsters go through the newspapers and find at least four stories about something evil/bad. They are to cut the stories out and paste them on the blank paper, then write short stories about something they did during the past year that was wrong; these are to be added to the stories from the newspapers. Have the groups share their findings. Collect the sheets and bind them together to make a newspaper, to be called "The Evil Times" or something similar.

Now ask the groups to go through the papers and find at least four stories about good things. This time the group members are to write personal stories about something good they did during the past year and add them to the newspaper stories. Again the groups are to share their stories with the whole class. Collect and bind these stories also, making a newspaper called, say, "The Good Times."

Talk with the students about: What was easy to do and what was difficult? What made it easy? What made it more difficult? (Unfortunately, you will find that the easiest thing to do was to find the evil stories.) As a closure, ask the students to think of one thing they could do to make more "good times." List their ideas, and in the next few weeks keep track of who has done that one thing.

GOOD AND BAD PICTURES

You will need magazines, scissors, glue, and 9 x 12 construction paper, folded in half.

Talk about Rosh Hashanah and Yom Kippur as the time to make amends for any wrongs committed during the past year. Elicit from the students some of the things they have done that were wrong—not the easiest thing to do, but some of them may be honest, especially if you lead the way by admitting a wrong you have committed. Ask the students to go through the magazines and find two pictures: one representing something bad/evil someone did, the other representing something good that could overcome the bad. They are to glue one picture on the top half of their papers and the other on the bottom half, then share their findings with the class.

Talk with the students about: What was most consistently done wrong? What different ways have they discovered to correct or overcome the wrong done? As a closure, have the students decide upon one thing they could do to avoid the wrong committed.

HIGH HOLY DAY CARDS

Planning on having your students make Rosh Hashanah cards this year? Try this for a change: Cut a sponge into the desired shape (e.g., Star of David, menorah, shofar, apple and honey jar). Dip it in poster paint and press to make designs on a sheet of paper. Then students can write their messages within the design.

JONAH AND THE WHALE MAZE

Each year, on Yom Kippur, we read the story of Jonah and the whale. Before you read or tell the story in class, create a picture of a large whale with a maze inside its body. The mouth is the opening where Jonah will enter, and also the place where he will leave the whale. Tell the story of Jonah; when it is time for him to be swallowed by the whale—stop! Give the students time to put Jonah inside the whale and move around the maze a little. Continue the story, but at the point where Jonah prays to God—stop! Let the students find a way for Jonah to get out of the whale. Then finish the story.

Chanukah

CHANUKAH GIFTS

If you get as many mail order catalogues as I do, you have a wonderful source for a fun activity. Cut out pictures of gifts students could give someone they love for Chanukah. Paste the pictures on small index cards. In addition, prepare some cards which state an action students could take as a way of giving of themselves to someone they love. Laminate or cover with clear contact paper. Take a file folder and place a library pocket on one side and the instructions on the other side. Put the "gifts" in the pocket. Be sure to include one or two "giving of oneself" cards in each pocket. The instructions could look something like this:

1. Select a gift from the pocket.
2. Write about: What made you select this gift? Who is it for? What do you think it would mean to this person? How do you feel about giving this gift?

Prepare gift files for everyone in class. Tell the students what they are to do. Upon completion, have them share their choices and their responses. Talk about giving: What is more important, the gift or the thought behind the gift?

Tu Bishvat

A TREE BULLETIN BOARD

Begin by reading Shel Silverstein's *The Giving Tree.* Discuss for what and how we use trees. What do trees do for us, and what can we do for trees? What kinds of trees are mentioned in the Bible? (See Deuteronomy 20:19–20, Genesis 2:9, 21:33, 35:4 for some examples.) Students can also research to learn about the trees mentioned in the Bible and about our responsibility to preserve what God has created. There is a great midrash about an old man who was planting a carob tree by the side of a road. Now the carob is a very slow growing tree, and it takes a long time for it to bear fruit. A passerby saw what the old man was doing and asked him why he was planting the tree, since he probably would not be around when it finally bore fruit. The old man said, "Someone planted trees for me to enjoy, and I'm planting this tree for others to enjoy."

Once the students have gathered the needed information, it is time to create the bulletin board. You will need colored construction paper, crayons and colored markers, white paper, scissors, pencils, colored yarn, background for the board, and a tree trunk made from brown construction paper.

Place the tree trunk on the background paper. Have outlines of different kinds of leaves available for the students to use as guides in cutting out leaf shapes. On each leaf, students draw a small symbol picture of the benefits we derive from trees. If the tree is found in the Bible, write the book, chapter, and verse number on the leaf. Place the leaves on the trunk and branches of the tree in an attractive manner. Students then prepare index cards telling how we can preserve trees and make sure there are plenty of them for future generations. On each side of the tree, arrange the index cards, attaching colored pieces of yarn from one index card to an appropriate leaf.

Other Activities

TREES FOR ISRAEL

Have the class organize a fund-raising campaign to purchase trees for Israel through the Jewish National Fund. One idea would be to have a walkathon around the synagogue. Youngsters sign up parents, friends, and relatives to pay a certain amount of money for each time they walk around the building.

TREE COLLAGE

What are all the different ways we benefit from trees? Use the bulletin board to make a giant collage of pictures of benefits derived from trees. Before beginning the collage, do some brainstorming, making a list of everything we get from trees. Then have the class cut out and draw pictures for the collage.

PROTECTING TREES

How can we save and protect trees? Do some brainstorming, listing all the different ways we can save and protect our trees. Then have the class design posters showing how we can protect our trees, and why we should do so. Post the finished products around the building.

Purim

WHO SAID IT?

Prepare a list of quotations from the story of Esther, the Megillah. Use quotations from all of the main characters: King Ahasuerus, Haman, Esther, and Mordecai. Place each quotation on an index card.

Prepare a posterboard or the bulletin board with four pockets, or more if you have quotations from more than four characters. Library pockets will hold a 3 x 5 index card. Label each pocket with the name of one of the characters in the story. Divide the class into small groups. Give each group a different set of quotations. The group members are to identify who said each quotation and place the card in the appropriate pocket. If they do not know who said it, they are to look up the quotation in the text to find out.

BE CREATIVE—USE YOUR IMAGINATION

By now the youngsters are familiar enough with the story of Purim for you to do a fun activity like this one. Gather together an assortment of "found" objects (e.g., tops of aerosol cans, empty plastic containers, paper-clips, rubber bands, string, yarn, flexible wire, popsicle sticks, nuts, bolts, screws, dried beans, scraps of cloth). Make sure there are enough materials to provide each group of students with a wide variety of objects to work with. Divide the class into small groups. Remind the students of the rules of brainstorming. Their task is to use the objects to make something that can be used for Purim. Then let their imaginations go to work! Give them enough time to complete the project. Let them show off their creation and tell how it can be used for Purim.

NEAT AND SIMPLE

STOMP ON HAMAN

Write the name *Haman* on the bottom of the students' shoes with chalk. Explain that when they go to hear the Megillah reading, they can erase Haman's name by stamping on the floor.

SHALACH MANOT BASKETS

Take a thin paper plate and fold it in the shape of a triangle. Staple, leaving the top open. Cut out a handle from construction paper and staple it across the top. Put a napkin inside and fill it with hamantashen, cookies, nuts, candy, and fruit. Make as many as you can for friends, teachers, and relatives. Or make them for the local Jewish home for the aged and arrange for the class to deliver them. The children could even dress up in their Purim costumes when they deliver the shalach manot baskets.

ANOTHER OPTION

According to tradition, Mordecai told the Jews to make Purim "days of sending portions one to another and gifts to the poor" (Esther 9:22). In that spirit, a nice classroom activity is making gifts for the poor. Get the parents involved by asking them to send in at least two cans of food: tuna fish, vegetables, fruit, hard candy. In addition, maybe someone would be willing to make hamantashen, or perhaps you can let the kids make them. (Simple and easy-to-make hamantashen can be prepared from the ready-made cookie dough available in most supermarkets.) The food can be placed in baskets or paper plates which the children have decorated and then wrapped in foil or plastic wrap. Plastic freezer bags are also good containers. These too can be decorated. Get some parents to take the children to the local food bank to deliver the gifts.

WRITE A DIARY

Have the students choose their favorite Purim characters and write a diary entry entitled "Three Days in the Life of _____." Upon completion, they share their diaries with the class.

THE BANQUETS

The Book of Esther describes four different banquets. Ask the class to read about each banquet and make a chart which includes the following:

The purpose of each banquet.

The people who attended each banquet.

Was the purpose of the banquet achieved?

What foods were served at each banquet? (This is not mentioned in the Bible, so the answers will be based on their imaginations.)

CREATE A NEWSPAPER

Ask the students to choose their favorite characters in the Book of Esther and decide on a name for the newspaper they will create, something like *The Shushan Times*. Tell them they have been granted exclusive interviews with their favorite characters and have them develop a list of questions to ask. Using these questions, they are to write stories based on the interviews. When the stories are completed, put together an issue of *The Shushan Times* and share with the whole class.

TELL A STORY

Using a topic selected from the list given below, students are to write a story based on the Book of Esther.

The most important moment in the story.

A seemingly minor incident that turned out to be important.

Their favorite part of the story and the reasons why.

The part they don't like and the reasons why.

Have the students share their stories with the whole class.

SEND ESTHER A TELEGRAM

Esther needs urging to go to the king to plead for her people. The students are to send telegrams giving reasons why she should go to the king. As telegrams, the messages are to consist of 25 words or less and begin with the words "I urge you to _____." Students share their telegrams with the class.

SPOTLIGHT THE STARS OF PURIM

Divide the class into small groups. Let each group choose one character from the Purim story, or assign each group a character. The group members are to write down everything they know, or imagine, about their character. Give each group a posterboard and colored markers. The members are to create a poster that tells everything they know or imagine. They can draw pictures, write bios, jingles, etc. Upon completion, the groups display their posters and tell about their characters.

PURIM COLLAGE

Here are some ways to begin this activity. Choose the one that best suits your class.

1. Tell the story of Purim.
2. Read a picture story of Purim, showing the pictures as you read.
3. Have the class do a round robin, each child in turn telling the story of Purim.
4. Have students choose parts and act out the story of Purim.

After the story, talk about what can be learned from it. What were Esther's strengths? Mordecai's? Provide a variety of arts and crafts materials, including magazines, scissors, glue or paste, facial tissues, tissue paper, foil, yarn, cotton balls, large pieces of colored construction paper, and colored markers or crayons. Each student is to make a Purim collage which represents the meaning of Purim today. Upon completion, the students explain what the collages represent, then hang them on the wall.

A Class Megillah

Make your own class Megillah! Tell the story of Purim. Assign different scenes from the story to the students. There are two options:

Option 1

Using 8.5 x 11 sheets of white or colored paper, give everyone in the class a sheet with a different portion of the Purim story printed on it. The students illustrate their pages, then take all the pages and tape them together in the right order. Tape or staple one end to a dowel and roll the taped papers around it. Your class now has its own Megillah.

Option 2

Take a roll of large white paper and roll it out on the floor. Have the students gather around the paper, each at a different assigned space. Staying within their assigned areas, the students draw scenes representing their portions of the story. Under their drawings, they explain what is happening in the drawings in a few sentences. When they have finished, place a dowel large enough to fit the paper at the end of the story and roll up (so that the beginning of the story starts when it is rolled out). Just another way to create your own class Megillah.

Pesach

The Four Cups of Wine

According to tradition, the four cups of wine we drink during the seder symbolize the four stages in the process of redemption mentioned in Exodus 6:6–7. The fifth cup of wine represents a wish for the future and is called Elijah's cup. Ask the students to list the biblical phrases associated with the various cups of wine. Take a very large piece of white butcher or art paper and mark it off in five large sections. Divide the class into five groups and assign each a section of the paper and one of the phrases. Each group, working in its assigned area, is to create a mural which explains the meaning of its phrase. Upon completion, display the mural in the school hallway for everyone to see.

Yom Ha'atzmaut

GO FLY A KITE!

Celebrate the birth of the State of Israel by making streamer kites and taking the class outside to fly them! For each kite you will need a sturdy paper plate (not plastic coated), 3 feet of yarn or string, cellophane tape, and six strips of 2 x 3 crepe paper. You will also need enough tempera paint and brushes or colored markers, glue, and yarn needles for everyone in the class.

To make the kite: Paint or draw designs on the top surface of the paper plates, using Jewish symbols, Israel flags, etc. Place a 2-inch piece of tape in the middle of the back of each plate. Punch a small hole, with a yarn needle, on either side of the tape. Thread the yarn, or string, beginning at the top of the plate, going around the tape on the back, and coming through to the top. Tie a knot, but not too close to the plate. Glue the streamers around the rim of the plate. Do not use too much glue. When both the glue and the weather are dry, go fly a kite!

Ideas for Any Holiday

WALL-HANGING COLLAGE

By the intermediate grades, the youngsters already know quite a bit about the Jewish holidays. Sometimes it is nice to let them express how they feel about the holidays. How do they feel about what they do on a specific holiday? For this activity you will need large butcher paper or burlap (if burlap is used, you will need wooden dowels for each end) plus all kinds of arts and crafts materials: scraps of felt, ribbon, yarn, foil, construction paper, pipe cleaners, popsicle sticks, flowers, tissue paper, magazines, markers and crayons.

Talk about the holiday. Let the students express what it means to them, and share some of your own ideas about the holiday; identify the different concepts and values associated with it. Ask how they feel about these ideas. Give them blank scrap paper to design a symbol to place on the wall hanging which represents what they feel is the essence of the holiday. Once they have their symbol designs, let them go to work creating the class wall hanging. To do so, they make their symbols out of the crafts materials and mount them on the wall hanging. When all the students have placed their symbols on the wall hanging, ask them to explain the symbols and what they mean.

A REVIEW OF THE HOLIDAYS

Get some large paper plates or 10- to 12-inch cardboard cake plates (from a bakery). Gather pictures of holiday symbols and ritual objects. Copy, cut out, and arrange the pictures for a holiday on a paper plate. Write the name of the holiday on the other side. Laminate. Cut into puzzle pieces. Do a number of the holidays in this manner. Put the pieces for several holiday puzzles in a plastic freezer bag. Divide the class into small groups. Give each group a plastic bag of puzzles. The group members are to put the puzzles together to identify the holiday.

CREATE TV COMMERCIALS

You will need either real ritual objects and symbols or pictures of them. If you use pictures, mount them on small index cards and laminate. Take file folders and put library pockets inside. Put at least three ritual objects/symbols or three pictures in the pockets. On the other side of the folder, place the instructions, which could look something like this:

1. Choose a partner.
2. Together with your partner choose one item from the pocket and think of three reasons why Jews would want to buy it.
3. Create a TV commercial that tells what is special about your item and why Jews would need to purchase it.
4. Choose one more item and repeat the process.
5. Share your TV commercials with the class.

If you use the real thing, display the ritual objects on a table. Assign one object to each pair of students.

ACROSTIC PLAY

Have the students head their papers with Rosh Hashanah written horizontally and vertically. On the vertical list they are to write one word, or a short sentence, beginning with each first letter, that describes the topic. If the topic has more than one word, they skip a line when placing the letters vertically. For example, a page could look something like this:

Rosh Hashanah
Raises our aspirations.
Opens our minds.
Spend time in worship.
Hope is created anew.

Haven for our deeds.
A chance to begin again.
Season of repentance.
Honey and apples to make life sweet.
Attentive to our laws.
None shall be afraid.
A salute to life.
High Holy Days.

MISSING LETTERS

Instead of giving the class a list of holiday words with which everyone should be familiar, distribute a list of words with letters missing. The students are to complete the words by placing the correct letters in the blank spaces. Then they do one of the following:

Write a short story using all the words.

Create a poster expressing the use of the words.

Write a poem using all the words.

Write a song using all the words.

For example, if you were reviewing Shabbat, your list could be:

C__ll_h

Ha_d_ll_h

-a_dl_s

-h-l_nt

K_ _d_s_

O_ _g S_a_b_t

HOLIDAY MATCH-UP

Gather enough shoeboxes for everyone in the class. Cover with colorful contact paper and label the boxes "Holiday Sets." Then gather pictures of holiday ritual objects, foods, and symbols. Do not limit it to one holiday. Copy a few pictures with Jewish content that have nothing to do with any holiday. Mount each picture on a small index card. Laminate. Place a complete set of pictures in each box.

Students choose partners and get their holiday boxes. They are to find cards related to each holiday and make a set of cards. Upon completion of the match-up, they take turns showing how they put their Holiday Sets together. They can also tell what each symbol and ritual object is, and how it is used during the holiday.

HOLIDAY BOOKS FOR YOUNGER CHILDREN

Plastic freezer bags make great books for the little ones. The older children can draw pictures, design games, puzzles, etc., about the holiday. Place two sheets of paper in one plastic bag with a piece of oaktag in-between to make each "page" sturdier. When all the pages of the book are completed, put the resealable side on the left and staple the book together on the left. Be sure to have the youngsters make covers for their books. Then give the books to the younger children to learn about the holiday.

STUDENTS WRITE A STORY

Divide the class into small groups. Prepare index cards with a variety of titles related to a holiday (e.g., "The Shofar Sings"; "The Candles Are Stars"; "Grandma's Challah"). Give each group one of the titles. The group members are to write a short story that goes with it. Once the story is written to their satisfaction, give them paper to print it nicely on several pages. Then they are to prepare illustrations in harmony with the story parts on each page. Finally, they are to design a cover for the story with the title and authors' names, and compile everything into a small booklet. Have the groups share their stories with the class. The booklets can be given to classes of younger children or placed in the library.

HOLIDAY MURAL

Divide the class into small groups. Assign each a different Jewish holiday. The group members are to find out all they can about their holiday, then create a mural to share what they have learned.

Take a long piece of white butcher or art paper and either roll it out on the floor or place it on the wall, whichever gives more freedom of movement for the students as they work. Provide colored markers or crayons, pencils, and old workbooks with pictures related to the holiday. Assign each group a section of the paper on which to work, but remind the youngsters that the holidays must appear in the mural in the sequence in which they occur in the year. Allow a few minutes for the group members to get in the proper order. Explain that they are to design scenes of how we celebrate the holiday, how it was once celebrated, and what it means to the Jewish people today. When their work is completed, each group explains its part of the mural. The mural can be hung in the school hallway.

PAST AND FUTURE

Invite three or four senior citizens from the congregation to come to your class as members of a panel to discuss how things used to be. The focus could be one of the Jewish holidays, including Shabbat.

Prior to the visit, have the class develop interview questions and decide which students will ask them. During the visit, everyone is to take notes. When the visitors leave, have the students summarize the discussion: what was different from, and what was similar to, the way the holiday is celebrated today? Take time for the students to write thank-you notes to each of the visitors.

As a closure, have the students write predictions of how they think the holiday will be celebrated 20 years from now. What will be different and what will be the same? Make sure they give their reasons. Share their predictions with the class.

WHAT DOESN'T BELONG?

This is good for a review of any Jewish holiday. On the blackboard list the items that belong to a certain holiday (e.g, symbols, rituals, foods, names of prayers). Include at least one item that does not belong (e.g., on a Purim list, Havdalah candle, candlesticks, etrog, spice box; on a Shabbat list, lulav, Megillah, matzah). Have the students copy the list and circle the item that does not belong. Below the list, they are to explain why it is wrong. Students share and defend their reasons.

SOMEONE IS COMING TO SHABBAT DINNER—OR ANY HOLIDAY DINNER

Ask the students to identify a famous Jewish person (living or dead) they would like to invite to dinner. Talk about the different reasons they would want this person as a guest. Once they have decided, the class is to plan the dinner. Divide into small groups and give each group an assignment for planning the dinner. Some things to consider could be:

Who else will they invite?

Make a list of guests so they know how many will be coming.

How would they set the table?

Make up a seating chart.

Who will sit on the right of the guest of honor? Who on the left?

What will they have for dinner?

What special foods will they prepare for this holiday?

What will they talk about?

What questions will they ask of the guest? List them.

Bring the groups together to share their plans. Make any adjustments as needed.

HOLIDAY REVIEW BULLETIN BOARD

You will need butcher or art paper to cover the board, tagboard, pieces of cloth, a stapler and small cards, magazines, old workbooks, scissors, and glue.

Cover the board, then make a pocket out of a piece of cloth. Staple it to the middle of the board so that it becomes a pocket in which you can place a card or object. Put something related to the holiday, or a picture of something related to the holiday, in the pocket. (Be sure the students cannot see what it is.) Put a card with a written clue next to the pocket; add additional clue cards, one at a time, until the class can identify the object in the pocket. For example: put a picture of a Havdalah candle in the pocket. The clues, added one at a time, could be: *ritual, flickering light, separation,* etc.

The students can get into the act too. Let them choose an object related to a holiday, then develop the clue cards. They can challenge their classmates to identify the object from their clues.

JEWISH IDENTITY

The "Jewish Me" Museum

With this project you can help your students feel good about themselves as Jews. Establish a space on your wall or bulletin board called The "Jewish Me" Museum.

Divide it into sections headed *Family, Holidays, Hobbies, Life-cycle events,* etc. To begin, put up a display about yourself! For each section, write a few sentences on a small index card; post the cards in the appropriate sections. Add some memorabilia and pictures to complete your Jewish

70

Me Museum. Take the students on a tour of your museum and explain that they will now have an opportunity to create their own Jewish Me Museums.

Leave your display up and assign a date when the students can put up their own museums. If you have enough space on your wall to leave the Jewish Me Museums up, the students will be able to add to them throughout the year as exciting events take place in their lives.

"Jewish Me" Hats

Every once in awhile it's good to let the kids toot their horns about how good it is to be Jewish and how unique they are as individuals. Make it a celebration of their Jewish uniqueness. You will need a sheet of 18 x 24 white paper for each student, tape, scissors, glue, markers, colored tissue paper, colored construction paper, felt, sequins, newspapers, magazines, and anything else that can be used for decorations. Talk with the students about what makes them special or unique as Jews. Brainstorm to make a list of their unique Jewish qualities, talents, and interests. Give out white paper, scissors, and tape. Show them how to make cone hats that fit their heads. Explain how their unique qualities as Jews can be transformed into symbols. Give the kids some scrap paper to play around with, designing symbols which represent their unique qualities and talents as Jews. When they are satisfied with their designs, they can begin to decorate their hats, turning them into great works of art. Show them some decorating tricks with yarn, ribbon, colored markers, how to cut out different designs, etc. Upon completion, students put on their hats to celebrate. One at a time, ask them to talk about their Jewish Me Hats with the class.

Using Your Senses

We always emphasize the use of the senses with younger children, but it can be done with older ones as well. Prepare a sheet, attractively decorated with Jewish symbols, with the following statements:

With my eyes (seeing)...

With my nose (smelling)...

With my hands (touching)...

With my ears (hearing)...

With my mouth (tasting)...

Ask the students to write about all the things they do through their five senses that are Jewish, making a list for each of the above statements. Share their responses with the class.

We Are One

This is a nonverbal activity that teaches the value of working together. Have the students choose partners. Give each pair *one* crayon and *one* piece of drawing paper. State that partners may not talk to each other or decide prior to the activity what picture they will draw as a team. Give the class a theme, based on your unit of study, so that there are some choices about what to draw.

If possible, have a tape recorder and play some music while the students are drawing. Both partners hold the one crayon simultaneously and without talking draw a picture together. Give them a specific time to complete the drawing. When the time is up, the pairs share their works of art. Then talk about:

What did you draw? What does it represent?

What was difficult? What was easy?

Was it difficult not to be able to talk to your partner?

Was it an equal effort?

How did you feel when you realized your picture was going to be something?

What did you learn about sharing and cooperation?

What is the most effective way Jews can accomplish specific tasks?

Of course, the discussion will depend on the students' responses.

Creating a "Jewish Me" Book

Ask students to bring a baby picture of themselves from home. Tell them to be sure no one in the class sees their picture. Mount the pictures on the bulletin board or wall and include a baby picture of yourself. Give each picture a number. Note: be sure to make a list of the numbered pictures and their owners.

Give out sheets of paper and have the students number a series of spaces corresponding to the number of pictures on the board. Give them some time to look at the baby pictures. Whenever they can identify someone, they are to place the name next to the corresponding number on the sheet. Ask them to tell how many classmates they have identified, but without revealing the names.

Have a "Jewish Me" worksheet ready, so that the students can list details that will help them create their own autobiographies. Include such things as birthplace, Berit Milah/naming, Consecration, favorite Jewish holiday, Jewish book, Jewish activity, Jewish song, prayer, etc. Once they have completed their worksheets, they are to write their autobiographies, telling about the Jewish aspects of their lives up to the present time. Upon completion, tell them to go over the drafts and remove any details that might reveal their identities (names). When they have completed the final draft, collect the stories, cover the names, and place them under each student's baby picture. Give the class time to read the stories and refine their original guesses about the identities.

Finally, let the students, one at a time, go to their picture and read their autobiography. Each time, ask the kids if any had guessed the correct identity and what clues helped them to identify the student. Collect the pictures and stories, and compile them into a book for the school library. (If parents want the baby pictures returned, copy them to include with the stories and return the pictures.)

Let's Do Some Jewish Shopping

If you are not already receiving them, get on the mailing list of some Jewish mail order catalogues (e.g., California Stitchery, Hamakor, The Source for Everything Jewish, Galerie Robin, and even some Jewish publishers). Write and ask for additional catalogues to ensure that you have at least two different catalogues for every pair of students. Then let the students do some Jewish shopping.

1. Have the students choose partners, and give each pair two different catalogues.
2. Tell the students to pretend they can buy five items from the catalogues.
3. Be sure they have paper and pencil. They are to list the five items they want more than anything else in the different catalogues. Next to each item they are to tell why they want each item.
4. Students share their lists and the reasons for their choices.

Your Jewish Self

You will need butcher paper, magazines, felt tip markers, glue sticks or paste, and scissors.

Divide the class into pairs. Give each pair a piece of butcher paper large enough to draw outlines of two bodies. See that each pair has some of the supplies. Each partner is to draw an outline of the other partner's body, then cut out the outline.

Working on the floor, the partners then cut out pictures from magazines or draw pictures which represent their Jewish selves: who they are as Jews, how being Jewish affects their lives, etc. The partners are to work on filling out their own outlines. When completed, they are to compare their outlines, then hang them on the wall to be able to share them with the rest of the class.

Secular vs. Jewish

Prepare a sheet that lists Jewish symbols, holidays, skills, rituals, etc., and items that could be either Jewish or secular. Place the list on the left side of the sheet. Add two other columns, one headed *Jewish*, the other *Secular*, with space for a check after each item. Your sheet could look something like this:

	JEWISH	SECULAR
Sabbath	_____	_____
Shofar	_____	_____
Anti-Semitism	_____	_____
Hebrew	_____	_____
Independence Day	_____	_____
Bible	_____	_____
Zionism	_____	_____
Rosh Hashanah	_____	_____
Ashkenazi	_____	_____
Presidents' Day	_____	_____
Circumcision	_____	_____
War	_____	_____
Exodus	_____	_____
People of the Book	_____	_____
Thanksgiving	_____	_____
Veterans Day	_____	_____
Immigrants	_____	_____
Sephardi	_____	_____
Messianic Age	_____	_____
Flag Day	_____	_____

Have the students classify the items and share their responses. Talk about the similarities and differences in the responses.

Draw a Jewish Symbol of Your Own Design

Each student will need a sheet of paper divided into six squares and a crayon or colored marker. Ask the students to draw in each square a symbol or drawing expressing their reaction to a statement you will make. Your statement could be something like this:

1. My favorite Jewish holiday.
2. Giving tzedakah to help others is the Jewish way.
3. Where a Jew should spend the Sabbath.
4. A Jewish historical event which has influenced you.
5. Jerusalem is important to all Jews.
6. A Jewish ritual object that is most significant to you.

Do this exercise together with the students. Upon completion, have the students share their responses and the reasons for them.

A Group Poster

You will need drawing paper large enough to be a poster and colored markers. Divide the class into groups of three or four. Talk about listening to one another, treating one another with respect and consideration, working together, who they are as Jews, what is important to them about being Jewish.

Ask the members of each group to create a poster that says something about them as a group and as Jews. They are also to come up with a name for their group that includes the first letter of each member's name; if necessary, they can create a new word, but it must reflect who they are as a group and as Jews. Tell them to place the group name down the left-hand side of the paper in large letters. Within the group, they are to talk about their positive qualities as Jews. Each member of the group is to decide on a personal Jewish trait or quality which begins with one of the letters in the group's name. Write each member's quality next to the appropriate letter of the group name. On the right-hand side of the paper, they are to design a logo which goes with the group name and personal qualities. Working together, they are to color and decorate the poster, explain it to the class, and then hang it.

Glad to Be a Jew

Prepare a sheet that looks like an outline of the front page of a newspaper, with the name of the paper and city, and space for a headline, the date, a picture, and an article. Distribute copies of the sheet. Ask the students to write a newspaper article describing a special Jewish activity they did this week. They are to include the headline for the article and draw a picture of the activity. Or they can write a letter to the editor, telling about the most important Jewish thing they have accomplished this week.

Word Portrait

Ask the students to write letters to a non-Jewish friend (real or pretend). In it they are to describe who and what Jews are, including what is important to them as Jews, family activities, their favorite times as Jews, things they do at the synagogue, and what Jews believe.

Have the students share their letters with their classmates. As the letters are shared, they are to make notes of any changes they would like to make: things to add and things to take out. Give them time to redo the letters. Share again, then talk about how the letters could be used. Some suggestions could be: sharing with visiting church groups, actually mailing them to non-Jewish friends, sharing with a church class of the same age group, which in turn would write descriptive letters to your class, etc.

Using the Alphabet to Build Jewish Self-Esteem

Using every letter in the alphabet, ask the students to describe who they are as Jews: their interests, favorite Jewish foods, holidays, activities, what they like, Bible, history, prayer, etc. If they have trouble coming up with a word for any letter, skip it and go back to it later. They can write short sentences or phrases, underlining the word that begins with the letter in the alphabet and placing it in the proper alphabetic sequence. Have the students share their results.

If you wish, divide the class into small groups for this project and have a few dictionaries available for their use.

Incomplete Sentences

Filling in the missing words in incomplete sentences can lead into some good group discussions on what it means to be Jewish. It can also help you to learn more about the students' attitudes toward being Jewish. The following are my ideas. Use them as a guide for creating your own.

Being Jewish is important to me because...

I expect my friends to be...

Openness and honesty are important to me because...

When some disaster happens in Israel, I...

Anti-Semitism concerns me because...

On Christmas I feel...

I will date only Jewish girls/boys because...

The religion of the person I date is important to me because...

Judaism teaches me...

Have the students complete the sentences with the first words that come to mind. This part is done individually. Upon completion, form the class into small groups and give some time for the members to share their responses with each other, as well as the reasons for their responses. Bring the whole class together after a bit. Share your own completed sentences with the class.

Talk about the differences and similarities between the responses. (Be sure to be accepting.)

What Makes Me Jewish?

Prepare a sheet on which the students can list the things that make them Jewish. It could look something like this:

What Makes Me Jewish?

You are to list 10 different answers to this question in the spaces provided below. Include those things that characterize you as Jewish today, things or deeds that made you Jewish in the past, and what will make you Jewish in the future.

[Number spaces 1 through 10, leaving them blank for the students to complete.]

Some answers you might receive could be:

1. I celebrate Shabbat.

2. I go to religious school.

3. I give tzedakah.

4. I go to Israel.

5. I was consecrated.

6. I control my temper.

7. I date only Jews.

8. I study Torah.

9. I learn Hebrew.

10. I was Bar/Bat Mitzvah.

When the students finish their lists, have them share their responses, talking about the similarities and differences.

Time Capsule Bulletin Board

Cover your bulletin board with brightly colored paper. Using white butcher paper, put up a time capsule cut in the shape of a big box or capsule so that it takes up a good part of the board. Head it with the words "Time Capsule" and the year. You will also need colored markers, writing paper, drawing paper, pens, and magazines.

Talk about the concept of a time capsule, its purpose and where time capsules are usually found. Find out if your congregation placed one in the cornerstone when the building was first constructed. Maybe someone in the congregation remembers what was put in it. The purpose of the time capsule is to show future generations what Jewish life and culture were like today. Ask the class to pretend that the time capsule on the board will be opened 100 years from now. What do they want people to know about the Jewish life and culture of today? Each student is to find a picture of one item to be included in the capsule, label it, and write a description of anything that is not apparent in the picture. The picture and the description are placed in the capsule on the board. Talk with the class about the different items included in the capsule: What makes them special? Why are they being included? And so on.

Being Different Is Okay! A Bulletin Board

Being able to accept differences helps to eliminate prejudice and discrimination. From newspaper cut out a string of six to eight paper dolls. Mount them in the center of your bulletin board. Cut out black cowboy hats and put hats on all but one of the paper dolls. On the one, put a yarmulke. Ask the students to talk about the paper dolls and what is different about any of them. Talk about the yarmulke: what it means and why some Jews wear it, how it makes a Jew feel different and special. Then ask the students what it feels like to be different, and how they feel when they are made to feel different. Let them give examples of situations when they felt different. What was happening at the time? How did they react to the feeling of difference? When is it okay to be different?

After the discussion, have the students cut out individual paper dolls. They are to write on their doll something that is unique and different about them as Jews, something that makes them feel good. (I did this once, and at the time I had a dog from Jerusalem which I thought was very special and unique, and it sure made me feel different!) Encourage them to decorate their doll, make a colorful hat out of construction paper, and place it on their doll. Finish up your bulletin board by having the students mount their dolls on it and tell what is special, unique, and different about them as Jews.

THE BIBLE AND JEWISH HISTORY

Words of Wisdom

Happy is the person who finds wisdom, the person who finds understanding (Proverbs 3:13).

The world is based on three principles, Torah, worship, and deeds of loving-kindness (Pirke Avot—Simeon).

Do not separate yourself from the community (Pirke Avot—Hillel).

One good deed brings on another (Pirke Avot—Ben Azzai).

There are three crowns: the crown of Torah, the crown of priesthood, and the crown of royalty; but the crown of a good name excels them all (Pirke Avot—Simeon).

These are just a few samples of the words of wisdom found in traditional Jewish writings. See how many more the kids can find. Pirke Avot (included in *Gates of Prayer*), the Book of Proverbs, the Torah, and *The Treasury of Jewish Quotations* are just some of the books they can use. Have the students list the words of wisdom they find. Go over the lists with them, discussing what makes the various statements words of wisdom, what benefits are derived from them, etc.

Ask the students to choose quotations they really like; each student should select the one that is most personally meaningful. When a student chooses a quotation, remove it from the list so that there are no duplications. Have the students design posters to "sell" their words of wisdom. Display their finished work in the school hallway.

Introduction to the Study of Torah

Prepare index cards, each one with a Jewish concept or idea on it (e.g., Shabbat, God, freedom, Torah, siddur, Hebrew, peace, holidays, Talmud, brotherhood/sisterhood, compassion, truth, holiness, menorah, Kiddush cup, challah, candlesticks/candles). You will need at least five Jewish concepts per group of students. Place the cards in a box. Divide the class into small groups. Each group is to choose five cards from the box, then *let's pretend*:

Tell the students that the members of each group are going to pretend they are the leaders of a new Jewish community being established on a new planet which has the same atmosphere as Earth. They are to determine how they would use their Jewish concepts/ideas to ensure the survival of the Jewish people in their new location. Give them time to talk it through, then tell them to create a skit to act out how they would ensure the survival of the Jewish people with what they have in their possession.

After each group has made its presentation, have the whole class discuss what was easy, what was difficult, and what key ingredient in Jewish survival was missing. Only the group that had the card headed *Torah* would really have had nothing missing. The idea is that the Torah contains everything else on the list and then some. It is the one item that has been there for the Jewish people over all the centuries. Hopefully, the students will reach this conclusion on their own. In your discussion, lead them in that direction.

Create a Newspaper for a Torah Portion

Divide the class into small groups. Assign a Torah portion to each group, or use one Torah portion and assign different parts of the newspaper to each group. The different parts of the paper could include:

News articles: human interest stories, major news reports, etc.

Editorials.

Weather reports.

Advice columns.

Sports events.

Cartoons.

Advertising.

Each group works on its portion of the paper. Upon completion, compile into a newspaper—headline and all, then make enough copies for the whole class.

A Biblical Collage

This is an old tool, but here is a somewhat different approach. You will need old magazines, colored construction paper, posterboard, pencils, scissors, glue, newspapers, buttons, crayons, markers, yarn, etc.

Before the students begin to work on their collages, discuss the subject from your unit of study. For example, if your unit includes the story of Joseph and his problems with his brothers, the many-colored coat, etc., consider such questions as: What was the root of the problem? What kind of relationship did Joseph have with his brothers? What problems did the brothers have with Joseph? What happened to Joseph? What about his dreams? And so on. Ask the students to think about how they would depict the various aspects of the story in a collage. Then divide the class into small groups.

On the posterboard, with pencils, the students sketch out enlarged shapes of their designs. These can be just shapes, nothing specific, because they are to serve as background. When the background design is finished, have the students cut out various shapes from the colored construction paper to fill in the designs. Once the background is filled in, they can begin to design the rest of the collage, identifying those shapes needed to tell their understanding of the story of Joseph. They can use any of the materials you have available, other than the construction paper, to fill in the rest of the collage. When the entire posterboard is covered and they are satisfied with their design, they are to share their creative work and explain the reasons for their design.

A Family of the Bible

Whenever possible, lead into the study of the Bible with an activity to which the students can relate on a personal level. For example: Teaching the story of Jacob and his family, Joseph and his brothers.

Begin the lesson by giving out clumps of clay and having the students make a perfect Jewish family of clay people; or give out drawing paper and have them draw pictures of perfect Jewish families. Upon completion, the students present their family works of art, telling who each person is and what role everyone has in family situations and events. Remember that children tend to talk about their own families; from this activity the class will learn that there are all kinds of families, and that all are important and perfect in the eyes of their members.

Now the class is ready to learn about another kind of family, from the Bible. They will be able to compare and discuss the different situations which evolve from the Bible story.

Jewish Family Wheel

Here is another approach in which the students look at their own families before studying families in the Bible. You will need a large piece of oaktag or posterboard cut into a large circle. Make it large enough so there will be space for a pie-shaped piece of drawing paper from each student to go around in the circle. You will also need drawing paper cut into pie-shaped pieces, one per child, so that when the pie shapes are attached to the large circle they complete the circle. In addition, provide crayons, pictures, scissors, and glue.

Tell the students they are going to make a Jewish Family Wheel which shows something special about each family. They are to think about all the Jewish things their families do together. Show them the pie-shaped papers that they will fill in with this information. Turn the children loose to fill in their papers with drawings about Jewish family life. When finished, they draw a decorative border around their pie-shaped pieces to distinguish each child's story. Assemble the pieces in the circle, gluing the drawings on to the Jewish Family Wheel. Let the children tell about their families as their pieces are glued to the Wheel.

Alternative Introduction to Families in the Bible

You will need a small picture of each child, construction paper, crayons or markers, and glue. On a sheet of construction paper, have the students draw a small box in the upper-right-hand corner and leave it empty for a picture to be placed later. Next have them draw portraits of their families taking part in a Jewish activity. Pets, relatives, etc., can be included. When the portraits are completed, they can glue their picture in the empty box. Give them small pieces of construction paper, cut the size of the pictures, to staple at the top as a flap covering the pictures. Place all the family portraits around the room. Give the students some time to look at them, then see if they can guess whose family is portrayed in each picture.

Bible Families Bulletin Board

Prepare your bulletin board space by covering the background with colorful construction or art paper. If you wish, students can create a decorative border to go around the sides. Have the students choose partners. Assign each pair a family in the Bible to research. Place the names of the family heads across the top of the bulletin board.

The teams are to research the family trees of their assigned families. This will encourage them to read the Bible in order to learn about the family's lineage. As they identify the different people born into their assigned families, they are to list them in the correct order. When the lists are complete, they can place the names on labels and put them in the correct order on the bulletin board, drawing lines from one person to the next to show the relationships.

Asking Questions

This is an example of how you can have your students read the actual text of the Bible and make the words come alive for them—something real, not just an old text written thousands of years ago.

After the class has read some stories about Abraham from the Bible, try a few of these questions:

What one or two words would you use to describe Abraham today? (Do some brainstorming and make a list. Discuss the reasons for the choices.)

If God called on you to leave home, how would you react? (Give the students some time to think about this, then let them share their responses.)

Abraham became one of our ancestors because...(Ask the students to respond with the first words that come to mind. Discuss and list Abraham's character traits. See if they can identify someone today who has many or all of the same traits.)

Abraham had a lot of faith in God. What kind of faith do you have in God? How did your faith develop? (The answers to these questions will be personal, so let the students write their answers, then limit sharing to those who wish to do so.)

The one thing I admire the most about Abraham is...(Give the students time to think about this, and then list the things they admire most.)

Quotations from Traditional Sources

Choose a quotation, based on your unit of study, and write it on the blackboard. Discuss what it means: what did it mean when it was written, and what does it mean to us today? Have the students rephrase the quotation in their own words. The new phrasing is to express what the quotation means to them in today's world. One quotation we use quite a bit, "Seek peace, and pursue it" (Psalms 34:15), could look something like this when the kids get through with it: "We must work for peace each in our own way."

Digging Deeper into the Text

On small paper strips, place one-sentence situations pertaining to your unit of study. For example:

Joseph was thrown into a pit.

Moses struck a rock.

Jacob "stole" his birthright.

Have the students choose partners and draw strips from the collection. Each pair of students is come up with a series of how and why questions related to the situation. Give some examples of what you want them to do:

How did Joseph get thrown into the pit?

Why did Joseph get thrown into the pit?

Who threw Joseph into the pit?

When the students have completed their questions, they are to write the answers and then share them with their classmates.

Bible Fill-Ins: When You Have Some Time Left

Haven't planned enough for the entire lesson? Need some quick learning experiences? Prepare a box of quickie activities on index cards so you can just pull one out and give it to a student. The index card should have everything on it that the student is to do for the lesson. A Bible quotation with instructions on what to do makes a good quickie.

For example: Put a quotation on an index card (Leviticus and Proverbs are good sources), accompanied by the words, "Write or draw what this quotation is saying to you."

The question or activity will depend on the quotation used. Always relate the question or activity to the content of the quotation. Students can take the index card and interpret its meaning. In addition to drawing a picture, they might also write a short skit or song—even create a game, or work in any other medium with which they are comfortable—to explain the meaning of the Bible quotation. If there is still time, the student can share it with the class.

Tips for Teaching the Bible

1. Have a student become one of the major characters in the story, taking on the role completely and telling the story in the first person. Before class, ask the other students to develop questions to ask the one who plays the role. Let students take turns role-playing the character.

2. Divide the class into groups of three. Assign a biblical text to be read. The group members are to read the portion and discuss its ramifications. The members of each group are to prepare three questions to ask the whole class. Then have a Bible quiz using the questions they have prepared.

3. When the Bible portion is exceptionally long, write a synopsis of the story for the class. Number each line. As the class reads the story, ask specific questions related to each numbered line.

4. Copy the Bible portion. Divide it into several parts and place each part on an index card. Mix the cards well and have students arrange them in the proper sequence. Alternative: Place the parts of the story on cards. Have students sort them according to your directions (e.g., the Story of Creation: sort the cards according to the different days; Prophets: sort according to who said what).

My Favorite Prophet: An Election

As the class studies the prophets, ask the students to make lists of the characteristics of a prophet and the qualifications to be a prophet. As a closure for your unit on the prophets, choosing a favorite prophet is a fun activity.

Have the students share their lists. From these, choose the best characteristics and qualifications of a prophet, making two lists. Divide the class into two teams, or parties. Based on the two lists, each team chooses the prophet it deems to be the best candidate to lead the Jewish people. Each party plans a political campaign to get its prophet elected. One of the members will act as campaign director, another as the prophet candidate, another as art director, and so on; in other words, there should be a role for everyone in the campaign. Among other things the parties can design posters, create ads, slogans, TV ads, songs, jingles and, of course, speeches. If you really want to have some fun with this, see if the campaign can't be directed to the entire religious school. Choose a date for the election, then plan an election rally where the candidates speak, advertising is displayed, etc., to be held before the date of the election. The day of the election, see that there are ballots and final campaigning, then the voting. The elected prophet gets to give an acceptance speech.

As the campaign progresses, keep in mind that the campaign material is to utilize what the students have learned about the characteristics and qualifications of a prophet.

You Are There!

When teaching a unit of study, have the students imagine themselves as participants in the event. Ask them to write letters to members of their families describing what is taking place and how they feel about it.

Into the Future

Once upon a time there were no TVs, radios, etc. The only pictures of Jewish life we had were drawings, mostly done by non-Jewish artists. See if the students can discover why there were no, or very few, pieces of art depicting Jewish life done by Jewish artists.

Now, let's pretend! We have no radio, no newspapers, no TV, nothing that can capture Jewish life today. The only means we have will be drawings. Have drawing materials available. Let the students choose an aspect of Jewish life they would like people to know about 100 years from now. Have them draw pictures depicting that aspect of Jewish life. Upon completion, share their drawings with the class and post around the room.

The Way It Was

Compare Jewish life in the past to today. This is a good activity when studying things like shtetl life, early Jewish immigrants, early life in Israel, etc. Look at foods/meals, famous Jews and what they did, children's games, clothing, ritual and synagogue life, school, everyday chores, symbols of wealth, care/compassion, work/jobs, etc.

Have the students pretend they come from that period of time. Divide the class into small groups. Each group is to write a short story about a particular event during that period. Or groups can write and put on a short skit about a particular event (e.g., celebrating Shabbat, a wedding, the birth of a child, a day in school). The presentation must be representative of the way life was at the time.

Interview the Parents

With the class, create a questionnaire for parents to complete about when they attended religious school. You can ask such questions as:

How did you get to school?

What was your favorite subject?

Who were your favorite teachers?

What was the highlight of your religious school years?

What books do you remember reading?

How did you celebrate Shabbat and other holidays?

Send the questionnaire home with the students, requesting parents to complete it and talk with their children about the "old days." Students bring the answers back to share with the class and compare what religious school was like in the old days and now.

Step Out of the Past

Many of our ancestors came from countries other than the United States. A unit on Jewish immigration to the States comes alive when it is about the families and relatives of the students. If, after some research into their family histories, there are no remaining memories, have the students develop memories of an imaginary family. If you wish, they can do this together with their parents.

Divide the class into small groups. Give each group a specific assignment to complete. For example:

Develop a procedure for interviewing newly arrived families.

Questions to be asked using the format of a TV talk show.

Research how people traveled to the States.

Where they embarked from and landed.

How they were received, and who greeted them upon arrival.

Where they first lived, what their first days in a new country were like.

Who helped them to get settled.

Difficulties and ease in adjusting to a new land and culture.

When all the groups are prepared, put on a TV talk show with members of each group role-playing the parts of the new arrivals, thus sharing the information they have gathered about their own families and some imaginary families.

NEAT AND SIMPLE

What Happened When?

Prepare a list of historical events. Place them in random order on a sheet of paper with space between the lines. Copy and give one to each student. The students are to read the list, then cut it up and paste the events in the correct order. See how many students actually place them correctly.

Begin with the Family

Personal information about their own families can bring Jewish history alive for the students. Here is an activity which will involve the entire family: parents, grandparents, aunts/uncles, cousins, etc. It is actually more than a one-day lesson and can be extended into quite a project.

Either have a large map of the world for the whole class or provide each student with a map of the world. You will also need index cards and adhesive colored dots.

With the students, prepare a list of interview questions to be used in their research. The questions could look something like this:

Where were you born?

What were the cities, towns, regions like where you were born?

Where did the different Jewish life-cycle events take place?

Names of people, places, and events: births, weddings, Bar/Bat Mitzvah, deaths, etc.

Students are to interview their families to obtain all the needed information. As they gather information, they use the colored dots to identify locations on the map where Jewish life-cycle events took place. As they identify a location, they write up the event briefly on an index card, color-coding it to match the map dot, or number the dots as well as color-coding to make them easy to identify.

Ask students to gather stories, pictures, memorabilia, letters, even stamps, anything relevant to family history. Make attractive displays of what they gather. You can turn the whole project into a family event by having a family celebration, inviting the families on a specific day to view the completed project.

ALTERNATIVE

Once the students have identified where their families come from, divide the class into small groups. Assign each group a different part of the world. Each group is to find out where Jewish communities once were, where Jews once lived and emigrated from to the United States or other countries. As they locate where Jews once lived, number and color-code a circle dot and place on the site. Prepare an index card with some information about the Jewish community that once existed in this place. Place on the board, color-coding and numbering to correspond to the site. Once they have located and identified past Jewish communities, where are the Jewish communities of today? Each group looks at its same area of the world and locates the Jewish communities of today. Number and color-code the locations; prepare an index card telling something about the Jewish community today and place on the board. This expands the dimensions of their research about communities of Jews in the world.

Jewish Family History: A Cluster Bulletin Board

Have the students interview members of their families. As they do so, becoming aware of who their relatives are, the relationships between them, the lines of descent over the generations, etc., they can create a cluster of their family history. For this activity, make a master sheet with at least 15 Jewish stars, large enough to write on. Make one copy for each student on yellow tagboard. In addition you will need 11 x 14 sheets of dark blue construction paper, scissors, glue, colored markers, glitter, and rulers.

Give these instructions to the class:

1. Cut out stars for each family member, including one for yourself.

2. Write the name of one family member on each star and how he or she is related to you (uncle, aunt, cousin, etc.).

3. Place the stars on the blue construction paper, in order of descent, to show how the family members are related to one other. Glue when you are satisfied with the arrangement.

4. Using a ruler, draw straight lines to show how the family members descend and are related.

5. Decorate with glitter to make the stars shine.

Jewish Family History: Immigration

Hang a map of the world on the bulletin board or wall, and ask the students to design coats of arms for their families. Create your own coat of arms as an example. In order to do so, they will have to find out the family's country of origin, then write two unique facts about the family or their ancestors on paper ribbons which are attached to the family's place of origin on the map with map pins. The family coats of arms which they create are placed around the map. Attach a thin piece of colored ribbon or yarn to each coat of arms, extend it to the family's place of origin, and attach to the map pin. A picture of the student could also be placed near each coat of arms.

Guess Who's Coming to Visit

With the students, pretend that a famous biblical or historical personality is coming to visit the class. You can decide on a figure, or have the students decide who they would like to have visit them (e.g. Moses, Aaron, Joshua, King David, David Ben-Gurion, Golda Meir).

Once they have decided, the students have to prepare for the visit. They will want to show the visitor everything there is about their Jewish life today: how they worship, the synagogue, holiday celebrations, Shabbat, family celebrations, their homes, modes of transportation, Jewish artifacts, books, etc. Divide the class into small groups and assign a specific task to each group. The bulletin board, wall space, and tables can be used to display the group presentations; if you wish, assign a group to prepare a book that will tell the visitor the whole story.

As an added dimension, get a member of the congregation to role-play the visitor in an appropriate costume. The students can prepare questions to ask the visitor, and you can assign several youngsters to be the spokespersons for the class. Be sure the visitor is prepared in advance and knows the answers to the questions.

Our Memories Are Making Jewish History

The week before this activity, ask the students to bring in Jewish objects from home that have special meanings for them and their families. The objects they select should reflect some part of the family's Jewish history. Tell the students to conceal the objects in paper bags before bringing them to school.

Have the class form a circle. Go around the circle and have the students, one at time, share their objects by showing them and telling about their special history and meaning. Once all have shared, talk about: How did you decide what to bring? What did sharing your family story tell you about Jewish history? How are all of us making Jewish history with our stories and memories?

Keeping a Diary

Take an event in Jewish history and let the students imagine they are there! Ask them to create a day-to-day diary which reflects their feelings and reactions, worries and concerns, about what is happening and how it has affected them.

Where Are We?

Divide the class into small groups or have the students do this individually. Each group (or student if done as an individual project) chooses a country, without revealing which one is selected. The group gathers information about the Jewish communities in that country: where Jews live, their role in society and the economy, their efforts in Jewish education, social work, and religious involvement. Once the research is completed, the members write up a series of clues, and using these their classmates try to identify the country.

ALTERNATIVE

Give the students large index cards. Draw an outline of the country with dots marking different places where Jews live, but do not give the country's name. On the other side, write at least six questions which are clues to the places marked on the map. The questions can be in different categories (e.g., Jewish history—an event that happened to Jews in this place, famous Jews who were born or lived here, religious background, etc.). Have the students answer the questions and then attempt to guess the name of the country.

Making History Come Alive

Senior adults, whether the grandparents of your students or members of the congregation, can be a great resource. Identify those older adults who were among the founders of the synagogue, came over from Europe or places other than the United States, have been involved in Jewish communal affairs, or were early "settlers" of your city. Ask them to come to class and share some of their experiences when they were growing up, telling how they became involved in Jewish life, why they came to America, etc. Ask them to bring pictures and memorabilia, if possible. Prior to their visit, work with the class to prepare some interview questions for the guests—things the students would like to know about the past. This is a great way to learn about the past, right from those who have lived it! (I suggest that this activity be videotaped or recorded for the synagogue's history archives.)

Role-Playing Historical Figures

Here is an activity that makes the study of the Bible or history much more interesting. Make a list of people from your unit of study. If you are doing Bible stories, for instance, the list would include Abraham, Sarah, Isaac, Rebekah, Leah, Rachel, Jacob, and Esau. Ask the students to choose an individual from the list, or assign someone to each student. The students are to try to determine what their assigned person would think about Jewish life today: What would he or she like or dislike? What would he or she think about how the Torah is interpreted or holidays celebrated?

Give the students some time to think about this and make some notes. Then let each of them play the role of the person they selected, talking to the class about such things as how present-day Judaism looks from his or her perspective.

After each performance, ask the student: Were you giving your own opinions or those of the person you were role-playing? Did your own ideas sift through? What can we learn from the person you role-played? Continue until everyone has done a role-play, then conduct a class discussion on the question of whose roles were really being played.

Students Become Part of History

History can come alive when you give the class problems to solve that are related to the history lesson. Dealing with these problems enables the students to better understand the problems encountered by people in the historical period they are studying.

Prepare index cards, each with a different situation or problem to solve. On the board, or on a separate page, list the instructions for the activity. They could look something like this:

1. Read the card carefully.
2. Decide what you would do if this happened to you.

3. Write down what you would do first, second, third, etc.

4. Determine the consequences of your action.

The students can work individually, in pairs, or in groups of three or four to solve the problems. Once you have given them the situation/problem and instructions, allow time for them to complete the problem. When the groups finish, have them share their results with the class. Here is an example: Your course of study is the Spanish Inquisition. The following are possible problems to solve:

What would you do if—

Spanish officials find you reading a siddur?

You return from school and see the police entering your home?

You and your family are celebrating Shabbat in the basement and you hear loud pounding on the door?

You see a Jewish friend being carried off by the police?

Where Do Jews Live?

Whether your unit of study is Jewish communities of the world, Israel, major Jewish communities of the United States, or places from which Jews emigrated, this activity can be effective and useful. It also makes an attractive bulletin board.

On a large posterboard, trace an outline of a map covering the area in your unit of study. Number the important locations and laminate. Next to each number, attach a small piece of magnetic tape or Velcro. Next, put as many Jewish stars as you can on colored construction paper. Label each star with the name of a location that matches your numbers, then laminate. Cut out the Jewish stars. Place a small piece of magnetic tape or Velcro on the back of each star. For your information: create an answer key. Fasten a pocket on the back of the map or in an out-of-the-way corner on the front, to provide a place to store the stars when they are not in use. Mount the map on the wall. As your class studies the different locations, ask the students to match up the place stars with the proper locations on the map.

The Clothes We Wore

Divide the class into small groups. Assign each group a different period of time in Jewish history to research. The group members are to find out what kinds of clothing men, women, and children wore in their period. If you wish, restrict the area of research to men only, women only, or what boys wore for their Bar Mitzvahs (if you do the latter, remind the students that Bat Mitzvah ceremonies were not introduced until the twentieth century).

Give each group a large piece of butcher paper. On it the members are to draw an outline of a human body, using one of their group as a model. Once they have the outline, they are to draw clothing on it in the style of the period under study. Place the finished product on the wall and compare the clothing worn in the past with what is worn now.

Form only two groups. One researches men's clothing, the other, women's clothing. Two pieces of butcher paper will be needed, one for a man's body outline and the clothing, the other for a woman's. With this alternative, only one historical period can be covered.

A Story from History

Whenever I do this activity, the kids not only get into it, but have fun doing it. Instead of teaching Jewish history from the aspect of a time sequence, cover a specific aspect of a past era. For example: Your lesson is about the Marranos during the Spanish Inquisition. Have the students "hide" themselves in the room. Give them time to become parts of the room—a chair, desk, window, drapes, and so on. Turn your back while they hide. Then turn around and pretend that you cannot see them, but admire the fine desks, beautiful drapes, clear, clean windows, tables, and chairs. Allow time for the laughing and giggling, then gather the students around you. Tell the story of the Marranos, the hidden Jews.

After the story, divide the class into small groups. Ask the members of each group to write a short story about how they would celebrate the Sabbath under these circumstances. Once, when I did this activity, I compared the Marranos to the Jews in the Soviet Union and assigned the students to write short stories about how the Jews there celebrated the Sabbath. Have the groups share their stories with the rest of the class.

Kids Love a Story—Especially One with a Twist

Add a dimension to a story by having the students do a related task before you tell it. For example: Yochanan ben Zakai escaped from Jerusalem during the Roman siege, and there is a delightful story about this incident. Because of it, he was able to preserve a living Judaism.

Assign the students to come up with a method of preserving a very important message for all human beings. It is a message which must not be lost, and they have to decide on the best way to save it. Allow them a few minutes to come up with their ideas. Then let them tell what they have come up with; be accepting, they all have great ideas (and I have heard some really good ones with this activity). Thank them for all the ideas, then tell them the story of Yochanan ben Zakai.

A Historical Newspaper

Bring in an assortment of newspapers. Ask the students to go through them and list all the different sections (e.g., news reports, sports, weather, ads, comics, political cartoons, letters to the editor, religion, feature stories). Divide the class into small groups and assign each a specific section of a newspaper.

Based on your unit of study, the groups are to research a period in the past: what historical events were taking place, etc. As they research, they make notes, as if they were reporters, so that they can create a newspaper from the era they are studying. When all the research has been completed, they are to put out a newspaper, headlines and all.

Famous Jewish People

Make copies of pictures of people who lived in the historical period covered in your unit of study. Mount the pictures on the bulletin board. As the students study this period, they are to write what they learn about these people on index cards and place the cards under their pictures.

Kids Use Their Imaginations

Draw a Jewish star on an 8.5 x 11 piece of paper. In the middle add lines for students to write on. Make enough copies for the whole class. Ask the students to imagine they are real people living during the period of Jewish history you are studying. Ask them to think about something they could do during this period which would be of value to the Jewish people. Give a few minutes for them to think about it, and then have them write their decisions on the stars. Share their ideas with the class, then post them on the bulletin board.

Footsteps of History

Instead of a time-line or trying to memorize facts, try this. You will need a box filled with colored markers. Cut out large footprints and place them in the same box. Whenever your class has a history lesson, the students take a footprint and label it with an important date or event. When all the footprints are labeled, place them in order around the room. Placement on the floor is fine, but they can also go up on the wall. Talk about what impact these events had on the Jewish people and what made them important enough to be remembered.

Voices from the Past

Mount a pocket on a posterboard. Take strips of tagboard and on each strip write the names of two Jewish historical figures. Under the paired names, write a short statement indicating what the two individuals might talk about. Put the strips in the pocket. Put the instructions next to the pocket. Your instructions could look something like this:

Pick a pair.

Write an imaginary dialogue between your pair.

If the students know the background of their chosen pair, they can begin writing the imaginary dialogue. If they do not, they will have to do some research before they can write the dialogue. Students can work individually or in pairs to accomplish this task. Here are some possible pairs and dialogue subjects:

Adam and Eve: coming out of the Garden of Eden.

Jacob and Esau: meeting after many years.

Joseph and his brothers: before they throw him in the pit.

David Ben-Gurion and Golda Meir: current issues in Israel.

Benjamin Netanyahu and Shimon Peres: peace with the Arabs.

Moses and your rabbi: Moses' Judaism and your rabbi's Judaism.

Jews Then and Now

Divide the class into small groups. Give each group a sheet of paper and have the members divide it into three columns. Head the first column *Topics*, the second, *Then*, and the third, *Now*. Distribute lists of topics to the groups, but make sure that each group's list is different. Topics you can consider are: food, clothing, recreation, religious practice, education, government, transportation, God ideas, social concerns, etc. The students are to research the past of each topic, writing a short paragraph about how it was in the past to be posted under *Then*. And for posting under *Now*, a short paragraph about how it is today. Each group shares its findings with the whole class.

Puzzle Maps and Where Jews Live

Copy maps of the countries you want to study from an atlas or geography book. Laminate or cover with clear contact paper. Then cut into puzzle pieces. Place each country's map puzzle in a separate envelope, marking the envelope accordingly. The students put the puzzles together and identify the places in the country where Jews have lived or are living. Depending on the country, they might have to do a little research to find out where Jews have lived. Have a map of the world on the bulletin board, so the students can see the location of their country in relation to the rest of the world.

Some Will Call This Bingo

Make Bingo cards by taking a sheet of paper large enough to divide evenly into nine squares. In each square place a heading, drawing a line under it. For example: Your unit of study is Israel. The headings for the top three squares will be *City*, *Religion*, and *Book*. The second three squares will be headed *Site*, *Desert*, and *Water*. The third three squares will be headed *Holy*, *Fruit*, and *Government*. Make enough copies for the whole class.

When you choose a story or give a reading assignment, distribute Bingo cards to the class. As the students listen to the story or read their assignment, they will hear or see words like "Holy Western Wall." When they do, they are to fill in the appropriate space; in this case, put the words "Western Wall" in the box marked *Holy*. When they hear about foods grown in Israel, like oranges, they fill in the *Fruit* space. The first student with three correct answers in a row, horizontally, vertically, or diagonally, is the winner. Using the same cards, you can also play games in which the winning combination of filled spaces has to be in the shape of a *T* or an *X*.

Let's Pretend

There are several options for this activity.

BREAK THE FAST

Divide the class into small groups. Prepare task cards outlining what each group is to do. For example: Pretend you are planning the Break the Fast for Yom Kippur. Whom do you invite? Write invitations. Make place-cards, organize your table setting, plan the menu, etc.

A VISIT TO NEW YORK

Pretend you are taking a trip to Jewish New York. Plan the trip. How do you get there? Where do you stay? Make a list of the things of Jewish interest you will see.

A FAMOUS DINNER GUEST

Pretend you are going to have a dinner for Moses (or any Jewish historical figure). Plan the meal. Whom else will you invite? What will be the seating arrangements? Plan the menu. Make a list of questions you will ask Moses.

Letters from the Future

Have the students pretend they are 15 to 20 years into the future. They have moved to _____ (whatever community or country you wish). They are to write letters telling why they decided to move, what life is like, and what they miss most about their homeland or hometown. Ask them to be specific, including such things as weather, economic conditions, physical features, landmarks, education, religious community, manufacturing, agriculture, health care systems, etc.

NEAT AND SIMPLE

Letters from the Past

Have the students pretend to be living in the historical period you have just studied. They are to write letters about their lives. Once again, ask them to be specific, as in the Letters from the Future exercise.

Missing Letters

Based on your study unit, choose a sentence you wish to use, then remove some letters from each word. Give out copies of the sentence. The challenge is to fill in the missing letters to make the sentence complete. For example: The sentence chosen is:

The Western Wall is a holy place in the Old City of Jerusalem.

After the letters have been removed, it would look like this:

_ _ e _ _ _ t _ _ n _ a _ l _ s a _ _ _ y _ _ _ ce in _ h _ _ l _
_ _ ty of _ _ r _ s _ _ _ _.

Make as many different sentences with missing letters as you wish, and challenge the class to complete them.

NEAT AND SIMPLE

A Time-Line

Hang a 6-foot piece of twine on the wall or across a portion of the room. Distribute 4 x 6 index cards. As you study a Bible portion or a period of Jewish history, have the students identify the main events by writing short statements or drawing pictures on the cards. Then attach the cards to the twine in the proper sequence, using clips or clothes pins.

Paper Time-Line

You will need a 25 x 3 strip of paper (the kind paper-fed adding machines use), two dowels, colored markers, and tape for each student. As you cover the unit of study, the students are to list the important events and number them in the correct order. To make the time-line:

1. On the long strip of paper, draw pictures of the events in the order they occurred, write a short account of each event, or affix cutout pictures representing each event.

2. Roll one end of the strip of paper around a dowel and tape it in place. Roll the other end around the other dowel and tape it in place.

Each student now has a personal time-line scroll.

Write a Story

Instead of testing the students to see what they have learned, prepare a list of words from your unit of study. Have the students write stories using the words on the list. If your unit of study was Israel, the list might look something like this:

Arab
beach
desert
Druse
Jerusalem
Negev
Never Again!
Old City
oranges
port
remember
Solomon

A Mural of History

Murals are always a fun way for students to show what they have learned about something. Include stick figures dressed in clothing of the period to make the mural two-dimensional. If you are studying the shtetl, the mural could be made up of homes in a ghetto, the synagogue, and the market-place. If a kibbutz, it could show the houses, farm buildings, and fields.

You will need four craft sticks per figure, glue, scissors, fabric of some kind, sequins, beads, button, paper and crayons, yarn for hair, and small circles for the heads. To make the stick figures:

1. Place a generous amount of glue on one stick and put another stick on top of it to form an upside-down *V*. Hold them together until the glue sets. These will be the legs of the stick figure.

2. Take two more sticks to form the body and arms, and make a cross with the top stick glued closer to the top.

3. Join the two sections together with glue.

4. Glue a small circle for the head to the top of the stick figure.

5. Dress the stick figure in the clothing of the period and decorate as desired. Glue on short pieces of yarn for the hair, and draw a face on the circle.

The mural can be put together on the floor, then mounted on the wall. After the buildings and scenery have been drawn as desired, students decide on the best places to glue their stick figures to make the mural more realistic. Glue on the stick figures, and when dry, hang the mural.

Paper Bag Dramatics

Use this for a review; it is much more fun than a test.

Divide the class into small groups. Prepare one paper prop bag for each group, with a variety of props that lend themselves to your unit of study. Include a few items that challenge the imagination. For example: Your unit of study was the Spanish Inquisition. You could put into the bag: masks, candles, a siddur, plates, silverware, hats, mirror, etc.

Give each group a bag and assign a topic (e.g., how Marranos observed Shabbat). Each group's topic should be different, and so should the assortments of props in the bags. Give the groups 5 minutes to plan a skit using all the props in the bag. Skits are to be performed for the whole class.

ALTERNATIVE

Prepare a box with an assortment of props. Give each group a different topic based on your unit of study. One person from each group goes to the prop box, blindly chooses a prop, and begins the skit. Another member of the same group goes to the box, chooses another prop, and continues the skit; and so on, until everyone in the group has taken part in the skit.

Create a TV Show

Watching television is a favorite activity, and your class can make a TV movie without using a camcorder! You will need plain computer paper, colored markers, old workbooks (for pictures), glue, scissors, dowels, and a big box—one that a TV set might have come in would be suitable.

For the TV: Cut out one side of the box for the "screen." Decorate the front to look like a TV set. Cut large vertical slits on each side through which the computer paper can slide easily.

With the students, choose a topic and outline the script. Divide the class into small groups. Assign each group a different portion of the script. Group members are to illustrate the episodes of their portion on a long sheet of computer paper. Remind them that each picture has to be the size of the TV screen. When each group has completed its episodes, tape them together. Be sure to have extra paper at the beginning and end to attach to the dowels. Slide the beginning through the slots in the TV until the first picture is seen on the screen. Attach the dowel, then attach the other dowel at the end of the paper and roll up. A student will have to stand on each side of the TV to roll the script through the screen. Other students can do the narration. Rehearse! Then your class can present its work to an audience of parents or young children.

Biblical/Historical Mobiles

This activity can be used to emphasize the concepts, ideas, people, or events in your unit of study. To make simple mobiles, you will need one wire hanger per student, tagboard patterns in various geometric or Jewish-symbol shapes (circles, triangles, rectangles, squares, Jewish stars, menorahs, shofars, etrogs, dreidels, Kiddush cups, etc.), yarn in a variety of colors cut in different lengths from 5 inches to 12 inches, glue or paste, scissors, colored markers, a hole-punch, and all kinds of decorating materials (bric-a-brac, glitter, sequins, ribbon, etc.).

To make the mobile:

1. Assign each student a different historical person.
2. The students are to research the assigned individuals and list their contributions.
3. Using the different patterns, they trace the number of designs they will need for their mobile (one for each of the person's contributions) and cut out the shapes.
4. They draw a picture representing a contribution on each shape, along with a word or two emphasizing it.
5. On the back of each drawing, they briefly tell what the picture represents; additional decorations are added if necessary.
6. They punch a hole in the top of each shape.
7. They take one piece of yarn for each shape, using different lengths, and tie the yarn to each piece. The yarn is attached to a wire hanger decorated with contact or tissue paper, or with yarn.

Have the students show off their mobiles and tell what they learned about their famous Jewish persons. Hang the mobiles around the room when everyone has shared.

Name a Picture

Gather some pictures related to your unit of study. If no other source is available, go through magazines and cut out pictures that, with a little imagination, can be identified with the topic. Or copy pictures from workbooks, enlarging them if they are too small. You will need one picture for each student. Paste the pictures on sheets of colored paper—not construction paper. Give out the pictures. Ask the students to study their pictures and come up with titles for them based on your unit of study. The students are then to write explanations for the choice of title. Share with the class.

Identify the Picture: A Bulletin Board

Use colored art paper for a background on the bulletin board. Prepare a pocket for the bulletin board large enough to hold at least an 8.5 x 11 picture. You will also need some index cards. You will need a picture, based on your unit of study, that lends itself to giving clues but is not too easy to identify. Or it can be placed face down so the content cannot be seen. Put the picture in the pocket. Each day write a few clues about the picture on index cards and pin them on the board. Students are to try and guess what the picture represents. Continue to add clues until they guess correctly.

ALTERNATIVE

Have students make their own pockets out of tagboard and mount them on the bulletin board. They choose pictures of Jewish objects and put them in the pockets, face down so they cannot be seen. Then they write clues about the objects on several cards and mount them around their pockets. Classmates have to guess what the objects are from the clues. If they do not guess in the first week, let them think about it and try again. If they haven't guessed correctly after the second go-round, the student tells what the item is and how the clues provided the information to help them identify it.

Let's Play Ball

Football, soccer, basketball, even baseball make good learning games. Draw the appropriate field/court on the board, or on a big posterboard, and laminate so it can be used over again. If you do not know all the specifics for making a field/court for one or another of these sports, ask the students; they would love to be involved in creating the game.

Prepare questions based on your unit of study. Base the rules on the game whose format you have adopted. Divide the class into two teams. Flip a coin to see which team goes first. Place the "ball" in the center of the field/court, or if baseball, on homeplate. The ball will be moved only when questions are answered correctly. It moves forward on the field as each question is answered correctly. If a team answers a question incorrectly or doesn't know the answer, the ball becomes the other team's and moves in the other direction. (If the game is baseball, the ball travels around the diamond clockwise.) The team continues until it gets a touchdown, field goal, basket, or makes it around the bases. Scoring would be: football—6 points; soccer field goal—2 points; basketball—2 points; baseball—1 point per run. The other team then takes over with the ball back in the middle or at homeplate.

Create a Book Based on a Study Unit

Instead of testing to see what the students have learned, let them create a book. Divide the class into small groups. Give each group a different list of questions to answer. Each group develops a story that answers the questions and illustrates the pages on which the story is written. The group members design a cover and title page, then compile the pages into a little booklet to share with the whole class.

Historical Mural

Instead of butcher paper, posterboard, or the like, get a full roll of wide white shelf paper. Divide the class into small groups. Keeping the roll of shelf paper intact, assign a portion of it to each group. Give each group 4 x 6 feet, or more if needed for its creative work.

Assign each group a different topic, based on your unit of study. Along with the topic, assign a list of questions the group is to answer. The students are to research the information, then determine what it is important to portray, what the message will be. They will need to discuss the design and who is going to do what, identify the materials they will need (e.g., crayons, chalk, paints, glue, cotton, foil, wallpaper samples, fabric). Be sure the kids have plenty of room within which to work. They begin by outlining the design of the mural in pencil. When all the materials are available, they work on the mural until completed. The groups share their work with the whole class, then place the murals on the wall or even in the school hallway for everyone to see their work.

Into Current Events

This activity aims at getting the kids more involved in what is taking place in the Jewish world. Bring in a selection of pictures of Jewish people who are or have been in the news. Include headlines involving these people. Mount the pictures on colored construction paper and place on the bulletin board. Number each picture. Take one at a time and ask the students what they know about the person depicted. If they know anything, let them write their information on index cards and put them under the proper picture. For additional information, they are to keep track of the news and bring in whatever they learn about each person on the bulletin board.

Radio or TV?

Divide the class into small groups. Give the groups copies of Jewish magazines and newspapers from which to gather information on current events. Each group can choose one of the following ways of presenting the news to the rest of the class:

Radio or TV newscast.

Radio or TV talk show.

Press release.

Radio or TV interview.

Role-play the situation.

Encourage the students to make their presentations more realistic by naming their station and giving it call letters. Let them prepare a place in the room for their presentations. When everyone is ready, give each group time to make its current events presentation.

Good News!

Sometimes it is depressing to read only bad news in the newspaper. There is some good news out there! Have your students create a monthly good news report. Tell them to read newspapers and magazines, and listen to the news on radio and TV, to gather the good news. In their good news report they can share stories showing that people do care, describe special events in the school, and tell about the good things kids do! To add a Jewish dimension, tell them to relate their reports to an appropriate Jewish concept.

Current Events File Folder

Keep a file folder of magazine and newspaper articles that cover events in the Middle East and other issues of concern (e.g., ecology, conservation, AIDS, abortion/right to life). When you have accumulated enough for your class, sort them according to issues and approach. For example:

Straightforward—just the facts.

Analysis—commentary.

One-sided—Whose side?

Presents both sides of picture.

Appeals to certain people—who?

Biased.

Mount the articles on tagboard and place in a pocket on the bulletin board. Next to the pocket, post instructions for the students, such as:

After reading the article, identify the Jewish source that calls for us to be concerned. Then do one of the following:

Develop a debate pro/con on the subject.

Write letters of support.

Write letters to the editor pointing out discrepancies in the articles.

Put on a one-act play that presents both sides of the picture and offers options for a solution.

Rewrite a biased article so that it is no longer biased.

Current Events Scavenger Hunt

Save issues of newspapers and magazines, both Jewish and general. When you have enough, develop a list of news items the students are to locate during a scavenger hunt through these materials. Divide the class into small groups. Place five to ten news items on each sheet, making the list different for each group. Your news item questions could look something like this:

1. What is the goal of the UJC?
2. What exhibit opened at the Jewish Museum in New York?
3. Who was elected mayor of Jerusalem?
4. What did the prime minister of Israel say about the recent meeting with the PLO?
5. Which South American country elected a Jewish legislator?

The group members search for the answers to their questions in the newspapers and magazines. When they have completed the assignment, share with the class.

Holocaust Museum

This is a challenge, but it is also an excellent way to culminate the study of the Holocaust.

When you begin your Holocaust unit, talk to the class about creating a museum right in the classroom. Discuss the purpose of the museum, who would be invited to view it, what items to include, how items would be displayed, etc.

As you go through the lessons in this unit, identify, with the class, what information could be presented in the museum and how it could be displayed. Allow time during lessons for students, working in small groups, to develop displays based on what they have learned. The displays could be in the form of posters, clay models, models made from boxes, ritual objects, etc. Put each project on display.

Continue until all the lessons are completed. Rearrange the display as necessary, then invite guests to visit your Holocaust Museum.

Holocaust Memorial: A Closure

When your class has completed its study of the Holocaust, have the students create a Holocaust Memorial. If your synagogue does not have one, they could send letters to the leaders of the congregation explaining why the synagogue should consider establishing a Holocaust Memorial. After they have sent the letters, have students design their concept of a Holocaust

Memorial, either for indoors or outdoors. For this purpose divide the class into small groups. Each group draws its ideas and shares with the class, then the class chooses a design (perhaps it will be a composite, with ideas from all the groups). They then construct a model of their chosen concept.

Role-Play a Famous Jewish Person

Have everyone in the class take on the role of a famous Jewish person who lived during the period covered in your unit of study. Give the students time to do some research about the individuals to be role-played. Encourage them to use their imaginations to create costumes, masks, and posters that will express the person's characteristics without revealing the name. Assign the students specific times to role-play. When their turns come, they put on their costumes, display their posters, and parade around the room. After the other students guess the character's identity, the role-player explains the design of the costume and posters.

More Role-Playing

This is more fun if the kids can dress up! Get a box from the grocery store, cover with brightly colored paper, and you have a costume box. From friends, parents, and members of the congregation, collect such things as old wigs, ties, costume jewelry, purses, scarves, shoes, gloves, sunglasses, clothes, hats, etc. Store these in the box.

Make the role-playing a special event so that the students will clamor to do a role. Let them take turns playing a part. They get to choose items to make up costumes from the box, dressing up to play the roles.

Making Role-Playing More Comfortable

Sometimes students feel uncomfortable when they have to speak in front of their peers, but a little practice in role-playing and it becomes easier for them. You can help them along with some warm-up role-playing. Use simple situations with a selected cast of characters to demonstrate the technique. Describe a situation briefly, such as: "Company is coming to dinner." The cast of characters would be: mother, grandpa, sister, brother, family dog. Once the students are chosen for the roles, just let them improvise the situation for a few minutes. If necessary, make a few suggestions: How do you react to the news that company is coming? Who is the guest? Who is going to do what? And so on.

Once they have had a warm-up, give them role-play situations from a Jewish perspective, such as: "Moses is coming to the temple." The characters could be: the rabbi, Moses, a student, a teacher, the president of the congregation. Suggestions could be: What will Moses encounter? How do we prepare for the visit?

You can role-play many different situations, both present-day and historical. Just let the students assume the roles and develop characters according to their own perceptions and styles.

Wanted Posters

Have your students identify all the famous Jewish people who lived in the time period covered in your unit of study. Assign one person to each student. On the board place a list of what should be included in a wanted poster; it could look something like this:

Name of person; occupation.

Last seen; wanted for what?

Always being...(ready to help).

Having strong ideas about...(social issues, freedom, etc).

Greatly values...(Jewish concepts, life, and rituals).

Lives by...(Jewish time).

And any other information you want the students to obtain.

The incomplete sentences are to be filled in by the students, but give them an idea of what they need to look for in their research. Once they have finished their research, they create their wanted poster and share the finished product with their classmates.

Biographical Sheets

You will need stacks of old newspapers, scissors, glue, and blank newsprint.
Divide the class into small groups. Assign each group a famous person from Jewish history, and give it a stack of old newspapers and several sheets of newsprint. The members are to research their assigned person's background and write a biography on the newsprint, decorating it with descriptive words, sentences, and headlines cut from the newspapers. Each group shares its bio with the whole class.

Helping Hands Bulletin Board

With the class, develop a list of famous Jews. Assign students different people to research, finding out where they were born, something about their families, the work they did, and their contributions to the Jewish community and the community as a whole. While the students are doing this research, prepare the bulletin board and make up a number of hands cut from colored construction paper. Have the students present their findings to the class, then write the important information on 3 x 5 index cards. Mount each completed index card on a hand, and hang the hands on the Helping Hands bulletin board.

Bible/History Riddles

Riddles are fun, and youngsters enjoy them. Let them make up riddles about people they have studied. Or you can write the riddles, if you prefer.
Ask the students to each choose someone covered in the day's lesson.

Give out 3 x 5 index cards. Each student is to draw a picture of the chosen person or a symbol representing the person and underneath it is to write a short riddle with clues to the person's identity. Here are two examples:

I am a man. I lived on a kibbutz.
It is located in the south of Israel.
I helped to found the State of Israel.
Who am I?

I am a woman.
I am a princess.
I raised a baby found in a basket.
Who am I?

Interviewing Famous Jewish People

Prepare a list of questions to be used for an interview with a famous Jewish personality. The person the students interview can be someone from either past or present. Here are some sample questions:

What are some of your favorite Jewish activities?

What would you like to see changed in the Jewish community?

What would you like to remain the same?

Describe the characteristics of what you consider to be a good person.

How were you able to achieve…(whatever made the person famous)?

Did anything take place during your lifetime that made you angry? What was it?

What happened to make you sad?

What happened to make you happy?

The list of questions can be generic or can focus on the individual or the Jewish people.

Have the students choose partners and research their assigned persons, finding out all they can. Then they take turns at being interviewer and interviewee, asking and answering the questions and taking notes. After the interviews, each pair of students writes a newspaper article based on it. Compile all the articles into a class newspaper.

NEAT AND SIMPLE

A Simple Puppet Show

Collect pictures of famous Jewish people from old workbooks, history books, and periodicals. Enlarge as needed so that the heads are large enough to make puppets. Have students cut out the heads and mount them on tagboard; laminate if desired. Glue the tagboard with the head to a tongue depressor or popsicle stick. Behold, you have a puppet! Students can put on a puppet show based on an event in the person's life.

This Is Your Life!

Some of you may remember the old TV show of this name. It makes a good format for the study of famous Jewish people. Have the class choose someone to be the subject of the program, and do research to find out as much as possible about this person.

Using large pieces of butcher paper, they draw scenes from the person's life (e.g., birth, making friends, going to school, major achievements, special events, what the person did to become famous). Those who do not feel comfortable with drawing can cut pictures out of magazines. In addition, include some quotations from the Bible or a history book about this person or related to this person's life. Upon completion, post the "This Is Your Life" program on the wall and go over the events in the life of this person with the whole class.

Wall of Names

The Vietnam Memorial commemorates those who died during that war. How about having your students build a "Wall of Names" of people who have made major contributions to Jewish life? As they find individuals who they think belong on the Wall, let them explain the reasons for their choice. If the class concludes that the choice fits its criteria, add the name to the Wall.

Hall of Fame

As an alternative, make a Hall of Fame. Cover the bulletin board with colored paper and put the words *Hall of Fame* at the top. With the students, do some brainstorming to develop criteria for enrolling people in the Hall of Fame (include lifetime accomplishments, what they did for the Jewish people, how their acts helped the Jewish people, etc.). As the class learns about famous Jews, have students advocate on behalf of those they especially like. Then the class as a whole is to decide whom to admit to the Hall of Fame.

ALTERNATIVE

Cut out Jewish stars large enough to have a library pocket mounted in the center. Label each star with the name of a different Jewish "star" (famous person) from some historical period. Arrange the stars on the bulletin board in an attractive manner. Give students 3 x 5 index cards. As they gather information about the historical stars, they write one important fact on each card. Collect the cards. Shuffle and mix. Students are then to match the cards to the correct stars and put them in the appropriate pocket.

Badges of Fame

Discuss and list the qualities of heroism. Give some examples of heroic achievements by Jewish people. Keep the list in view as the lesson continues.

Divide the class into small groups, each to read a different story that has characters from Jewish history. Using the list, the group members are to decide which characters were heroic, stating their reasons.

Give each student the following supplies: a 5 x 7 piece of white paper, colored markers, a 6 x 8 piece of construction paper, and a 20-inch piece of yarn; in addition, each group will also need a holepunch, clear contact paper, and glue.

Each group member draws a picture of someone who played a heroic role in Jewish history, and around the picture writes a brief sentence that tells about the person selected. Paste the picture on the construction paper. Cover with clear contact paper. Punch holes in the construction paper, and pull the yarn through the holes, knotting to make a necklace. Have the students wear these "badges" when they tell their classmates about the heroic individuals shown in the pictures.

The Mystery Guest

Each student chooses a Jewish personality, but does not tell who it is. The person selected should be someone the student admires (e.g., a character from the Bible, a great sage, a figure noted for courage or a heroic contribution of some kind). The students are to find out as much as they can about the persons they have selected, listing mystery clues that could help others to identify their choices.

Upon completion of their research, the students make posters which offer clues about the persons selected but don't fully identify them. Set a specific time when each student's Mystery Guest is due to arrive in the classroom. Each student is to prepare a 2-minute speech about the Guest's life and accomplishments, and deliver the speech in the first-person ("I am so-and-so. I was born in...," etc.). The class has to identify the Mystery Guest.

ALTERNATIVE

Choose someone from your unit of study and describe this person to the class without revealing the name. Draw students into the mystery by providing clues (e.g., a postcard sent by this person to a friend describing a historical event). After each clue, give the class a chance to identify the person. If several clues don't work, try reading a letter written by this person to the class, providing additional clues. If the students still can't identify the person, have them write letters asking for more clues. They can ask for such things as a physical description, the person's occupation and contribution to Jewish life, where the person lives, etc. As each clue is provided, the class is to try to identify the individual. With each step, the students will learn more about what made this person famous. After they finally guess the person's identity, conclude the activity by reading aloud a farewell letter from the person.

Who Goes with What?

You will need construction paper, colored markers, and scissors. Cut out as many Jewish stars as you need. On one star write the name of a famous Jewish person, on another, write the name of a Jewish historical event with which this person is identified (e.g., David Ben-Gurion—creation of the State of Israel). Or choose biblical characters who go together (e.g., Abraham and Sarah, Moses and Aaron, Jacob and Esau). Scatter the stars on the table or floor, and have students match them up, putting the correct pair of stars together.

Oscar-Winning Performance

Jewish history is full of people who have played important parts on the stage of life. Have students nominate candidates to win Oscars for achievements in Jewish life and history. You can have Oscars in different categories (e.g., producer—behind-the-scenes facilitator; director—big macher; best actor and actress—male and female mensch; and the list can go on and on). Let the kids develop a list of as many as eight or ten categories, or have just three or four categories and make them really special. The class can also develop a list of qualities that nominees in each category must have before they can be considered. They will have to know their favorite Jewish figures very well, either through classroom study or research, in order to nominate them for any category.

Once students have nominated people, have them develop campaigns to "sell" their nominees. These should include posters, TV and newspaper ads, fliers, etc, giving the reasons for their choices. The Oscar project can involve the whole school, or at least several grade levels. Prepare ballots and have the election. After counting the ballots, have the presentation of awards.

Want more fun? Have either kids or parents role-play the winners and make acceptance speeches just like on an Academy Awards show.

To include an arts and crafts activity, have students make the awards to be given.

Past and Present

Divide the class into small groups. Let the members of each group choose two famous Jewish people, one from the past and one from the present. Provide a list to prevent duplications. Have the groups research the lives of these people, comparing the differences and similarities in their family backgrounds, growing up, education, and whatever professional training they might have had. Contrast their efforts on behalf of humanity and the Jewish people, and the strategies they used to effect change.

When the research is completed, the students are to prepare reports to be shared with the class. The reports can be in the form of a series of posters, a drama, a TV show, a news report, a slide show, or any other creative means of sharing the information.

Filling the Shoes

Provide the class with a list of famous Jews, with one or two words describing their accomplishments. Ask the students to choose one person they admire, making sure there are no duplications. They are to research the persons they select, listing their qualities and background. Give each student a large sheet of construction paper, scissors, and colored markers. Ask them to draw a shoe, or give them an outline to trace; color the shoe and cut it out. On the inside of the shoe, write the name of the famous Jewish person and list all the qualities needed to fill the person's shoes. Students share their "shoes" with the class, then display them in the school hallway for everyone to see.

My Dinner with...

Ask the students to pretend they are going to have a dinner party for a famous Jewish person from your unit of study. Divide the class into small groups and give each group a task (e.g., guest list and seating arrangements, menu, table setting and decorations, ritual, intellectual pursuits). The groups are to decide whom to invite, what food to serve, what Jewish rituals are appropriate, who sits next to whom, and what questions to ask the guest. To make all this more realistic, ask a parent or a member of the congregation to role-play the guest. Give the guest the questions ahead of time. On the date of the "dinner party," the guest arrives, the students do their thing, and the guest answers the questions, etc.

ALTERNATIVE

Write the name of some famous Jewish persons on strips of colored paper. Make enough strips for the whole class. Have the students choose strips and, without revealing what is written on them, find out as much as they can about the persons they have chosen. When the research is completed, ask for a volunteer to be the "guest of honor." The guest sits in a chair in front of the room. The class asks yes or no questions to try and identify the guest of honor. Those who guess wrong do not participate again until the next guest arrives. The student who identifies the guest correctly becomes the next guest of honor.

ISRAEL

A Time-Line

Stretch a wire or clothesline across a portion of the classroom. Tell the class that this is a time-line which they will add to as they study the State of Israel. Provide index cards, colored markers, and clips to be used whenever needed during lessons. The students are to draw or cut out pictures to represent various events in Israel's history, then place them on the time-line. As more and more cards are added to the line, it will be necessary to keep them in the proper sequence.

Story with Missing Words

This activity can be used with any city or historical site in Israel. Create a story about the historical site, leaving blank spaces where the students are to place the correct words. Give them a list of the missing words, but not in the correct order. Here is an example of what you can do:

The Story of Masada

In the first century C.E., the rulers of the Roman Empire decided to prohibit all groups from following their own lifestyles and _____. A group of Jews called _____ refused to give up their rights and _____. They made their way up to _____, an old fortress on a _____ top in the middle of the _____. Though they were surrounded by the _____ legions, they held out for three years. The Romans, though, were fed up with the fight and built a _____ to reach the _____. The Jews knew they could no longer hold out and decided on _____ instead of being overrun by the Roman soldiers. The story of the Zealots' last hours was related by _____, a Jew turned Roman historian. Masada is located on the edge of the _____ Desert. It was originally built by _____ as a royal fortress for himself. Today, in _____, there is a slogan, "_____ will not _____ again." Masada is not only a _____ attraction, but the army swears in new _____ there, and it is a popular place to celebrate one's _____.

Words you can use to fill in the blank spaces:

beliefs	King Herod	ramp
rebelled	Masada	mass suicide
mountain	tourist	Judean
Roman	Bar Mitzvah	Israel
fortress	Zealots	fall
Josephus	desert	recruits

ALTERNATIVE

This approach will show you what the students know and don't know about Israel before you begin to teach the subject. Prepare a short paragraph about Israel, but leave 10 words blank for the students to fill in. Give them a list of 12 to 15 words that can be used, but be sure the words are not in the correct order. Your paragraph could look something like this:

Today nearly _____ Jews live in the State of Israel. More than _____ Jewish immigrants were helped by the Joint Distribution Committee and the United Jewish Appeal to come to live in Israel soon after World War II. Israel officially became a nation in _____. The _____ offers every Jew automatic citizenship. Operation _____ brought 50,000 Jews to Israel from _____. All over Israel _____ dig for links with Israel's past. Arad is an example of a _____. After the Six-Day War Jews could once again pray at the _____. The last Arab-Israeli war took place on _____. Before he was assassinated, the president of Egypt, Anwar _____, and the prime minister of Israel, Menachem _____, worked hard to find a just and honorable _____ for everyone. In 1994, Shimon _____, Yitzhak _____, and Yasir _____ received the Nobel Peace Prize for their effort to make peace in the Middle East.

Words you can use:

peace	Rabin	1947
Kotel	development town	1948
Begin	moshav	Yemen
1973	Magic Carpet	archaeologists
Arafat	2,000,000	Sadat
1966	250,000	Yom Kippur
Law of Return	3,000,000	
kibbutzim	Peres	

Another Fill In the Missing Words

Here is an exercise for teaching students about cities in Israel. Prepare incomplete sentences and place them on the left-hand side of the paper. On the right-hand side, put a list of words which can be used to fill in the blanks. Put them in the wrong order and include a few words that do not belong, not to confuse the class, but to make them think about what they are doing. This is not a test. If they do not know the correct word to complete a sentence, have resources or textbooks available in which they can look up the answer. For example (the following is for the city of Jerusalem):

1. The _____ Valley is the site of ancient tombs near the Old City.

2. Jerusalem is the _____ city in Israel.

3. _____ is the location of Chasidim and very religious Jews.

4. _____ were the first homes built outside the Old City by Sir Moses Montefiore.

5. Jerusalem is the holy city for these three religions: _____, _____, and _____.

6. You can enter the _____ and go directly to the Western Wall in the Old City.

7. The building where Moslems pray is called a _____.

8. The holy place where Jews pray and place written prayers between the cracks is called the _____.

9. The _____ is the Israeli legislative body that makes all the laws.

10. The Dead Sea Scrolls are kept in the _____.

11. The largest medical center in the Middle East is in Jerusalem

110

and is called _____.

12. Hebrew University is located on _____.

13. _____ contains artifacts found in the many archaeological digs.

14. There are a number of gates into the Old City; the one used mostly by Arabs is called the _____.

15. The Citadel of David is located by the _____.

The following are the words which can be used to fill in the blanks:

holiest	Shrine of the Book	Dome of the Rock
Moslem	Mount of Olives	Hadassah Medical Center
Dung Gate	Kidron	Israel Museum
Knesset	Mea Shearim	Damascus Gate
Mount Scopus	Mishkenot Sha'anaim	Eilat
Jaffa Gate	Christianity	mosque
Western Wall	Judaism	
	Islam	

NEAT AND SIMPLE

Identify Jews of Israel

Prepare short paragraphs about at least five different people who were instrumental in or important to the history of the State of Israel. Do not include the names. The students are to identify each person based on the information given. Make one or two fairly easy to identify, but see that the others need a bit of research. If the students cannot identity anyone on the list, they are to seek further information in the text or other books.

Qualities to Be Admired

Divide the class into small groups. Give each the name of someone who played an important part in Israeli history. The members are to find out as much as they can about the individual assigned them, listing the person's accomplishments in order to understand why this person is admired by other Israelis. Each group reports on its findings. When the groups have reported, make a composite list of the qualities that Israelis admire. With the students, go over the list and see if they can identify anyone today who has the same qualities.

Learn Where Sites Are in Israel

Trace a map of Israel on posterboard or mount a large blank map of Israel on the bulletin board. Number those sites/cities you want the students to be able to locate. Place a small piece of magnetic tape or Velcro beside each number. Cut out Jewish stars from tagboard. Label each star with the name of a numbered site or city. Laminate. Place a small piece of magnetic tape or Velcro on the back of each star. Store the stars in a pocket attached to the posterboard. Make and keep an answer key. As you study the State of Israel, have students identify the different sites and place the appropriate star in the proper location on the map.

Jewish Geography

This activity has been adapted from a popular PBS TV show "Where in the World Is Carmen Sandiego?" It is a fun way to familiarize students with locations and sites in Israel. Here are some examples of what you can do. Assign each student a specific question to research, or prepare 100 questions (more or less) and make it a baseball game. You can also develop geography questions based on Jews around the world, Jewish history, and even the Bible. The students become detectives as they identify the locations where a person or people might be found. So, here is a sample:

1. You are tracking Shlomo Gomo, and you know he is either in Haifa, Jerusalem, or Eilat. Then you get a tip that he is in the city with Israel's largest port. Where do you go? _____.

2. It turns out that your tipster was a native Israeli who lives in a kibbutz in northern Israel. What is a native Israeli called? _____.

3. Sarah Farah is lying low in the south of Israel where David Ben-Gurion had his home. Name the area where you might find her. _____.

4. If Shlomo wanted to steal the Dead Sea Scrolls, which city would he have to hit? _____.

5. Joe Shmoe is taking a train to Israel's holiest city. Name his destination. _____.

6. Jake and Joe Faker are great fans of art and mysticism. In what city in Israel will they find an artists' colony and the place where Jewish mysticism began? _____.

7. Jake and Joe Faker are chased out by the mystics and run to the mountains near the Mediterranean. Name the mountain they seek refuge on. _____.

8. Mo Brutus is hunting for more scrolls like the ones found near the Dead Sea. Name the caves where the Dead Sea Scrolls were found. _____.

9. Amos Camus begins heading south of Jerusalem to find what is considered the world's oldest city. Name it. _____.

10. Shlomo and Amos meet up with each other in the final stronghold of the Jews against the Romans. What is its name? _____.

11. Moe and Joe end up having coffee in a famous area of the modern city of Tel Aviv. What is this area called? _____.

12. Avi Novi goes prospecting for copper and finds it near the desert town of Eilat. Name the desert. _____.

13. Moshe, a very religious Jew, comes to Israel to study and live. He settles in one of the first Jewish settlements built outside the Old City's walls. Name this area. _____.

14. David Wavid begins hunting for the oldest-established vineyards and winery in Israel. Name this area. _____.

15. Leah and Rachel look for the beautiful lake in the north of Israel. They know it is near a city that has a Roman name. Name the lake. _____. Name the city. _____.

Locate This Site!

Hang a large map of Israel on the wall. Prepare paper strips with the names of Israeli cities or historical sites. Put the strips in a paper bag. Tell the students to take one strip each without letting anyone see it. Next have them check the locations of their sites on the map, but warn them to make sure no one else can tell which site they are looking at. Then they are to find out not less than five important facts about their sites. The facts are to be written on a sheet of paper headed with the name of the site—don't let anyone see it! Upon completion, each student shares the information, but without revealing the name. The other students have to guess what city or historical site it is. Whoever guesses right goes up to the map and marks the location.

Postcards from Israel

If any friends or fellow congregants are going to Israel, ask them to bring back a selection of postcards. Have the class browse through your collection of Israeli postcards and a map of Israel. Each student is to choose one card to write about.

First, locate the place on the map—without indicating the name to anyone else. Then write about what the card shows, using any of the following methods:

A letter home.

A story about the place.

A newsflash.

A commercial.

A press release.

The students are to keep in mind that the rest of the class will try and identify the card's location based on what they have written. Students write away, then share with the class. The class has to figure out where the postcard came from.

Reading a Map

Instead of pointing out Israeli locales on the map, copy enough small maps of Israel for each student or pair of students. Distribute a list of questions that will help the students to learn some Israeli geography; for example:

Is the Dead Sea north or south of Jerusalem?

Locate the moshav where David Ben-Gurion lived.

What big city is it near?

What is the desert called where this moshav is located?

Locate the oldest kibbutz in Israel.

What lake is it near?

And so on—the questions are limitless.

Game of Israel for Review

The class can work on creating this game throughout the unit on the State of Israel. Draw an outline map of Israel on a posterboard. Use colorful round sticky dots for the trail. Place a library pocket on the board to hold the cards, then laminate. Slit open the library pocket with an Exacto knife. Students write two or three review questions about Israel, check their work, then write each question on the front of a 3 x 5 index card and the answer on the back. Store the cards in the pocket. As new material is covered, the students add additional cards. By the end of the unit you will have your game for review all ready to go.

To play: The first student draws a card and answers the question. The player turns the card over to see if the answer given was correct. If it is, flip a coin and move the player's piece: heads—3 spaces; tails—2 spaces. If incorrect, the piece is not moved.

A Glossary

As you go through your unit of study on Israel, have the students create personal books of newly learned terms. In it they should list the words, and next to each word draw a descriptive or explanatory picture. By the end of the unit they will have a nice glossary of terms to remind them of important aspects of Israel.

Land of Israel Wall

After you complete your study of Israel, divide the class into small groups. Have prepared a list of different locations in Israel which you have studied (e.g., the Galilee, the Negev, the beach at Tel Aviv, the port of Haifa, the Old City of Jerusalem, Ein Gedi). Each group is to choose a location and create a mural showing all its highlights. Give each group a large piece of butcher or art paper, colored markers, construction paper of all colors, tissue paper of all colors, etc., to complete the task. Post on the wall.

Students Become Detectives

Prepare a short story about some aspect of the history of Israel. Include at least five mistakes. The students are to read the story, locate and circle the errors, and make the necessary corrections so that the information in the story is accurate.

Billboards

Creating a billboard can be quite a challenge. Advertisers have to create billboards that sell products with as few words as possible, because people usually see the billboard very quickly as they flash by in a car.

Divide the class into small groups. Challenge them to design billboards to sell some aspect of Israel and encourage people to visit the state. Assign each group a specific subject, or let the members use their imaginations to identify a subject that would induce people to visit Israel. Provide them with pencils and scrap paper to work on proposed designs. When the members of a group decide on a design, give them a large sheet of butcher paper and colored markers, and let them make the billboard.

Upon completion, the groups share their work, then place the bill-boards in the school hallway.

Create a Giant State of Israel Book

Divide the class into small groups. Give each group a different topic (e.g., government, industry, recreation, tourism, education, climate, flora and fauna, bodies of water, minerals, major cities, religious activities). Either have resource books available in the classroom or arrange for your class to use the library for research.

Cut, from butcher paper, a very large shape of the State of Israel—at least 6 feet in size. You will need one such sheet for each group. Have index cards in all colors, construction paper and lined paper, pencils, colored markers, glue, and scissors available.

When the research is completed, the groups begin putting the information together for their maps of Israel. The group members can use any of the materials you have provided, and the presentation of information can be in the form of poetry, prose, lists, drawings, etc. When the information is compiled, the members place it on their outline sheets of Israel in an attractive manner. When all the groups have completed their maps, prepare to bind the sheets together into a booklet. Before binding and to make the booklet sturdier, get a parent or friend to cut out of cardboard two outline maps of Israel. One will be used for the cover, on which the students create a design, and the other for the back. Bind cover and pages together with the back, and allow the kids to ooh and aah over their work. Place it on display in the library.

Tourism is big business in Israel. Using the same approach as above, have the students gear their research and findings to arousing interest in visiting Israel. Their giant travel brochure can be an incentive to visit the State of Israel.

Along the Same Lines: Travel Posters

As a closure for the study of Israel, let students choose their favorite cities or historical sites and design travel posters that highlight the main attractions to be seen there. Or, have them work in pairs designing general posters that encourage travel to Israel.

Some Role-Playing Opportunities

The students can take turns role-playing different situations that could or did take place in Israel. Give them the situations one at a time, asking for volunteers. Let them role-play what they think will happen during a given situation. Here are some possible situations:

Theodor Herzl and Ahad Ha'am discussing the question of Uganda.

A kibbutznik and an Israeli city-dweller comparing their lifestyles.

An American Jew and an Israeli discussing the question of aliyah.

Do You Know Your Neighbors?

Trace a map of Israel and the surrounding countries. Give copies to the students. Ask them to write in pencil the names of the countries around Israel. Display a map of the Middle East and let them see how many neighbors they got right and how many wrong.

Hidden Messages

Just a few different ways you can hide some lessons and have the students decipher the messages:

RUN SENTENCES TOGETHER

Run several sentences together without spaces between the words. To avoid making it too easy, do not capitalize proper nouns. Pretend the sentences have a secret message. Have the students decipher them. For example:

Injerusalemyoucanfindthewailingwall.

Intelavivyoucanvisitthemuseumofthediaspora.

Themuseumofthediasporaisthehistoryofthejewsoutsidethelandofisrael.

BROKEN TYPEWRITER

This activity is simple to create, and the kids have fun deciphering the message. Write a short story on a typewriter (or computer), but with an *x* whxrxvxr thxrx should be an *e*. You can even change every *a* to a *?*; this makes it a bit more difficult, but more fun. Distribute copies of the story. For example:

> Jxrus?lxm is ? grx?t pl?cx to sxx. Thx city bxlongs to our Jxwish hxrit?ge. You c?n sxx the W?iling W?ll ?nd pl?cx ? pr?yxr or wish right into ? sp?cx in thx w?ll. You c?n w?lk ?round thx w?ll of thx Old City and sxx m?ny nxw buildings in thx Jxwish Qu?rtxr.

MIRROR MESSAGES

If you really want to get ambitious, try writing the messages backwards. You will need to practice writing sentences or questions backwards, and provide a mirror in case the kids can't read your backwards writing. Each sentence should have either an action to perform or a question to answer.

Mural of Cities in Israel

Have the students choose partners. Assign each pair a specific city in Israel. They are to find out as much as they can about this city (e.g., size, population, historical sites, geography, government, agriculture, manufacturing, education, religious sites). While they are doing their research, gather the materials they will need for their mural: a very long piece of white butcher paper—allowing about 6 feet for each city—colored markers, colorful travel brochures about different cities in Israel, old workbooks, magazines, and newspapers with pictures of Israel.

Upon completion of the research, roll the piece of butcher paper out on the floor. Assign a portion of the paper to each pair of students. They are to transform all their information into a colorful mural which tells all about their city. They can draw, write, cut out pictures to highlight the information. When the mural is complete, hang it on the wall to be admired. Have each pair of students share what they have learned about their city.

Plan a Trip to Israel

A fun way to learn about Israel is for the students to plan a trip there. Divide the class into pairs or small groups. Assign a different task to each group or pair. Tell the students to think about: What time of the year should they make the trip? How will they get there? What will they do when they get there? What will the weather be like? What clothes will they need? Which cities should they visit? What is there to see in each city?

After the groups gather the information, the class, working together, develops an itinerary and a day-to-day agenda of places to visit and what to see.

A Book about Israel

As they study the unit on Israel, the students can be compiling a book on it. Begin by making a cardboard outline map of Israel. Have the students trace the map on construction paper. They will need two pieces, one for the cover and one for the back. Use white paper for the pages of the book. Let the students decide whether they want to have different sections (e.g., government, agriculture, historical sites, political parties, kibbutzim and moshavim, religion, lifestyles). These could be distinguished by using different-colored paper for each section or by separating the sections with dividers made from colored paper.

As the students learn the locations of different sites in Israel, they are to mark them on their maps. The separate sections can be filled with pictures they draw or cut out from old workbooks, as well as with written material, puzzles, and games. By the end of their study of Israel each student will have a complete book of the information learned.

Children of Israel

Ask the students to list their free-time activities. From their lists, they are to rank-order six things they like to do more than anything else. Put the lists aside. Now have them research what Israeli youngsters their age do in their free time and list these activities. Have them compare the activities on the two lists. What are the similarities and differences? What are the reasons for the differences and similarities? Once your students have become interested in the life of Israeli youngsters of the same age, you could move from this into proposing that they join a pen pal program with Israeli peers.

Fact Sheets

Another way students can teach themselves is to prepare fact sheets about two cities in Israel. Let the students choose the cities. This is not a test. If they do not know an answer, they can look it up; just make sure you have textbooks and other resources available for this purpose. For example, below is a list of sites and facts pertaining to Safed and Jerusalem. The students are to place an *S* on items pertaining to Safed, and a *J* on those that tell something about Jerusalem.

_____ site of the Davidka

_____ center of Jewish mysticism

_____ Kidron Valley

_____ artists' colony

_____ Israel Museum

_____ burial place of Joseph Caro

_____ Cave of Shem and Eber

_____ Mount of Olives

_____ Shrine of the Book

_____ first printing of a Hebrew book

Fact or Fiction

True-and-false questions are always good and can also be called fact-or-fiction questions. This method can be used both to review and to learn. If for learning, it is not a test. If the students do not know an answer, they can look it up. Here is an example of what you can do:

1. Throughout 19 centuries of foreign rule, Jewish life continued to exist in the land of Israel. Fact_____ Fiction_____

2. The State of Israel was established by a declaration of the United States on May 14, 1948. Fact_____Fiction_____

3. All the Israelis living in Israel today are Sabras, born in the State of Israel. Fact____Fiction_____

4. Tel Aviv is the capital of Israel. Fact____Fiction_____

5. Today in Israel, buses stop running and most shops close down on Friday evening for Shabbat, remaining closed until Saturday at sundown. Fact_____Fiction_____

6. An activity which occupies much of the spare time of a lot of Israelis is archaeology. Fact____Fiction_____

7. The city of Safed was once where many studied Kabbalah, mystical Judaism. Safed is also where the song we sing on Friday night, "Lechah Dodi," originated many years ago. Fact_____Fiction____

8. The moshav and kibbutz are agricultural communities in Israel where all the profits of the community are shared. Fact_____Fiction_____

News Report

Divide the class into news teams. Assign each team a city or place in Israel to investigate and report on. Give each team a list of questions that need to be answered in its newscast. The teams do their research, then create a telecast from that location in Israel.

Celebrate Yom Ha'atzmaut

Celebrate Israel Independence Day with a tabletop parade that is not only a commemoration of Yom Ha'atzmaut but the culmination of the study unit. Divide the class into small groups to make parade "floats." As the students study different aspects of Israel, they are to list the information they will want to share with others in the school through the parade. Their floats should be designed to display important facts and features of Israel (famous landmarks, agriculture and industry, geography, religious and historical facts of interest, etc.).

To design the floats, have the students lay them out on paper first, then identify the materials they will need. These could include such things as colored markers, scissors, match boxes, glue, styrofoam trays, checkers, empty thread spools, corks, even sand, yarn, etc. Also determine what size table will be needed, and whether more than one is needed. Arrange for a table or tables to be available on the appropriate day. When their work is completed, the students set up their parade on the table or tables for all to admire.

Create a Wall

On brown butcher paper, or using 9 x 12 gray construction paper, create a simulation of the Western Wall in the Old City of Jerusalem. Place it on the wall of the classroom or in the hallway of the school. Decorate it by putting plants, flowers, etc., in some of the cracks. After explaining the history of the Western Wall and the custom of placing prayers in the cracks, ask the students to write prayers or wishes for themselves or others, and attach them to the cracks in the simulated wall. If the wall is placed in the school hallway, invite other classes to do the same thing. Discuss with the students what they might do to make their prayers/wishes come true.

SYMBOLS, RITUALS, AND CONCEPTS
Tikun Olam: The World Is in Our Hands

The world may be in our hands, but it is really a very big place. Thinking in terms of "our world" can sometimes be discouraging for children. What difference can they make in such a big world? So let's make their lives simpler and give them a chance to make a difference in their own smaller worlds.

In Genesis 1:26–28 we are told to "rule the earth." Scholars say that this also means to preserve the earth, because if we destroy it there will be no one to restore it. Recycling is one way kids can make a difference, even in a small way, because every little bit helps.

Provide your class with an assortment of magazines and newspapers. Ask each student to cut out at least 20 pictures of household products. Then have them choose partners, and give each dyad two lunch bags. They are to label one lunch bag *Can be recycled*, and the other, *Can't be recycled*. Have the students sort through the pictures and put them in the appropriate bags. If they run across an item they are not sure about, encourage them to ask questions. List the questionable items to be researched later.

After sorting the pictures, the class is to make up a composite list of recyclable and nonrecyclable items. The students are then to develop a campaign to encourage the congregation, their families, and their friends to use only items that are recyclable. The campaign can include posters, letters to the synagogue president, sisterhood, brotherhood, families and friends, articles in the temple bulletin, and even letters to the editors of the local and Jewish newspapers.

For the nonrecyclable items, the class will need to investigate different ways they could possibly be made recyclable. The students might want to write the manufacturers, asking what they are doing to make their products recyclable or encouraging them to do so. They can do some brainstorming and make up a list of alternative products that are recyclable and could be used instead. Even if they discover an answer for only one item, they have made a difference in their small world.

Preserving Our Environment

Preserving the environment involves more than just clean air, recycling, and saving energy. Also consider unnecessary uses of materials from animals. Here are a few activities which you can do in your classroom:

READ LABELS

Check the labels on pet foods and cosmetics. If they contain horse meat or whale meat, or if animals are used for testing, the students can encourage people not to buy these products and can write letters to the manufacturers requesting that they discontinue the objectionable practices.

CLEAN AIR AND WATER

Have the class contact factories and processing plants in your area to find out what steps they are taking to clean up the air and water. When the students find an environmentally concerned company, have them write letters to your local and Jewish newspapers commending it.

SAVING ENERGY

Have the students take an inventory of the items in their homes that use electricity. Discuss what items they could do without or use less of as a means of saving energy, especially if there is a power shortage. Have a debate, pro and con, on the proposed policy of having utility companies charge *more* as a home's use of electricity increases, instead of reducing charges for each kilowatt hour as consumption decreases.

OIL SPILLS

Oil spills are becoming too common. Divide the class into small groups. Ask the members of each group to write an imaginary story describing an oil spill from the underwater vantage point of a fish, or from the point of view of a bird caught in the oil.

RECYCLE OLD PAPERBACK BOOKS AND NEWSPAPERS

Ask the class to collect old magazines and books in their own neighborhoods. Get the entire congregation involved in the campaign. The old magazines and paperback books can be donated to a nursing home, VA hospital, AIDS hospice, etc.

LEFTOVER FOOD

What happens to leftover food from a congregational *simchah*? What effort is made to redistribute it to a food pantry? Let students investigate the congregation's policy, and if the food is tossed, have them encourage the congregation to make arrangements to take any leftovers to the nearest food pantry.

PAPERLESS LESSON

Try doing a lesson without using paper. Do some brainstorming with the class to come up with ways to do a paperless lesson (e.g., using the chalkboard, playing games, what else?). See how creative the students can be, then determine how many trees you have saved by not using paper for one lesson. Relate the whole lesson to the Jewish responsibility to preserve the environment, including trees.

Rebuilding the World

This idea originated at the Conference on Alternatives in Jewish Education (CAJE) Conference in Seattle, Washington, in 1989. It has been adapted for use in a fund-raising activity for a whole school.

Jews help to "fix the world" by doing mitzvot. We work with God to make the world a better place. First, have students in several classes identify different organizations in your community whose efforts are directed toward helping the homeless and hungry, fighting injustice, pursuing environmental concerns, helping abused children and battered wives, etc. You might prepare a list for the students to begin with and include Jewish organizations, both local and national. The students can add to the list if they find other worthwhile organizations that they want to consider. They are to research the background of each organization and determine the value of its contribution to "fixing the world."

Upon completion of their research, the students are to choose several organizations they wish to support. You might even want to create a Tikun Olam Council of students to make this decision. Depending on the size of your school and congregation, limit the list to four to six organizations.

Make a large map of the world, at least 24 x 48 inches. Mount it on thick posterboard (available at any art store), then get a parent to cut it into small puzzle pieces with a jig-saw. Use a frame the same size as the puzzle and insert the same-size cardboard. On this board draw an outline of the map that was cut into puzzle pieces. Now you have a base on which to place the puzzle pieces. Put this in a very visible location in the synagogue/school. Each day of religious school have students staff the map puzzle and sell pieces of it. The purchasers, by placing the pieces they buy on the map outline, will be acting symbolically to "fix the world." Sell the pieces of the puzzle for about $2 each.

Meanwhile, have other students design and create posters and fliers to let everyone know about the project. When the puzzle has been completely filled in, the funds raised can be distributed to the organizations chosen by the students.

What Have We Done to Our Earth?

Here are a few activities that will help the students to learn how we have polluted our world:

DOES IT BIODEGRADE?

Have the students bury some potato peels, a tin can, a bottle, and a plastic bag in their backyards. Ask them to identify the spots where the items are buried, using sticks with identifying signs. They are to check the items after a few weeks to see what has happened to them, then report their findings to the class.

WASTE FLOW CHART

Have students design a chart on which to record what is thrown away in their homes in one day. They are to post their charts in a convenient place and ask every member of the family to record everything thrown into a waste container during one day. Do this for a week. Bring the results to class and determine how much waste is created in the homes in just one week. Then multiply this by the number of people in your city. WOW! Discuss to cut down on solid waste disposal.

WHAT'S OUT THERE

Cut discarded nylon stockings into small equal squares. Fasten each square between two sticks to spread the hose apart. Place the samples in several outside locations and keep one inside as a control. Check the samples after one week to see what has happened. (My grandson did this for a science project and it was amazing how much crud accumulated in one week's time!) Discuss ways to control pollution.

And, of course, relate all these activities to the Jewish tradition of caring for our earth (*tikun olam*).

Feeding the Hungry

According to Jewish tradition, we are always to leave a corner of the field to be gleaned by the widows, orphans, and poor. In today's world many of our children, because their stomachs are always full, do not understand that there really are hungry people out there. Here are a few ways to alert them to the needs of the hungry:

GARBAGE CANS

Ask the students to list the types and amounts of food thrown out after at least one meal during the week. From the lists they submit, determine what sorts of meals could have been prepared from the leftovers. Emphasize that some people survive by eating what they find in garbage cans.

JUNK FOOD

Ask the students to list how much money their family spends in one week on junk food like soft drinks, chips, and candy bars. When they bring their lists in, total up how much money is spent on junk food during the week by just one class. Multiply by 52 to find out the approximate yearly cost of this junk food. How many hungry people could be fed on that amount of money?

A Bowl of Rice

This could be a tough one. There are people in the world who survive on one bowl of rice a day. Ask your students to try an experiment to find out what it's like. On a given day they are to eat only one-third of a cup of cooked rice and water for each meal—no snacks in between! Ask them to share their feelings during the day's experiment.

Here are some other activities related to hunger. Do these or similar activities to help the students become aware of the hunger problem in their own city, if not the world. You might even have someone from your local hunger pantry or food bank come and talk to the class after the activities to explain the local problem. Then have the students develop "Beat Hunger" projects. Be sure the projects are doable and will have results that can be seen.

Canned Food Drive

Designate one day a month as canned food day for the entire school. Students organize, publicize the event, and set up collection sites at the synagogue. Get some parents to deliver the canned goods to the food pantry each month; even better, establish a crew of kids to help the food pantry organize and shelve your school's delivery each month.

Walk for Food

Even if it is just around the synagogue building. Students get people to sponsor them, and each time they make a circuit around the building the sponsor donates a can of food. This can really add up when the whole school is involved. (I sponsored my grandson several years ago and had to hand over 18 cans of food when he was finished!)

Plant a Vegetable Garden

Get the synagogue to give the class a plot of ground where the students can plant vegetables and care for them. When the vegetables are harvested, deliver them to the local food bank.

Gathering the Sparks

Divide the class into small groups. You will need one large piece of butcher paper for each group, lots of magazines, scissors, and glue. Prepare the following midrash to share with the students (it can be on paper for them to read or can be told aloud as a story).

> Said the Besht: "A king dropped a gem out of his ring, and gave his favorite son a clue as to its whereabouts. By finding it the son would be able to show his diligence and sagacity in pleasing his father. Likewise, God has dropped sparks of holiness upon the world. Through God's Torah, Israel is given clues regarding the places they have fallen on earth, so that the people of Israel may gather up the sparks and return them to God."

Talk about: What are the sparks of holiness? Where might they be located? How can we find them? How can the Torah help us? How can gathering the sparks help us to be partners with God in completing creation?

Lead into the following activity: Have the members of each group draw an outline of a human body on butcher paper—one of the students can lie down on the paper as a model to be outlined. Then have the students go through the magazines and cut out pictures representing ways they can gather the sparks to repair the world: the process known as *tikun olam*, showing that Jews are fixers, God's partners in completing the creation. Using these pictures, the students are to make a collage on the body outline. Upon completion, the students in each group explain its collage and how the pictures represent how we can gather the sparks. After they have explained, mount the collages on the wall.

Caring for the Elderly: Performing a Mitzvah

It is part of the Jewish tradition to respect and care for the elderly. Prepare several traditional quotations that tell us how to treat the elderly. Some good ones can be found in the Book of Leviticus and in Proverbs. Share them with the class. Here are several activities the students can do:

BIRTHDAY CARDS

Contact your local Jewish home. If there is none, let it be any home for the elderly; the activity would still be a mitzvah. Obtain the names and birth dates of the senior citizens in residence. Have the students write poems and stories, design birthday cards, or draw pictures to help the senior citizens celebrate their birthdays. Send their work to the home on each person's birthday.

VISIT THE HOME

Set a date with the center, then get the students involved in planning a program: songs, a short play, poetry readings, etc. Also consider making little gifts to give each resident.

ANOTHER KIND OF VISIT

Plan two trips to the home. The first trip is to meet and interview the senior citizens. Let students choose partners and assign one senior citizen to each pair of children. Prior to the visit, brainstorm with the students, making a list of questions they should ask in order to learn more about the elderly persons to whom they are assigned. The questions could include:

What was the funniest thing that happened to you as a child?

What did you enjoy playing?

What was a typical school day like?

What did you and your friends do for fun?

What was the best thing that ever happened to you?

What was the worst thing that ever happened to you?

What was your mode of transportation? How did you get around?

What is your favorite Jewish holiday? How did your family celebrate it?

Also ask questions about religious school, worship services, how they celebrated Shabbat, etc.

On the first visit, the students should have their questions and notebooks ready and interview their senior citizens. Bring a camera and take pictures of them with the seniors. Before the next visit, the students are to write a story about their seniors based on the answers to the questions. They decorate the pages, design a cover and title page, and place the picture you took on the title page. Compile the pages into a booklet and it becomes a gift the students can bring to the residents when they visit the home again.

"Love Your Neighbor as Yourself"

Ideally, we would like to see our children grow up to be part of a loving, caring community. A positive self-image is important, and so is the ability to tolerate differences. The following is a true story:

> A member of the Ku Klux Klan was told by his leader to learn all he could about the enemy—the Jews. The Klan member began reading about what Jews believed and practiced, and he liked what he read! He studied for a year with a rabbi, learned Hebrew and prayers, Bible and Jewish history. After a year of intense study he converted to Judaism.
>
> We can't touch every member of the KKK in this manner, although it would be nice, but we can prepare our children. Before we can love our neighbors, we must love ourselves. Unfortunately, young people have the very bad habit of putting their peers down, and this certainly doesn't build positive self-esteem. If children are to love themselves, we must encourage them to think positively and not allow put-downs.

The following simple exercise helps young people to think positively about themselves and others. Give a large sheet of newsprint and several colored markers to each student. They are to write their names in the center of the sheet and then, using the markers, are to encircle their names with all the things they like about themselves. As they do this, go around the room and encourage anyone who has a negative self-image by pointing out positive attributes you have noticed. Allow time for the class to complete this task, then have the students pass their sheets to the next person. The recipient is to write one positive quality or thing about the person whose name is on the sheet. Continue this process until the sheets have gone all around the room and are returned to the owners. Post the sheets on the wall. One at a time, the students are to stand by their sheets and read off all the nice things that have been said about them. The class applauds when each student finishes.

Process the activity. Let the students talk about how they feel when positive things are said about them. Also talk about how they feel when negative things are said about them. Ask them what effort they will make to avoid making negative comments. Remind them of the talmudic saying,

"Unless you have something nice to say about someone, don't say anything." Also from the Talmud: "Rabbi Nechuniah ben Hakaneh was asked: How have you merited long life? He replied, I never tried to elevate myself at the expense of my neighbor." Baruch Spinoza said: "I have made a ceaseless effort not to ridicule, not to bewail or to scorn human actions, but to understand them."

Discuss discrimination and prejudice. Do some brainstorming with the class and list the factors that cause discrimination and prejudice. Have the students list occasions or situations when they discriminated against someone. Talk about why they did so. How do they think the victim felt? Remind them of how they felt when positive and negative things were said about them. Let them talk about ways they can avoid discriminating against others. As a closure, ask everyone to write down one way to avoid discriminating against other people or putting them down.

Rank-Order What They Value

The lessons you teach usually embody valuable Jewish concepts. Prepare, in advance, a sheet with pictures, symbols, and words that represent Jewish concepts. Copy one for each student. After a lesson has been completed, give this sheet to the students along with a blank sheet of paper, scissors, and paste. Students are to cut out the pictures, symbols, and words, and place them in order of importance to them—the most important at the top of the page, and the least important at the bottom. Next to each one, they are to write their reasons for ranking them in this order. Have the students share their orders of importance and their reasons with the class.

The Missing Word

Write several quotations from your study unit on index cards, one word to a card. Prepare enough sets of quotations so that each group will have a different quotation. Divide the class into small groups. Give each group a set of cards, minus one word. Give the missing-word card to one member of the group, to be retained until you authorize using it. The members of each group form the quotation minus the missing word. They take turns showing the unfinished quotation, and the class tries to guess the missing word. When someone comes up with the right word, the person with the missing card joins the group to place the missing word in the quotation.

Collage of Jewish Concepts

Give each student a magazine, scissors, glue, and a sheet of 9 x 12 construction paper. Based on your unit of study, the students are to choose a Jewish concept that they feel very strongly about. Using the magazine, they cut out pictures that represent the essence of the chosen concept. Once they have created a collage from these pictures, they are to cut out words and phrases which explain the message of the Jewish concept. Place the message attractively over the collage. Upon completion, they share their work and the reasons for their choices. When each student has shared, compare the differences and similarities between the collages and messages based on the same Jewish concept.

A Story Can Lead to a Mitzvah

Choose a story with a major Jewish concept to either tell or read to the class. Kids like to be told stories, but if you are going to read aloud, make copies so they can follow along.

After the story, ask the class to identify the Jewish concept it embodies. Divide the class into small groups. Each group is to write its own story based on the same Jewish concept. This will give the students an opportunity to make the concept personal and a part of their everyday life.

After the students share their stories, form a circle. One at a time, have the students tell how they would fulfill the Jewish concept. For example: the concept is to feed the hungry. Each student suggests a project that would achieve this goal, and you keep a record of their proposals. After everyone has participated, let the students choose a project they would like to take to the end. Now you have taught a lesson and in addition have the potential of *doing* something that will actualize the concept.

Creating Mottos

As a lesson closure, ask the students to take the idea of the major Jewish concept you have taught and create a motto expressing its essence. Divide the class into small groups. Give each group paper and pencil to be used in designing the mottoes. When the group members are satisfied with their design, give them drawing paper and colored markers. Each group draws the design on the drawing paper. The groups share their designs, giving the reasons for their choices, and post around the room.

Investigating Jewish Symbols

Let the class take a deeper look at Jewish symbols and discover what they mean, where they came from, etc. The Star of David and the seven-branched menorah are the best-known Jewish symbols. The seven-branched menorah is probably the older of the two, for it is described in the Bible (Exodus 25:31–36). The olive tree is also a Jewish symbol, dating back to the story of Noah. Today the Israeli national emblem is a menorah with an olive branch on each side. Did you know that there is a plant found in Israel which sometimes looks like a menorah with seven branches? It is the moriah plant.

Ask the students to find out as much as they can about the various Jewish symbols. A good topic would be, How the Israeli flag was created and the reason for its design. Another would be the design of Israel's national emblem. Have them share their findings. As a closure, have small groups design Jewish symbols using the concepts discovered during the research phase of the activity.

Using Midrashim to Teach Jewish Concepts

Many midrashim are excellent teaching tools. The activity in this section is based on the commandment found in Leviticus 19:16, "Thou shall not go up and down as a talebearer."

Begin the session by whispering in a student's ear something like, "The synagogue is going to create a dress code for religious school and everyone must abide by it." The first student is to whisper the message in the next one's ear, and so on, until the message goes all around the room and back to the first student. The last person repeats the message out loud. How does it compare to what the first student heard? Is it the same message? How does it differ? (From experience I can tell you that it will be different from whatever it was you said to the first student.)

When this exercise is over, hand out copies of the following two midrashim:

A young woman came to the rabbi of her community and confessed that she had been in the habit of telling falsehoods and spreading lies about her neighbors. She asked his help to enable her to make amends. "Pluck a chicken," he told her, "and scatter the feathers all the way from your home to mine. Gather them up again and bring them to me, and I will then give you my answer." Eagerly she promised to do this and left. The following day she returned and said, "Rabbi, I did as you instructed me. I plucked the chicken and scattered its feathers, but I regret that I couldn't bring them here, because when I tried to pick them up I discovered that the wind had blown them in all directions." "Yes, my child," replied the rabbi sadly, "lies are like feathers; once scattered, it is impossible to retrieve them. Nor can the damage they have done ever be recalled or completely amended. Henceforth, resolve to speak only the truth."

A man invited some friends to dine with him and sent his servant to the market to buy the best foods he could find. When dinner was served, every course consisted of tongue richly prepared with different kinds of sauces. After dinner the master angrily said to the servant, "What do you mean by serving tongue for every course? Did I not tell you to buy the best foods that could be found in the market?" The servant replied, "Have I not obeyed your orders? There is nothing better than a good tongue. It is the organ with which we speak kindness, pray to God, and spread love and friendship among all people."

The next day the master sent the servant to market for some food to feed to his dogs. "Get me the worst things you can find," he ordered. When the servant brought tongue again, the master cried out, "What! You dare bring tongue again!" "Most certainly," replied the servant. "There is nothing worse than a bad tongue. It is the organ that speaks lies and spreads gossip. It says mean things that make people angry with each other. There is nothing as good as a kind tongue, and there is nothing as cruel as a bad one."

Read the two midrashim with the students. Compare the opening activity to the problem the woman encountered in the first midrash. Ask the students to list the ways one can hurt others with words. Get them to give examples of times they have been hurt with words, or of people they know who have been hurt by words. Do some brainstorming and list the ways lies, slander, and gossip cause distress, anger, and dismay. Divide the class into small groups and have each group create a 3-minute skit that gives an example of how disastrous lies, slander, and gossip can be. (Believe me, these skits will be based on their own experiences.) After each group has performed its skit, ask the students to complete this sentence: "I will do my best to refrain from spreading gossip and telling lies because..."

For your information, here are a couple of midrashim that will tickle the kids and can be told orally:

Why does the human finger fit precisely into the opening in your ear? It was created in this manner so that, if you hear words to which you ought not to listen, such as gossip and slander, you can insert your finger in your ears and refuse to hear them.

And why did God create the ear lobe soft even though the rest of the tissue surrounding the ear is hard? The lobe is made of a pliable texture for the sake of someone exposed to evil speech (gossip and slander). One should bend it upwards to cover the eardrum, thus shutting out all *leshon hara* (slander and gossip).

Another Use for Midrashim

Choose a story (or several stories related to the same topic) and make enough copies for the whole class. Ask the students to read the story and identify the Jewish concept the writer was teaching. Once they have done this, they are to make posters that explain the story's meaning. Or they can write short stories of their own that teach the same concept, but in contemporary language. Share what they produce with the whole class.

More Uses for Midrashim: Create a Compliment Tree

Remember the saying from the Talmud, "If you don't have something nice to say to someone, don't say anything"? Make a Compliment Tree to emphasize this idea. Stick a branch from a tree in a bucket of sand, or draw a tree with branches on butcher paper and mount it on the wall or bulletin board. Prepare a bunch of cutout leaves in different colors. Give the students a leaf each and ask them to write something nice about someone in the class and hang it on the tree. To be sure there is a leaf for everyone, write the names of everyone in the class on leaves and fold them in half. Put the leaves in a box and have each student draw a leaf out. The messages the students write are to be directed to whoever is mentioned on the leaf—and it should be something nice, of course. If any students have problems writing compliments, give them some examples. Sometimes writing a compliment is easier than saying it. Get the kids in the habit of saying something nice and we just might eliminate the put-downs.

At the beginning of school, have the students write their names on slips of paper. Put the papers into a box. Each week choose a name from the box. Only positive things may be said about the person whose name is chosen. One by one, everyone in class makes a positive statement about this person. The list is written on large newsprint, with the entire class signing it, and the chosen one gets to take the paper home after it has been on display. Continue each week until everyone in the class has been chosen. Besides enhancing the students' positive self-images, you can relate this activity to the idea of being chosen: How does it feel to be chosen? What responsibilities go with being chosen?

A Book of Jewish Concepts for Today

This can be a homework assignment involving the parents. Have the students prepare notebooks in which they collect articles from newspapers, magazines, etc., as well as comic strips and pictures pertaining to Jewish values or concepts. As they compile their collections in their notebooks, they are to identify the value or concept for each item. Specify a time by which the notebooks are to be completed. Then have the students share their findings with the whole class.

Ritual Objects Come to Life in a Story

Display some ritual objects or pictures of ritual objects. Ask the students to think of a story they could tell that would involve three of the objects on display. The story is to include some active use of the objects selected and must be told as though the student were one of the objects. When the stories are completed, have the students share with the whole class.

Jewish Values in Comic Strips

Kids like to read the comic strips, so why not let them read and collect them for a purpose: a lesson on some of the concepts and values of Judaism! Make a list of the concepts and values you have covered in class. It might look something like this:

Helping to care for others.

Respecting and honoring parents.

Peace.

Compassion and mercy.

Truth.

The Law.

Value of life.

Ecology.

God ideas.

Have everyone in class choose a concept or two. Over the next few weeks the students are to collect comic strips that are related in some way to the concepts they have chosen. Assign a date when they are to bring their collections of comic strips to class.

On the assigned day, the students share their comic strips, identifying the Jewish concepts in each one. From what they have collected, let them choose the six to ten comic strips which they think are the best examples of a Jewish concept or value. Place each of these at the top of a blank sheet of paper and copy. Divide the class into small groups and give each a set of the copied pages of comic strips. The group members are to write a short paragraph on what each comic strip is teaching and find a quotation from Jewish sources that confirms the concept. Have the groups share their work, and make a composite booklet of the best descriptions from each group. Copy the finished booklet and send it home to the parents. One copy could be placed in the library for viewing by other students.

We Are One: A Lesson in Cooperation

The people of Israel—Kelal Yisrael—are one, even though we are all individuals with our own ideas and characteristics. When we work alone, we are able to do some tasks, but we can accomplish much more when we are united and work on something together. This is a group activity; it could be done by one person, but the results are much more gratifying when a group works on it. Thus it is a good exercise to emphasize the "We are One" principle. You will need lots of 3 x 5 index cards and paperclips.

Divide the class into small groups. The task will be to construct an object that can only be built with index cards and paperclips. The group members may bend the cards, shape them in any fashion, and use them in any manner. The members will need to discuss their options in order to decide what their object will be, its purpose, and even its name. Give the groups a total of 15 minutes for discussion and construction. Upon completion, take a class vote on the different objects to determine which is the neatest, which the most creative, which the most humorous, etc. Hopefully each group will win in some category. The prizes will be a standing ovation and loud applause from the whole class. Then, emphasizing "We are One," talk about the effort they made working together, what was easy or difficult, and their success.

ALTERNATIVE

Prepare several different large Jewish symbols on posterboard or tagboard. You will need one symbol for each student. Cut the symbols into five pieces, using different cutting patterns for each puzzle. Provide one envelope for each group, and in it put one puzzle for each student in the group (thus, in a group with three members, there will be three puzzles in the envelope).

Divide the class into small groups. Give each group an envelope. Tell the students that each person in the group is to put together a Jewish symbol without talking to the others. Group members may give pieces to each other, but no one may take or ask out loud for a piece. Give the students a specific time limit to complete their puzzles. Begin with a signal and end with a signal. When they are finished, give the students some time to discuss what they did. Then talk about: What was easy or hard to do? How did they cooperate with each other? Compare this activity to the way the Jewish community works together to accomplish a task.

A Treasure Hunt in the Sanctuary

Take the class for a walk through the sanctuary, pointing out different objects. Give the students some time to really look at the sanctuary and what it contains. Back in the classroom, divide the class into small groups. Assign each group a different object that is found in the sanctuary, not letting any other group know what it is. Give the students time to find out everything they can about their object. Then have them come up with clues for a treasure hunt in the sanctuary. When they have written their clues, they exchange them with the other groups, and everyone goes to the sanctuary to find the treasures.

ALTERNATIVE

Write short silly letters to your class in which you provide the clues for a scavenger hunt. Use silly, funny headings like: "Dear Smarter Than We Thought" (or "Dear Getting Too Close," or "...Too Clever for Words," or "...Got to Be Getting Help from Someone," or "...Very Lucky People," etc.); just make the headings positive. Each letter is to be signed by two persons who are providing the clues about where the objects can be found. Use names like "Finky Joe" and "Shiny Susan." Prepare an answer sheet, each line with a number corresponding to a clue letter, and on each line enough spaces for all the letters in the answer. For example: two clue letters could read like this:

Dear Very Lucky People,

We got out! You couldn't keep us for very long, could you? Now let's see how smart you are and see if you can find us this time. The place where we are hiding is very special. Indiana Jones was looking for the ancient one from the Bible and he found it, could you? It is a receptacle for a treasured possession of the Jewish people, and there are usually more than one. It has been treasured for hundreds and even thousands of years. If you should find this place, enter the name of it in the first blanks on the answer sheet.

—Goodbye, You Poor People!

Dear Too Clever for Words,

You-all sure got lucky with that one, but we saw you coming and made it out just in time. But you will never find where we are now. It's warm and always will be, and we have enough light to read by so we can keep occupied while you stumble around below us. So hunt around, high and low, look as far as you can go; in the Bible

133

you will find a clue, 'cause Moses told Aaron what to do. Have fun hunting.

Finky Joe and Shiny Susan

The answer sheet would look something like this:

1. _ _ _ _ _ _ _ _ _ _ _
2. _ _ _ _ _ _ _ _

And so on.

The Synagogue as a Second Home

The synagogue can be a place where students feel good about themselves, feel comfortable and at home. Several simple activities create a positive self-image and only take a few minutes.

BAG OF GOOD STROKES

You will need a lunch bag for everyone in the class. Ask the students to place their names on the outside of the bags. Prepare and distribute strips of colored paper, making sure that everyone has as many strips as there are students in the class. The students pass their bags to the person next to them. The recipient writes on a strip of paper something positive and nice about the person whose bag it is and places the slip in the bag. Keep passing the bags until they have gone to everyone in the room and everyone has had a chance to add a positive statement about each student in the class. When the bags return to the owners, they open them, read the messages, and qvell!

FEELING WELCOME

Let students take turns each week saying hello and goodbye. They come to school a few minutes early when it is their turn. Standing at the door, they greet everyone with a warm smile and "good morning." At the end of the class they stand at the door and shake each person's hand, wishing each one well for the rest of the day.

The Glory of God's Creation

Take the class outside and give everyone a few minutes to look around and see the glory of God's creation. When you return to the classroom, distribute construction paper and colored markers or crayons. Tell the students to draw a picture of everything they saw that exemplifies or reveals the glory of God's creation. Upon completion, they share their drawings and the reasons for their choices.

Hebrew Flashcards

Make your own Hebrew flashcards with white paper plates and press-on Hebrew letters. Stack the cards when they are not in use. The cards are large enough for the kids to make words out of the Hebrew letters if you wish.

Introduction to a Prayer

Depending on the length of the prayer to be studied, either write each word on a separate card or write whole phrases on strips of paper. Mix them up so that they are totally out of order. Have the students arrange them in the correct order. After they put the prayer together, talk about the meaning of the prayer and where it fits into the worship service.

ALTERNATIVE

Take a short prayer (7-8 lines), preferably one familiar to the class. Place the verses or phrases from the prayer in random order on a sheet of paper, with a dotted line after each sentence. Distribute copies to everyone. Have the students read the paper, then cut out the phrases on the dotted lines. They are to arrange them in the proper order, then glue them to another sheet of paper. Check to be sure this has been done correctly.

Review of Prayers

You will need white butcher or art paper, sentence strips, pins, colored markers, tape or glue. Prepare the prayers you wish to review by placing one part of a prayer on one sentence strip, using both Hebrew and English, and the other half of the prayer on another sentence strip. For example: On one sentence strip put "Hear, O Israel"; on the other, "*Adonai* is our God. *Adonai* our God is One." Follow the same procedure until you have used all the prayers you want to be sure the students know. Mount the butcher paper on the wall.

Place the first part of each prayer on the butcher paper's left-hand side. Mix the other sentence strips up well and spread them on the table. Tell the students to match the ending of each prayer to its beginning.

A Prayer Pictograph

Not all prayers lend themselves to this activity, but among those that do are *Ve'ahavta* and *Ma'ariv*. Take a prayer, in Hebrew and English, and make copies for the class. Tell the students to read it and underline the most important words and/or phrases. Share with the class along with the reasons for their choices.

Divide the class into small groups. Ask each group to design a pictograph of the prayer, using pictures and symbols. The pictography is to have as few letters and words as possible. The resulting pictographs will be the students' own interpretations of the prayer, and making them will help the students to find meanings they may not have been aware of before. As each group shares the results of its creativity, encourage discussion. Share the traditional meaning of the prayer and have the class compare the similarities and differences between their interpretations and the traditional meaning.

Pirke Avot

There are many editions of *Pirke Avot* ("Ethics of Our Fathers"), and in addition you will find selections from this text in *Gates of Prayer*. Glean from *Pirke Avot* about a dozen sayings to share with the class.

Divide the class into small groups and distribute a copy of the sayings to each of them. Ask the members to read through the *Pirke Avot* selections and choose the one that they find most meaningful. Have them write a group story containing the essence of the selection. When the story is completed, they are to lay it out on several pages and illustrate them. Next the members are to design a cover and title page for the story, placing their names on the title page as the authors. Upon completion, the groups share their stories and explain how they arrived at the essence of the story.

Life-Cycle Wheel

This activity introduces the idea of life-cycle events. Each student constructs a Life-Cycle Wheel out of oaktag or a round pizza or cake board. Show the class an example of what you want them to make so they see how it is done. Label each spoke of the wheel with a life-cycle event: birth, Berit Milah, Consecration, Bar/Bat Mitzvah, Confirmation, marriage, death. Ask the students what life-cycle events they personally have celebrated. For those life-cycle events they have personally celebrated, ask them to bring in pictures of themselves participating in the events to place on the appropriate spokes of the wheel. If there is no picture available, they can draw one. For events yet to come, have them draw a picture on the appropriate spoke.

Life-Cycle Acrostic

After finishing the study of a life-cycle event, have the class compose an informational acrostic using the transliterated Hebrew name of the event. The acrostic is to convey what the life-cycle event means. For example:

BERIT

B is for Baby.

E is for Enjoyment.

R is for Relatives.

I is for the people of Israel.

T is for the Torah, which teaches us to keep the covenant.

"Important Events in My Life" Booklet

This activity will help your students to understand the sequence of life-cycle events and its relationship to special events in their lives. They will need to interview family members to find out about events in their past. Ideally, they should each try and find out about at least one major event which took place in every year of their lives up to the present time. Help the students prepare a fact list to be filled in during the interviews. It could look something like this:

Name _____.

Year One _____.

This is where I was born _____.

I was born at _____o'clock A.M./P.M.

My birthdate is _____.

I weighed _____ pounds _____ ounces and was _____ inches long.

My Hebrew name is _____.

I was named after _____.

My Hebrew name means _____.

Special events which took place when I was _____.

Year Two _____.

(List each year, until the present time.)

Prepare a 9 x 6 piece of tagboard or construction paper for each student, allowing 6 inches for each year of their lives, plus 6 inches for the cover. Fold each piece in 6-inch sections, accordion style. Or mark in advance where the paper is be folded and let the students do the folding. Have one already folded as an example. If the folds are creased with a ruler, they will be crisper. Staple a 20-inch piece of yarn to the last fold for a tie.

Explain to the class that each fold represents a year in their lives. They are to title each section at the top of each fold. They can either write their age or the year. They are now ready to create their own "Important Events in My Life" booklet. In each section they draw pictures or write short summaries of the significant events in their lives for that year, then decorate the cover and add the title. Relate this activity to the life-cycle events that take place during the life of a Jew and the sequence of these events. Let the kids talk about the life-cycle events they have already experienced.

Create a Dictionary of Hebrew Words

Provide the class with booklets made up of blank pages. In these they are to record Hebrew words as they learn them—one word on a page, with illustrations and a definition of the word. They can also design covers for the booklets. This "dictionary" will serve as a quick reference/resource book.

Peace Begins with Me

"Seek peace and pursue it" is a major Jewish concept. Well, peace wears many different colors and hues. Take some time, once in awhile, for the class to think about peace: how it can be achieved, what it means.

On the blackboard draw three separate areas. Label them *Me*, *My Community*, and *My Country*. Discuss the concept of peace with the class, then brainstorm all the different aspects of peace, placing the students' responses in the appropriate areas on the board.

Distribute 9 x 12 piece of papers which the students are to fold in three sections and label as on the blackboard. In each section, they are to draw a picture representing ways peace can be achieved and what they can do to help achieve peace. Or have lots of magazines available, along with scissors and glue. They can cut out pictures to make a collage in each area representing what they can do. Upon completion, share the work with the class, explaining what everyone can do in each area to contribute to the efforts to achieve peace. As a closure, have each student choose one thing to do. Encourage the students to create a time-task schedule to accomplish this thing.

ALTERNATIVE

World peace is much too broad a concept for some students. If they do not see results, they become discouraged. Let them develop an "In Pursuit of Peace" bulletin board. They can identify a theme (e.g., balloons, space, Jewish symbols). Do some brainstorming with the class, listing things young people can do to achieve peace, but limiting it to one area at a time (e.g., at home, with siblings, with neighbors, at school). Have the students make and cut out the symbols they have chosen for their theme, and as they develop their lists, write the goals for peace on each one. Place these on the bulletin board. All of the students are to identity a goal they would personally like to achieve in the pursuit of peace and place it on the bulletin board under the appropriate area. They are to set a time limit for their goal and each week report on their progress. When a goal has been achieved, the students report how they achieved it and how long it took them. Place a star next to the goals that have been achieved.

The Peaceful Classroom

Making peace can begin with the creation of a peaceful classroom community. Talk about what it takes to make the classroom a community of caring individuals. Ask the students to define *community*. Do some brainstorming: What makes a community? How does one create a community? Lead into the idea that the classroom can be a community and can be peaceful.

Again, do some brainstorming: How can a peaceful community be achieved? Make a list of what they can do, or cannot do, to make their classroom peaceful. Ask students to be specific (e.g., "People won't call other people names"). See how long a list they can create. As a closure, ask them to go over the list and choose one quality of a peaceful classroom they could improve upon. Make their choice the goal for the next few weeks. Ask them to suggest ways this goal can be met and how to assess their progress. Good luck!

Picture of Peace

Peace can be an elusive subject, but this activity will help the students to define it based on their own personal experiences. You will need drawing paper and crayons or colored markers.

Ask the students to think of a time when they really felt at peace. Try to think of that time as a photograph, remembering the colors, smells, who was there, and how their bodies were situated. Allow a few minutes for the students to think about this. Then have them draw pictures of peace with as much detail as possible. Those who find it difficult to recall a time when they were at peace can draw a picture of their idea of peace, being as descriptive as possible.

Have the students share their pictures of peace, describing how they felt. After everyone has shared, talk about: What are the similarities and differences between the pictures? How might other people in the picture feel? How could you capture that peaceful moment again? Be sure to post the pictures around the room.

Protagonists of Peace

Ask the students to choose a Jewish person (living or dead) whom they consider to be a protagonist of peace. They are to find out as much as possible about the persons they choose. When the research is completed, they are to create posters that tell about the persons they have selected, emphasizing their peaceful qualities. Share with the whole class.

Verbs of Peace

Divide the class into small groups. Ask the students to think about verbs that describe and express peace. Ask them to make lists of peaceful verbs for each letter of the alphabet. (Have some dictionaries available.) When their lists of verbs are complete, ask them to write poems which express peace, using some of the verbs. Once the poems are written, they are to design posters to go with their poems of peace.

NEAT AND SIMPLE

A Peace Tree

Brainstorm with the students, making a list of all the peace symbols they can think of (e.g., hearts, doves, olive branches, yellow ribbons, joined hands). On white butcher paper, draw a large, leafless tree. Have the students cut out different-colored large leaves. After drawing peace symbols on the leaves, they attach them to the tree.

Helping Hands: Deeds of Loving-Kindness

Every time we pick up the paper it always seems to be full of bad news. The good news, where we find people helping other people, is always way on the back pages. There are people, though, who offer a helping hand to others in need.

With the class, talk about the Jewish concept of helping others, doing deeds of loving-kindness. List all the different ways we can help others. Then ask the kids to design a class "Helping Hand" certificate. Let groups of three or four work together to design the certificate. After each group shares its design, have the class either choose the one it likes best or make a composite certificate taking the best from all that are offered.

As a homework assignment, ask the students to read the newspaper during the week and bring in articles about individuals or groups offering a helping hand to others. Take a few minutes each week and write a class letter to the people or groups mentioned in the paper, thanking them for what they did and sending them a "Helping Hand" certificate.

Another Kind of Helping Hand

Have each student trace a hand on color paper and cut out the outline. On the cutout hands the students are to tell about a way in which they have helped their family, their friends, or their community. The individual hands are stapled together in a circle of helping hands. If you find the students haven't been very helpful, do some brainstorming and make a list of all the different ways they can help others. If each student chooses one thing and does it during the week, the students will be able to make their circle of helping hands at the next class session.

Helping One Another

This activity is based on a midrash where a good person was shown heaven and hell. In hell people were sitting at a table laden with good food, but they were starving because their arms were tied in such a manner that they could not bend them. In heaven the people also were sitting at a table laden with good food, and their arms too were tied. The people in heaven, though, were happy and able to eat all they wanted, because even though the bonds on their arms made it impossible for them to feed themselves, they were still able to help someone else to eat, and they had learned that if they fed each other they too could partake of the food.

You will need two rulers per student, and enough old ties or twine to bind the arms of all the students in the class so that they cannot bend them at the elbow.

Ask parents or sisterhood to have some nice snacks laid out on a long table. Place chairs around the table, so that the students can sit across from each other. In another room, bind the students' arms. Bring them into the room with the table and tell them to sit down and enjoy the treats which have been prepared for them. Then back off. Let them figure out how to enjoy the snacks without being able to bend their elbows. It will take a few minutes, with much groaning and then giggling and laughing as they figure out that if they feed each other they can enjoy the snacks.

Untie the students' arms and tell the story about heaven and hell. Talk about the exercise they have just experienced. What did they learn from it? What is the lesson to be learned? Then do some brainstorming: Who are some people who are currently in need? Make a list of the students' ideas. Based on the list, ask them to identify ways these people can be helped— real projects the class could do to help them. Have the students choose one project they would like to do to help others. Have them develop a plan for its completion, assigning specific tasks to be accomplished and a time-line of when each task is to be completed. This way they can learn and then do deeds of loving-kindness.

Tzadik Award

Explain what a tzadik is. Do some brainstorming with the class and list the qualities of a righteous person. Once the list is made, talk about who they consider to be a righteous person today. Based on the list of the qualities of a righteous person, have them name some righteous people and talk about what they have done to be considered tzadikim. Could there be other people out there that they don't know about who are also righteous? Ask the students, during the week, to be aware of what actions people take, what they might do that would make others feel good. It could be something simple, like the secretary of the religious school smiling and greeting a student. It could even be something nice a family member did without being asked. They are to use the list of qualities of a righteous person as a guide. Ask them to bring the names to class the following week and describe the actions that made these individuals righteous.

How did the students recognize their righteous persons? Divide the class into small groups. Ask each group to design a Tzadik Award. Groups share their designs, and the class either chooses the one it likes best or makes a composite of the best from each design.

The next week students share their names and prepare a Tzadik Award for each person. They write a class letter to go with the awards and mail them to the individuals they have decided to honor.

The Caring Community

Many congregations have "caring community" committees that perform tasks showing concern for others. The Jewish tradition urges us to care for the less fortunate by feeding the poor, visiting the sick, helping people to help themselves, etc.

We hear enough of the bad, so let's be positive for a change. To help the students become aware of the good things people do, create a Caring Center in a corner of your room, or on a bulletin board, or on a wall in the hall of your school. This is to be a visual display of people who help. Have students, during the week, collect articles from newspapers and magazines about people who help other living things. Each class session, devote a few minutes for the sharing of their findings. Post articles in the Caring Center. An additional step, if you have time, would be for the students to write letters to these people, praising them for whatever they have done to care for others.

Secret Pals

There is more to giving then just money. According to Maimonides, one of the highest forms of *tzedakah* is to give to someone without the recipient knowing the identity of the donor. It says nothing about money. Students can give something nice to someone and make the recipient feel good at the same time. Try the following activity as another form of *tzedakah*:

Write all the students' names on individual slips of paper. Put these slips into a box or hat. Each student is to draw a slip out without revealing the name on it. The person named on the slip becomes the student's "secret pal" for the next few class sessions. The names of the secret pals are not to be revealed to anyone. During the next few class sessions, the students are to give at least three nice and special things to their secret pals. They must give them in such a way that the secret pal does not discover who is giving them.

Here are some suggestions:

Write a note to your secret pal telling what you like about him/her. Slip it in your pal's desk when no one is looking.

Write a poem especially for your secret pal and deliver it without being seen.

Slip a piece of gum or candy into your secret pal's desk with a note about how special he/she is.

At the end of the time period designated for this activity, the students are to reveal the identity of their secret pals. Discuss the feelings they had about being treated so nicely, and compare the way they gave gifts to their pals to Maimonides' form of *tzedakah*.

ALTERNATIVE

Give each student the name of another student which is to be kept secret. Prepare a large Jewish star out of light-blue construction paper for each student. Tell the students that in each corner of the star they are to write a positive statement about their secret classmates (i.e., six statements). They are to write the name of their secret classmate on the back of the star. Collect the stars and hand them out to the appropriate students. Give everyone time to qvell about all the nice things that have been said about each of them. Then ask the students to talk about how they feel when nice things are said and what bearing this has on giving *tzedakah*.

Helpful Words

Giving positive feedback to their peers may prove difficult for some students because they do not know what kinds of words make people feel good. Give them a list of positive words. For example:

Athletic	Cute	Mature
Attractive	Graceful	Neat
Bubbly	Handsome	Smart
Caring	Happy	Stunning
Clever	Helpful	Talented
Confident	Honest	Thoughtful
Considerate	Humorous	Trusting
Courteous	Intelligent	Well-groomed
Creative	Kind	

This is a beginning; add any other words that provide a feeling of positive self-worth.

Create a School Tzedakah Council

Some schools have a student Tzedakah Council which identifies the different charities that are to receive funds collected during the year. If yours doesn't have one, please consider this option. It will enable the students to learn about the different Jewish organizations and what needs they meet through their efforts. There is also no reason why your class can't investigate the different organizations on its own. If the students decide they especially like one organization, they could designate their funds for it.

To help with your class efforts, here is a simple *tzedakah* box your students can make:

You will need one pint or quart milk carton per student, scissors, staples, construction paper, crayons or colored markers, and glue or tape.

At the top, cut a hole for the money to be slipped in, then staple the top shut. Cut pieces of construction paper of a size to fit around the milk carton. Let students decorate the pieces as desired. Tape or glue them on the milk carton and it then becomes a personal *tzedakah* box. When the box is full, the students turn it in and make another one for their donations.

Giving More Than Keren Ami

The word *tzedakah* is from the Hebrew word *tzedek*, which means "justice" or "righteousness." Today, to most youngsters, *tzedakah* means no more than giving money to charity. But there is a deeper meaning to *tzedakah*, and the following activities will help the class learn other ways of giving.

Talk briefly about *tzedakah* and what the students think it means. Then do some brainstorming, making a list of giving words—things that can be given but not taken. Start the students off with a suggestion of your own, like *caring*. Other words could be: *assisting, belief, cooperating, courage, friendship, helping, integrity, love, patience, praise, respect, sensitivity, sharing, sincerity, smile, support, sympathy, trust, truth,* etc.

143

From the list of giving words, the students are to identify the three they consider the most important. Since these are all forms of *tzedakah,* the next step is for the students to come up with ways to give the three things, and to whom they can give them.

An Extension: Tzedakah Words

Only English words are used in the preceding activity. Hebrew words add another dimension to the understanding of *tzedakah.* Prepare a list of Hebrew words and English definitions. Place the Hebrew words on the right-hand side of the paper and number them. In the middle of the left-hand side place the English definitions, not in the same order as their Hebrew counterparts. The students are to match up the Hebrew words to the English definitions. But this is not a test; help them as necessary. In the list that follows, I have placed the English definitions opposite the correct Hebrew words. Remember to mix them well when you prepare your *tzedakah* word sheet.

Tzedakah Words

ahavah re'ut	love and friendship
bikur cholim	mitzvah of visiting the sick
bushah	insult
derech eretz	decency, acceptable behavior
emet	truth
gemilut chasadim	deeds of loving-kindness
hachnasat orchim	mitzvah of hospitality
hekdesh	community shelter for the needy
kavod	mitzvah of granting honor
kenah	jealousy
Keren Ami	Fund of My People
leshon hara	evil tongue (gossip, slander)
mensch	a good human being
mitzvah	commandment
nekamah	revenge
pushke	*tzedakah* box
rachamin	mercy, compassion
simchah shel mitzvah	joy of fulfilling the commandment
tikun olam	repairing the world
tzadik	a righteous person
tzedek	righteousness, justice

Note that the list includes some negative *tzedakah* words. We are also commanded *not* to do certain things. Have the students identify the negative words and give examples from their own experience of why they are negative. Compare the Hebrew list with the English list. How are they the same? How are they different?

Gemilut Chasadim Booklet

Creating a booklet of ideas for deeds of loving-kindness will help the students become more aware of what they can do to help others. You will need six sheets of plain paper and two pieces of blue tagboard or construction paper per student, scissors, glue, magazines, newspapers, catalogues, and old workbooks. To make:

1. Staple pages and cover together or punch two holes on the left-hand side and use two brads to secure booklet.
2. Have students look through the selection of magazines, etc., and cut out pictures representing deeds of gemilut chasadim (loving-kindness).
3. Decorate the covers and share their deeds of loving-kindness with the whole class.

Be accepting of the choices the students make, but if you are in doubt about any of them, ask for clarification. The act of clarifying will help students to be more sure about what they have chosen to depict.

Creating a Gemilut Chasadim Tree

The students can watch their tree grow as they perform deeds of loving-kindness throughout the year. Use a good-sized tree branch with a number of leafless branches; stick this in a pail with plaster of paris to set the branch, then decorate the pail. If a real branch is unavailable, draw a good-sized tree with leafless branches on butcher paper and hang on the wall. In addition you will need "deed leaves" cut from construction paper of all colors. If you use a real tree, you will need a hole punch and yarn to tie the leaves on the tree. If you use a butcher paper tree, you will need tape to stick the leaves on.

Discuss the concept of gemilut chasadim with the class. Brainstorm, listing as many examples as possible. Point out the tree and the deed leaves. Tell the students that whenever they perform a loving deed during the week, they can fill out a deed leaf describing it and put their name on the back. Hopefully, your gemilut chasadim tree will really begin to blossom and bloom all year long.

A POTPOURRI OF USEFUL IDEAS

Let Students Ask the Questions

When you haven't had time to fully plan a lesson, you probably turn to reading a textbook in class. That is sometimes a deadly way to spend a class session, but here's how to make it more palatable. First, talk about asking the right questions: questions that require thought before they can be answered, questions that require more than a yes or no answer, etc. Divide the class into small groups. Assign a different portion of the text and a reader to each group. The other members of the group are to listen carefully and write one or two questions for review. Upon completion, the students ask the questions and discussion can take place.

ALTERNATIVE

At the beginning of class, write on the blackboard the main topic from your unit of study. Prepare a colorful box ready to receive questions. Place some cards or slips of paper next to the box. When students arrive, ask them to write one question they would like answered about the topic. Save some time at the end of class and take the questions out and read them aloud. See if anyone can answer the questions. If no one knows the answer, including you, place the question on the bulletin board. Ask the students to discover the answer for the next class.

What Students Want to Know

Your curriculum is set, your lesson is planned, but sometimes students have questions that are not part of the curriculum. Take a shoebox and decorate it. Label the box something like "Things I Want to Know" and place a pen/pencil with slips of paper next to it. When students have a question that has nothing to do with your lesson, ask them to write it down and put it in the box. Read their questions and prepare yourself to answer them during spare minutes of classroom time. Read the question to the class and see if anyone knows the answer; embellish on whatever response is offered.

Students Teach Younger Students

Have your class plan lessons for younger children and work with them. By creating worksheets and workbooks on a specific Jewish subject, they will be learning while they teach the younger children. Talk with the teacher of the first- or second-grade class to make arrangements for each of their students to be assigned to one of yours. Plan a schedule for the year when the two will meet and work together—maybe once a month for about 30 minutes. Identify the subject matter for each session. Make a list of resource books for your students to use in creating their lessons. Spend a little time talking about the goals and objectives of the lessons, and supervise their work. Not only will your students be learning while they are teaching, they will also be developing a very positive self-image.

Create a Comic Strip Story

Your students become the models for a comic strip story based on your unit of study. You will need a Polaroid camera and film, felt tip pens, white drawing paper, and glue. First, with the students, identify the theme of your story.

Divide the class into small groups. Give each group a topic to discuss, one that stimulates an animated discussion. This is to set the stage for the pictures that will be taken for the comic strip story. As the groups talk, go around and take pictures until you have enough for the comic strip. Share the pictures with the students and let them decide whether there are enough for a comic strip. Take more pictures, if necessary.

Let the students arrange and rearrange the pictures until they are satisfied that the sequence can be used to create a comic strip story based on their chosen theme. They then use their imaginations to determine what the people in each picture are saying and doing. They write what each person says in a speech balloon for each picture until the story is completed. Have them mount the pictures in the proper order on the white drawing paper, with the speech balloons over each picture. You will probably use several pages for the comic strip. Once completed, copy it so that each student has a copy.

NEAT AND SIMPLE

Students Turn Comic Strips into a Jewish Lesson

Collect some comic strips. When you have enough for each student, blank out the words in the speech balloons and copy. Students are to write their own captions for the cartoons based on your unit of study. You can place emphasis on a major Jewish concept, a historical event, the meaning of prayer, etc. They share their comics and hang them on the bulletin board.

Comic Strips as Launching Devices

Comic strips make great launching devices for lessons or study units. Keep your eyes open for comic strips that have something to do with a Jewish concept or an issue of concern. Over the years there have been a good many comics of value, the best coming from "Hi and Lois." "Charlie Brown," "Hagar," and "Broomhilda." When using a comic strip, have the students read the comic. Then do some brainstorming with them as to what the hidden message might be. By using comic strips you help the class to learn to look behind the written word, just as they often need to do when studying Jewish texts.

Student Creative Writing

Cover a box with colorful contact paper. Collect pictures from magazines and old workbooks related to your unit of study. Paste them on index cards and laminate. Prepare sheets big enough for a title, a story, and an accompanying picture. Put these in the box with the pictures. Print the directions on the inside of the box lid. Your instructions could look something like this:

Select a picture and take a sheet of paper.

Paste the picture in the space provided on the paper.

Write your own story to go with the picture.

Title your story.

Share your story with the whole class.

Create a Rebus

You will need one sheet of white butcher paper per group, small pictures of a variety of items, sentence strips, colored markers, and enough wall space for several groups to create different stories. Prepare the butcher paper by drawing horizontal lines the same size as the sentence strips. Glue the cutout pictures here and there on each sheet of butcher paper, leaving enough space between the pictures for sentences written by the students. Hang the prepared sheets on the wall.

Divide the class into small groups. Give each group some sentence strips and colored markers. Assign each group to a prepared story sheet. Tell the students they are to create a short story, based on your unit of study, which incorporates the pictures. Their story must make sense. They write the story on the sentence sheets, cutting them as necessary to fit in between the pictures. Remind the students that the pictures are part of the story. Upon completion, groups share their stories with the whole class.

Complete a Story

Prepare a short story, but leave out some words and don't write an ending. Divide the class into small groups. Copy the story for each group. Ask the group members to complete the story by filling in the missing words. After they do this they are to finish the story by giving it an ending. For example:

Today is _____ and Susan is helping _____ get ready for _____. Joey is helping, too. Susan puts the _____ on the table, and Joey places the _____ next to the _____. Both Susan and Joey _____ their rooms and their _____ in order while Mother is making _____. The children place the _____ cups on the table and pour the _____. (Finish the story—what else happens?)

When the groups finish, have them share their stories with the whole class. Talk about how they arrived at their endings. What other alternatives were there?

Overhead Projector Stories

Divide the class into small groups. Each group is to write a story based on your unit of study. The story should have one or two characters and a specific setting, like a play. After writing the stories the group members are to draw the setting on wax paper with black crayon. Then they prepare shapes of their characters and glue them on popsicle sticks, to be used as silhouettes over their setting. They share their stories in a silhouette production by moving the characters above the setting, which has been placed on the overhead projector.

A Sandwich Bag Story Book

Here is an entertaining way to make story books for younger children, using plastic sandwich bags for the pages. Have the students write poems, draw pictures, cut out pictures, write letters or stories, etc., for young children to enjoy. The pages are glued to each side of card stock cut to the same size as a sandwich bag. Slip the finished page into the bag. Design a cover for the book. When all the pages are completed, place the open side of the bag on the left-hand side and sew or staple the pages together on that side. The students now have a finished book to give to young children.

Grab Bag Stories

Prepare a lunch bag for each group. For each bag you will need a set of instructions, pictures related to your unit of study, and a list of 10 or 12 words related to your unit of study (if possible, a different list for each group). Glue the instructions on one side of the bag and a picture on the other side. Put the list of words inside the bag. Give a bag to each group of students. The instructions for grab bag stories could look something like this:

1. Look over your word list. Use each word in your story.
2. With the words in mind, draw and color some pictures to go with the words.
3. With the pictures and words in mind, think of a story line.
4. Write your story, using all the words on your list.

Have the groups share their stories with the whole class.

ALTERNATIVE

You will need paper bags, 3 x 5 index cards, pencils, and lined paper. Prepare a set of index cards based on your unit of study for each group (a different set for each group). The index cards could read something like this:

1. Main characters: Give the name and description of each character.
2. Story setting: Give the location, time, and place of the story.
3. A major problem: To be solved in the story.

Put the index cards in the paper bag. Divide the class into small groups. Give each group a bag of cards and some writing materials. After the group members read the index cards, they are to discuss a story line based on this information and develop a story. Each group shares its story with the class.

Another Story Idea: You Provide the Ending, the Students Write the Beginning

Prepare a sheet with the ending of a story based on your unit of study. If you wish, include some words that are clues to be used in the story. Have the students choose partners and together write the beginning and middle of the story and give it a title. Their part of the story, of course, must tie in with the ending you have provided. They can illustrate their stories if time permits. They then share the stories with the class and talk about the similarities and differences between the different beginnings and the story lines leading up to the end.

Description of Pictures

Give out pictures related to your unit of study. Have the students choose partners and together try to identify the main ideas of the pictures. They are to list whatever details they think are important, then write a paragraph which describes the picture and what is taking place. When they are finished, they share their work with the class.

"Cut Up" Story Line

You will need a collection of magazines and newspapers, scissors, glue, and large newsprint. Divide the class into small groups. Give each group some magazines, newspapers, and other materials along with a sheet of newsprint. In advance prepare a list of at least a dozen possible story themes based on your unit of study. If your unit is on Israel, these could include:

My first trip to Israel.

Moses celebrates Shabbat.

Joshua goes hungry.

And so on.

Have the members of each group choose a theme and talk about a possible story line. Once they have an outline of their story, they cut out words and phrases that can be used in telling it. The size, shape, and print type of the words they cut out can vary—the story is what is important. As they cut out the words, they are to group them on the newsprint until they are ready to put them together. When they have enough words cut out, they begin to lay out their story. When they are satisfied with the layout, they paste up the cutout words on the newsprint. Decorate the page as they desire. Share the finished work with the class.

Adding Words to a Wordless Picture Book

Collect pictures related to your unit of study. Glue them to the top of a sheet of paper. Make as many picture pages without words as you think the students will need to write a story. Copy the pages, making enough for each group of students.

Divide the class into small groups. Give each group one copy of the wordless picture book. Assign each group a specific topic related to your unit of study. Tell the group members to discuss the different story ideas they see in the pictures and how the pictures go with their assigned topic. The members of each group write a story, based on their topic, to go with the pictures in their book. They can work on the draft of the story on plain paper before placing it on the pages of the book. Once the members are satisfied with the story line, they transfer the story to their wordless picture book, placing the portions of the story underneath the corresponding pictures. When finished, they share their new stories with the class.

Group Writing: A New Twist Using Pictures

Collect pictures related to your unit of study. Mount them on tagboard. Divide the class into small groups. Give each group one picture. Tell the students they are to write a story to go with the picture, but here is the twist: each member of the group gets to write three sentences of the story. The first person writes the first three sentences, then passes the page to the second person, who writes the next three sentences, then passes it to the next, continuing until each group member has added three sentences. The whole group then writes the ending. Each group shares its story with the class.

I Didn't Know That!

"I didn't know that" is something you learn that you never knew before. Have students keep a record of what they have learned that they didn't know before. Provide them with sheets of 8.5 by 14 paper which they can fold in half to make their own "discover" books. Students decorate the cover and each page as they develop their books. During the year, as you take them through a lesson, have them head each page with the title of the subject. Under the title, the students write those things that they never knew before. This becomes a good resource book.

Extemporaneous Speech

Need to fill a few minutes? Prepare a number of index cards with topics for brief speeches. Cover a box with colorful contact paper and put the index cards inside. Some of your topics could be:

> Pretend to be a parent explaining to a child why going to the movies on Yom Kippur is forbidden.

Describe the difference between a menorah and a chanukiah.

Explain the importance of the Kiddush.

Teach the class how to play the dreidel game.

Tell the students their speeches must be off the top of their heads and not more than one minute in length. Ask for volunteers at first, but as the kids get used to the idea of making speeches, choose randomly. Those who don't feel up to speaking can be allowed to "pass" a few times, but be sure every student has a turn during the year.

Paper Bag Dramatics

You will need to plan ahead for this one. One week, divide the class into small groups. Give each group an assignment for a 3–5 minute skit using subject matter from your unit of study. The group members are to write outlines of the skit and determine what props they will need from home. These are to be placed in a paper bag but must be large enough to be seen by the audience. Safety pins, paperclips, rubber bands are not acceptable. The members of each group must decide what each member of the group will bring from home.

The next week, the group members bring in bags filled with the planned objects. Here's the switch: each group is to exchange bags with another group. After examining the items in the new bag, and based on the items and the assigned topic, the group members are to write a brief description of the skit they will perform. Each item in the bag must be used! Allow a few minutes for rehearsal, then let the groups perform their skits. After each presentation, the members of the group that prepared the paper bag are to tell the class what they had planned to do as a skit. The class compares the different scenarios.

Tell a Story

When giving a reading assignment, instead of the old "write a report" instructions, have the students tell stories based on what they have read. Make it more realistic by using a tape recorder to record their stories. Even make a "microphone" for them to speak into while telling their stories. To make a microphone, take a cardboard tube from a roll of paper towels. Crumble up newspaper into a ball and stick it in one side of the tube. Cover it all with heavy aluminum foil and add a piece of yarn to the bottom for the cord and just let it hang down.

Fix a time limit for the stories. Have the students take turns telling their stories to the class. You can even let them take turns at being the "master of ceremonies" who introduces those who are about to tell their stories.

Puppets Masks Tell the Story

The students can make simple puppets for skits they create based on your unit of study. Divide the class into small groups. Give each group a different topic for which to create a skit. The group members outline their skits, identify the characters, and write the plays. Then they make puppet masks for each of the characters. Allow time for rehearsals.

To make the masks you will need one paper plate per child, enough yellow chalk or yellow pencils for the whole class, yarn in hair colors (red, black, brown, yellow), crayons, glue, paste, tape, scissors, and one popsicle stick for each mask.

1. Use yellow chalk or pencil to lightly draw eyes, a nose, and a mouth on the paper plate. Very carefully cut out the eyes so you can see when you put the mask up to your face.

2. Peel the paper off a crayon the same color as skin, and using the side of the crayon color the plate.

3. Color around the eyes (lashes), place the eyebrows, glasses, add freckles, etc.

4. Choose the color of yarn needed for the hair, and glue pieces of yarn along the top and sides of the plate.

5. Tape a popsicle to the bottom of the plate.

Student Storytellers

Ask the students to choose stories of Jewish content which they like or which contain a Jewish concept based on your unit of study. Be sure there are no duplications. Give them time to read the stories silently. Discuss some of the fine points of storytelling with them. Give them time to practice, in school and at home, asking parents to coach them if necessary. Then have a storytelling contest. The class will be the judges, or bring in some unattached adults (not related to the children). For this contest, though, everyone must be a winner! Instead of having first-, second-, and third-place awards, create some alternative awards (e.g., most dramatic, most creative, most visual, funniest). Use different-colored ribbons for the awards. After each story is told, ask the class to identify the Jewish concept it contains. When the contest is over, the students can go on to tell their stories to groups of younger children.

In the Beginning

Begin to tell or read a story. After a minute or two, stop, and ask a student, without seeing the material, to continue. After that student continues for a minute, move on to another student. Continue for several minutes, with each successive student adding to the story. Stop, and read the story as written. Have the students compare their version with the original.

Turn a Children's Story into an Operetta

This project will take more than one class session and could even include more than one class. It will give the kids a chance to work together and do something for the younger children in school.

With a teacher from the lower-level classes, choose a story that is a favorite of the younger children (one with Jewish content, of course). Have the students read it and divide it into three acts. Challenge the students to identify some popular music to go with the story. If they wish, let them rewrite the lyrics of some of the songs, creating a parody. To prepare, you might want to enlist the assistance of some parents to help with the production. Rehearse the "operetta," and when ready perform it for the younger children in the school.

Sketch a Story

Ask the students to draw a picture which shows their understanding of what they have learned from your unit of study. Collect the pictures and pass them out again, making sure that the students do not get their own pictures.

Have each student write a short story based on the picture. Then have the artist and the story writer come together. The writer reads the story and the artist explains the picture. How do they compare? What are the similarities and differences between the story and what the artist drew? Continue until everyone has shared. Compile the pictures and stories into a class storybook on your unit of study.

Advertising Sells

The students are to prepare an advertising campaign to encourage families to celebrate Shabbat. As part of the campaign, they will have a brand-new design for Shabbat candlesticks which are different from any others. (This is an example; the content of the advertising campaign can be any subject based on your unit of study.)

Divide the class into small groups. Each group is to design Shabbat candlesticks that differ from all other candlesticks. Then have the group members create pictures of their candlesticks, a written description, and a slogan or musical jingle. They plan the campaign, deciding on the kind of customer who will purchase the product, the media they will use, and the price of their candlesticks. Each group makes its presentation to the class.

Fabric Mural: A Yearlong Project

Don't let the fact that this is a project for the entire school year scare you. Just think of the end product and the visual effect it will have on parents when they view it at closing programs. It also makes a good closure to a unit of study, because each time you come to the end of a unit the students add to the mural.

At the outset you will need a large white sheet, fabric crayons in all colors, an iron, and white drawing paper. To make:

1. Using the fabric crayons, draw pictures on the white drawing paper. Press down with the crayons and fill in the drawings completely. This helps to make the drawing dark and colorful when transferred.

2. Place the drawings, one at a time, face down on the sheet, and gently iron back and forth until the entire picture has been transferred.

At the end of the school year, the students can add any additional decorations or information they deem necessary to make it more complete. They can even add a title to the mural. Hang the mural by stretching it across a wall and tacking it at the sides, or make a hem at the top and insert a dowel. Place eye screws so the mural can be hung on the wall.

What Do You Think?

Collect pictures of men, women, and children. Copy or cut out and paste a few people on the bottom of a sheet of white paper. Prepare one sheet for each student. Over each picture of a person, draw a large thought balloon. Give sheets to the students and ask them to draw a picture of what they think the people might be thinking about (related to your unit of study) in the thought balloon. Ask them to exchange their papers with one another. From the drawing, each student is to try and guess what the people are thinking.

Matchbook Art

This is a good way to review or culminate a research project. You will need construction paper, white drawing paper, and crayons or colored markers. Cut construction paper into one 7 x 3 piece per student. Cut the drawing paper into six to eight 2.5 x 3.5 pieces per student. More can be cut as needed. Students fold up the bottom inch of the construction paper and the drawing paper fits into this folded portion. The top part of the construction paper is to be folded over the drawing paper into a simulated matchbook. When they have completed their art work, the "matchbooks" can be stapled at the bottom so they stay intact. Based on your unit of study, the students write one sentence to a page and illustrate each page to match the written sentence.

Charades

Have some fun while learning. Create a number of charades on 4 x 6 index cards. Have each student, in turn, draw a card. After a few seconds to decide how to portray what is written on the card, the student does a charade and the class has to guess what it is—just like any game of charades. The charades you create are to be based on your unit of study. Some suitable ideas, depending on the unit, include putting on a talit, blowing a shofar, getting ready to read the Torah, and participating in an archaeological dig in Israel.

Fortune Cookie Charades

Buy some fortune cookies. Using a tweezer, take the fortunes out of the cookies. Write the scenes you want your students to act out on tiny pieces of paper, fold them, and insert in the cookies. In class, hand out the restuffed cookies and watch your class have a great time! (And have a snack too!)

Questions and More Questions

Here is a question-and-answer game with a different twist. Students write questions, based on your unit of study, on index cards. The question cards are collected and read aloud. Divide the class into small groups. Give each group several of the question cards. The members of each group are to determine where they can find the answers to their questions (e.g., library, prayer book, the cantor). Give the groups a specific amount of time to research the questions, then they must present their answers.

Detective Game

This is a game to be played in the library, so be sure to get the librarian's approval and cooperation. The students will be the detectives. They must find Shimon Sefer. Shimon Sefer is a paper cutout you will need to make. Give Shimon Sefer a funny face and a colorful costume. Hide Shimon Sefer in a book on the library shelves, then give clues as to his location. For example: for Purim, some of the clues could be:

Find me, my name is Shimon Sefer. I am hiding in a book. My book is about a Jewish queen.

The Jewish queen saved the Jewish people.

My queen has a favorite uncle.

And so on.

Messages in Code

Having students decipher a code is more fun than just reading plain text. The codes don't have to be complicated. Here is an example of a simple code: Move each letter ahead one in the sequence of the alphabet; thus *anx* is code for "boy." Here is another: Assign each letter a number in sequence: *a* = 1, *b* = 2, and so on.

Three Corners

Prepare a list of statements based on your unit of study about which you think students will have a variety of opinions. Here is an example:

Synagogues should have dress codes for religious schools.

Students should serve on the religious school committee.

Students should be required to attend Shabbat services each week.

Parents should attend religious school at least once a month.

Make up three signs: *agree, disagree, undecided.* Place these signs around the room. One at a time, read the statements. After each reading, the students are to think about the statement, and with no talking, go stand under the sign which most reflects their thoughts. In each group area, the students are to work up a statement which explains their position. These statements are to be shared with the whole class. Remind the students to be accepting of other people's views. Continue until all the statements have been read and reacted to, then discuss the different statements.

It's in the Bag!

Divide the class into small groups. Give each group a paper bag and some pictures related to your unit of study. The members of each group are to place three or four pictures in the bag as clues to a site location, a prayer, an historical event, a Jewish concept, etc. The members of each group write a set of clues to help their classmates solve the mystery of "What's in the bag?" For example, if you are studying Jerusalem, the bag should contain pictures of the menorah, the Western Wall, the Dome of the Rock, and the Knesset. The clues could be:

I sit in front of the Knesset.

I'm the oldest Jewish symbol.

Bar Mitzvahs take place here.

Site holy to three major religions.

The seat of government.

Once they have created their clues, the students are to try and identify the sites based on the clues and the pictures.

Tic-Tac-Toe

An old game, and still fun to use in the classroom. Prepare a list of questions. Place the Tic-Tac-Toe design on the blackboard. Divide the class into two teams. One has the X and the other has the O. Ask your questions, and if the members of one team get the right answer, they mark their spot. If they don't answer correctly, the other team gets a chance. Continue playing until all your questions are used and one team wins.

Indy 500 Car Race

To remain on track, the students must answer questions correctly. Design a simple game board—an oblong track with pit stops, a place for the question cards, start and finish, and a place to put five or six small cars. Laminate.

Write one question on each 3 x 5 index card. Laminate the question or cover with clear contact paper. If the game is part of a unit on the Bible, some of your questions might look like this:

Where did Moses receive the tablets?

How many books are in the Pentateuch?

Which story in the Bible explains the origin of different languages?

Name the two women in Abraham's life.

Name the Five Books of Moses.

Terah was the father of which patriarch?

Add some penalty cards—you can call them "pit traps." For example:

You have a flat tire, go back to the last pit stop.

You didn't slow down for the last flag, lose a turn.

You're out of gas, go to the last pit stop.

Information Experts

Divide the class into small groups. Assign each group a different topic from your unit of study. If the topic is Israel, assign each group a different city (e.g., Jerusalem, Haifa, Tel Aviv, Beersheva). Break down each city into four different areas, or a number which matches the number of students in each group. For a group of four, the breakdown could be: historical sites, government, religion, economy.

The group members are to gather all the information they can on their subjects and are to display what they have learned, using pictures, maps, charts, and posters. While they are doing their research and preparing their materials, find some large appliance boxes, one for each group. If your room isn't large enough for each group to have its own Learning Center box, get at least two and the groups can take turns. Or obtain permission to set up the boxes in a larger assembly-type room.

Help the students cut a door and windows in each box, leaving plenty of room to display their work. Each group sets up its Learning Center in an attractive display. Once they are set up, invite other classes to come visit and talk with the "information experts." The students take turns staffing the center to answer questions and share what they have learned.

Set Up a Simple Learning Center

Create an area in your classroom (e.g., a small table or desk) that can be set up and remain in place all the time. Use "real" props to draw students to the scene and invite them to get involved with the variety of activities. For example:

1. A flower pot with artificial flowers. Place colorful strips of paper in the pot with an activity on each one (e.g., pick a story and draw a picture about it).

2. A Teddy bear which has a sign on it that says something like "I celebrate Shabbat by _____." The students write how they celebrate Shabbat.

3. Place empty food containers with directions in them to plan a holiday meal.

4. Place Jewish symbols or items on the table with instructions to research and write about their meaning and when they are used.

5. Place pictures of clothing from different periods of Jewish history with instructions to write about that period.

Change the items in the Learning Center from time to time so that the students can choose from a wider variety of activities.

A Puzzle Story

Collect pictures related to your unit of study. Mount on tagboard, laminate or cover with clear contact paper. Cut each picture into a puzzle and place each puzzle in an envelope. Prepare one for each student.

Each student chooses an envelope with a puzzle and writes a story based on the picture of the puzzle, then returns the puzzle to the envelope. Collect the stories and place in a folder. Take one story at a time and ask the author to read it. Ask the rest of the class to go through the puzzles and find the one they think the story represents. After they assemble the puzzle, the author tells whether they chose the right one.

A Self-Correcting Activity

Divide two pieces of 8.5 x 11 tagboard into equal squares large enough to write questions or answers on. The facing squares have to match each other. Prepare a list of questions and answers for each square. Put the questions on a tagboard, one to each square. Put the answers on the other tagboard in the corresponding squares. The tagboard with the questions must match the tagboard with the answers. Place a picture related to your unit of study on the other side of the tagboard with the questions. Laminate. Cut into pieces by the squares. When the students match the question to the correct answer, they turn the piece face down. If all their answers are correct, they will put together a pretty picture.

Picture Postcards

When you have completed a unit of study, have the class make postcards expressing some of the major concepts from the unit. You will need magazines, old workbooks, scissors, glue, and 4 x 6 index cards. On one side of the card the students can mount pictures found in the magazines or workbooks. These will tell something about the unit of study just completed. Tell them to leave room for a caption relating the pictures to the unit. The other side of the card has to have room for an address and a message. When the card is completed, the students write a message about their lesson and address the card to a member of their family or a friend.

Instead of a Test

I always hated to test the kids on religion, yet we do need some means of finding out if they are learning anything. For a change from the usual, try providing the answers and letting them give the questions. Yes, this is a form of Jeopardy, and students enjoy the challenge. Here is an example of what you could do:

Answer: Sukot, Passover, and Shavuot.

Question: What are the Three Pilgrimage Festivals?

A Jewish Quilt

This is a good closure for just about any unit of study. Assign everyone in the class a letter of the alphabet, more than one if necessary for all the letters to be assigned. Ask the students to write a short statement based on your unit of study which begins with each alphabetical letter. For the first draft, let them use plain paper. When they are satisfied with what they have written, give them 8.5 x 11 construction paper in different colors, one sheet for each statement.

Have the students write their sentences on each piece, illustrating and decorating the paper as they desire. Collect the finished papers and arrange them in alphabetical order. Stitch all the sheets together with yarn to form a "quilt." Hang in the room, or in the school hallway so that everyone can see the Jewish quilt.

JUNIOR AND SENIOR HIGH SCHOOL

THE BIBLE AND JEWISH HISTORY
Using Biblical Texts

Many years ago a teacher I studied with showed me how to make it possible for students to get the most out of their reading when we used the Bible in the classroom. It was so long ago that I do not remember the teacher's name. All I have are the notes I took, which I am sharing with you. When using this approach, keep in the mind the age of the students and adapt the questions to suit their capabilities.

Prepare the following questions on index cards, one question to a card:

161

1. What's happening?

   Category: fairy tales/myths, fiction, historical, biographical.

   Themes: people, animals, travels, absurdity, magic, nature, seasons, wisdom, beauty, decisions, conflict, mystery, exploration, self-esteem, festivals.

2. What/who are the significant characters?
3. What is the setting?
4. What objects, if any, play important roles?
5. What new words does the text contain?
6. What perspectives regarding God do we gain from the text?
7. Can I retell the episode?
8. Can I identify key outcomes?
9. Can I relate a value message to a key outcome?
10. How do I feel about the characters?
11. What images are most impressive to me, and how would I translate them into an artistic form?
12. Who or what would I have liked to be in the text?
13. What do we know about the author?
14. Why was the text written?
15. If this particular text did not exist, what other texts would communicate a similar message and/or serve a similar purpose?
16. As a Jew, am I proud to be "related" to the text?
17. How do I react when hearing the text?
18. What is the relationship between this text and other Jewish writings?
19. How does this text help me understand Judaism?
20. How does this text help me understand myself?
21. How could this text be changed so as to significantly change its outcome?
22. What would be the purpose of changing the outcome of the text?

Arrange the question cards on a table. After the students read the text, ask them to go around the table and choose one or two questions they like and want to answer. Ask them to explain their choices. Give them time to think, then have them write their answers on paper or on large sheets of newsprint that can be displayed around the room. Take one question at a time and discuss the answer. If on newsprint, write down any additional answers other students offer for the same question. Continue until all the questions chosen have been discussed and answered.

Before Studying the Laws of the Torah

Begin with a brainstorming session. With the class, list all the different ways laws govern life today: What influence do laws have in our lives? What kinds of laws rule our lives from the very beginning when we are born? You will get the usual answers: driving laws, laws against stealing, etc. But point out that birth certificates are legal documents; that doctors are licensed before they can practice, and so are nurses; that drivers have to be licensed, and the pharmacist, etc. The list can go on and on.

Have ready a list of some laws from the Torah that relate or correspond to present-day secular laws. For example, "You shall not falsify measures of length, weight, or capacity" (Leviticus 19:35) corresponds to the law that the scale at a butcher shop must be checked regularly for correctness of weight. Have the students identify other laws in the Torah that relate to secular laws.

Another Introduction to the Study of Torah Laws

With the students do some brainstorming about what a law is, the purpose of laws, and our need for laws. List their answers.

Divide the class into small groups. Give each group two laws from the Torah. Choose laws that deal with community or relationships to others. After reading the laws the students are to discuss:

What purpose did the law fulfill?

What did the law do for the community? For the individual?

How does the law protect the community? The individual?

How does the law apply to today's needs?

After the discussion, the students are to rewrite the laws in contemporary language.

AN EXTENSION

As an extension to this lesson, invite an attorney or a judge to visit the class. Prior to the visit, give the guest a list of the Torah laws that will be discussed. Ask the guest to talk about the similarity between the laws of the community or government and the laws found in the Torah, with special reference to the laws the students will be discussing.

Another Beginning

Begin the lesson by brainstorming with the class, listing the many ways laws influence our lives. You will get the usual answers (e.g., driving laws, tax laws). But ask the students to consider birth certificates. What purpose do they serve? They are actually legal documents. Ask when the need to show a birth certificate might arise (e.g., obtaining a passport, proof of citizenship, proof of age). What other kinds of licenses does the law require? Mention doctors, nurses, pharmacists, business establishments of certain kinds. The list can go on and on; why does the law require licenses in these instances?

Have ready a list of a few laws from the Torah that relate or correspond to modern secular laws, such as: "You shall not falsify measures of length, weight, or capacity" (Leviticus 19:35). Compare this to the law requiring that the scale in a butcher shop be checked for accuracy on a regular basis. Ask the students to identify other laws in the Torah which relate to secular laws. Leviticus is a good place to begin. Have them share their findings with the class.

A Play to Introduce the Study of Torah

The following story is based on one originally written by Jamie Kyle. I found it in *Creative Classroom* (March 1993). With the use of this story and the related activities you will set the stage for studying the laws of the Torah. This can be done as a story or as a play, with students playing the different parts. It takes place in a diner. A person is sitting in a booth and waiting for the waitress to take the order. Another person comes in and sits at the counter.

Waitress:	What'll it be?
Person 1:	Roast beef sandwich, a large soda, and fruit salad, please.
Waitress:	No beef sandwiches, only beef and turkey together.
Person 1:	Well, if you have beef and turkey, then you have beef. I'll take a beef and turkey sandwich, but hold the turkey.
Waitress:	No can do. It's not on the menu. We only serve what's on the menu—beef and turkey sandwich.
Person 1:	Very well. I'll have a turkey and pastrami sandwich.
Waitress:	Can't do it. It's not on the menu. We have only pastrami sandwiches, not turkey and pastrami, just pastrami.
Person 1:	Can't you take the turkey from the beef and turkey sandwich and add it to the pastrami sandwich?
Waitress:	First rule of thumb. Rules are rules.
Person 1:	May I see the manager?
Waitress:	You're looking at her.
Person 1:	You're the manager?
Waitress:	I happen to be the waitress, the cook, the manager, and I work the cash register. How can I help you? What's your beef?
Person 1:	I'm very hungry. I don't enjoy turkey with my beef, but I like pastrami with my turkey.
Waitress:	Rules are rules.
Person 1:	It's not fair.
Waitress:	Who said life was fair?
Person 1:	What am I supposed to do?
Waitress:	I've got an idea. You can order a pastrami sandwich.

Then you can order a beef and turkey sandwich. Take the turkey from the beef sandwich and add it to the pastrami sandwich. I'll have to charge you for two sandwiches, though.

Person 1: *(confused)* I'll just have a baloney sandwich.

Waitress: Very well. *(And goes off to the kitchen)*

Person 1: You can't always get what you want. Sometimes you have to settle for what's on the menu. Some rules just don't seem to be important. I wonder why they exist.

Person 2: Are you talking to yourself?

Person 1: Yes.

Person 2: There's a rule about that!

Person 1: There is?

Person 2: *(laughing)* I'm just pulling your leg. You're allowed to talk to yourself in this diner. But it's against the rules to throw or complain about the food, argue with the help, or leave a small tip.

Person 1: Rules bother me. Do you ever wonder why we can't do whatever we want to do?

Person 2: Rules are important. They protect us. For instance, where would we be without:

(Stands up and recites) No parking, no stopping, no talking, no pushing, no shouting, no spitting? How about no boys allowed or no girls allowed?

Person 1: *(Stands and recites)* No one under 17 admitted without a parent, no tank tops, no fishing, no smoking.

Person 2: No smoking is a smart rule. So is not riding a bike without a helmet.

Person 1: No hunting, no fighting, no climbing, no picking flowers, no bare feet, no trespassing, no meat with milk, no bread on Pesach, no . . .

Waitress: *(returns)* Bad news. No turkey!

Person 1: *(with disbelief)* Excuse me!

Waitress: We ran out. *(Points to the other person)* That person got the last of the turkey. No more left. How about a nice roast beef sandwich? It's not on the menu, but I'll bend the rules for a cute kid like you.

Person 1: *(puzzled)* No. Thank you.

With the students discuss: How realistic are the "rules" of this diner? Do some brainstorming and list the rules they follow at home, at school, and in the community. Talk about: What makes it necessary to follow these rules? What would life be like if we didn't have rules? Ask the students if they have ever broken a rule. What happened?

Here are some other activities to do before you begin to study the laws of the Torah:

1. Working in small groups, have students create a list of classroom rules.

2. Have groups create new rules for safety purposes and discuss how people would be affected by each new rule.

Torahthon

You've heard of walkathons and danceathons; well, here's another one. It can be a fund-raiser as well as an opportunity to learn.

Set aside a weekend, or plan a Friday evening through Saturday until *Havdalah* (yes, overnight), to study the Torah. Invite special guest speakers (e.g., the rabbi, the cantor) to teach the Torah through storytelling, drama, and song. That will make it more interesting then just sitting there hour after hour. Encourage members of the congregation to sponsor students at, say, 50 cents and up per hour. The proceeds can be used for youth activities, repairing Torah scrolls, or any tzedakah fund you and the class choose. You can even set a minimum number of hours that the students must study Torah.

Deuteronomy 20

Did you know that the twentieth chapter of Deuteronomy is one of the earliest military manuals? Take a few moments to discover the rules of battle, the concern for soldiers and adversaries, the care of the ecological system, and the other issues it raises concerning war. It also includes a description of the two types of warfare permitted in Jewish tradition: the *milchemet mitzvah*, or necessary war, and the *milchemet reshut*, or optional war. A necessary war is waged either in self-defense or against a nation deemed to be totally evil. An optional war is related to the expansion of Jewish territory, but eight requirements must be met before it can be waged.

Either copy chapter 20 for the students or have them read it in a Bible. Here is a sampling of the kinds of assignments you can give them to consider while they are reading:

1. List the rules regarding the care of land and trees. What kinds of rules exist today regarding land and trees during a war?

2. List the rules regarding human life: how the soldiers are to be treated, who can serve and who cannot. Compare it to the rules in effect today for soldiers.

3. List the eight requirements that must be met before a *milchemet reshut* war can be fought. Compare the different wars of our recent past, including Israel's wars, to the two kinds of wars described in this chapter. What kinds of wars were they? If any of them could be considered a *milchemet reshut*, were the eight requirements met?

Ten Commandments

Make copies of the two versions of the Ten Commandments (Exodus 20:1–4 and Deuteronomy 5:6–18). If possible, use the versions in *The Torah: A Modern Commentary* published by the Union of American Hebrew Congregations. This text is an excellent resource for background materials for this exercise. Ask the class to compare the two versions, identifying the similarities and differences. Discuss the reasons for the differences and their implications.

Ten Commandments: Fill in the Missing Words

The students are to find the missing words and fill in the blank spaces to complete the Ten Commandments. Use graph paper to create the puzzle, then copy:

S	M	C	O	V	E	T	A
A	U	H	O	N	O	R	D
B	R	S	F			B	U
B	D	T	A			E	L
A	E	E	L			S	T
T	R	A	S			I	E
H	L	L	E			D	R
D	O	T	F			E	Y
A	R	E	S	G	O	D	S
Y	D	S	W	E	A	R	M

1. I am the _____ your God.
2. You shall have no other _____ _____ Me.
3. You shall not _____ falsely by the name of God.
4. Remember the _____ _____ and keep it holy.
5. _____ your father and your mother.
6. You shall not _____.
7. You shall not commit _____.
8. You shall not _____.
9. You shall not bear _____ witness.
10. You shall not _____.

Students can check the Bible to see if they have answered correctly.

Ten Commandments Interviews

With the class, develop a list of questions that can be used to interview parents, relatives, other adults, and peers (other than fellow religious school students). Specify what you want the students to find out in the interviews. Your list of questions could look something like this:

How many of the Ten Commandments do you know?

How many people live by the Ten Commandments today?

Which commandments are the most frequently broken?

Which are the most important commandments?

Do you know that the Ten Commandments are repeated twice in the Bible?

Where are the Ten Commandments found in the Bible?

Does following the Ten Commandments help us to be good people or good Jews?

If you were to change any of the Ten Commandments, which would it be? How would you change it?

If you were to add to the Ten Commandments, what would you add?

Give the students a week or so to do their surveys/interviews. Compile the results and discuss the implications. If you wish, publish the results in the temple bulletin or share them with the parents. As a closure for the activity, divide the class into small groups and have each group compile its own list of Ten Commandments for Jewish youth today. Or, and this is an oldie, have each student individually write an eleventh commandment.

The Holiness Code: Leviticus 19

At one time, Leviticus was the first book of the Bible to be taught in religious school. It's not difficult to understand why; it was taught first because it contains so many laws that help us to be good people as well as good Jews. To begin the study of the nineteenth chapter of Leviticus, the Holiness Code, I always liked to see how the kids would define *holiness*. There is a very simple activity to initiate this process; you will need one strip of colored paper and a dark-colored marker for each student.

HOLINESS IS...

Pass out the paper strips and the markers. Ask the students to complete the phrase "Holiness is . . ." in one, two, or even three words. Allow a few minutes for them to complete the phrase. They are then to share their responses and the reasons for them. Remember to be accepting of all responses whether you agree or not, and this goes for the class too! As the students share, take their colored strips and tape them to the wall in a multicolored "quilt" pattern.

Either place on the blackboard or copy on paper the following quotations:

O God, Your way is in holiness (Psalms 77:14).

Everything created by God contains a spark of holiness (Baal Shem Tov).

Holiness is the essence of all moral perfection (Kohler, *Jewish Theology*).

Holy, holy, holy, is the Lord of Hosts (Isaiah 6:3).

When the Bible says "be holy," it means the same as if it said, "Do My commandments" (Maimonides).

Read and discuss these quotations with the class. How does the traditional Jewish definition of holiness compare to the students' definitions? Do some brainstorming, listing the things the students think they can do, personally, to achieve holiness. The answers you get might be something like this:

Holiness is—

helping the disadvantaged.

being nice to one another.

lighting the Sabbath candles.

taking the trash out without being asked.

hanging up my clothes.

And so on.

Now have the students create a "Holiness is . . ." booklet. First they write out statements explaining what it means to be holy, using ideas from the brainstorming, and then they illustrate them. Compile the sheets into a booklet to be copied and sent home.

ALTERNATIVE

After the discussion of what it means to be holy, ask the students what a Holiness Code for today would be like if they were creating one. What would they include in it? Divide the class into small groups. Assign each group a specific area about which to write its own version of a Holiness Code for today. Here are some examples of the areas you could assign:

Relationships with others.

Business, honesty, and responsibility.

Charity.

Caring and compassion.

The following version of a Holiness Code was written by an eighth-grade student at Temple Beth El in San Antonio:

Understand your religion no matter what it may be. (All religions are holy.)

Spend time with the people you love.

Don't dislike people unless they dislike you first. (Don't prejudge. You may lose a future husband, wife, or friend.)

Listen to others. Give everyone a chance to shine. Speak your mind, but let others speak theirs.

Help the needy. Give food to the hungry and find shelter for the homeless.

When stepping up in society, don't step on others on your way.

Don't do drugs, don't drink alcohol (unless you are old enough), don't smoke, and don't be pushed into anything you don't want to do.

Believe in everyone. He or she may be an angel in disguise.

Teach people to read.

Believe in yourself, for you may be all you have.

Don't fight (with fists or weapons) unless that is the only option available.

Another Way to Look at the Holiness Code

This activity requires several days' accumulation of newspapers as well as a Bible or a copy of Leviticus 19 for everyone in the class. Divide the class into small groups. The students are to read Leviticus 19 and list the different ways it says men and women can help each other. Then give newspapers to each group. The students are to go through the papers and find articles about relationships between men and women. They are to make notes on the articles: What happened? In what ways did the men and women help, hinder, or hurt each other? Which situations if any are related to the lists made from Leviticus 19?

Upon completion, ask the students to share what they have discovered. Talk about: What kinds of relationships exist between men and women in our society? How much "Love your neighbor" is there is in our society? What makes it possible, or impossible, to love your neighbor? If we are commanded to love our neighbors, how are we going to do this? Here do some brainstorming with the class, listing the different ways the students think we can love our neighbors.

Ask the students to go over the lists they have compiled and choose one thing they could do to improve a relationship with just one person. Then have them create a time schedule of how and when they will do this. Give them a few weeks for some progress to take place and then ask for a progress report. Talk about: How easy was it to do? How difficult was it? Will they continue to try and improve the relationship? Ask for their reasons for continuing. (This is all worth a try—good luck!)

ANOTHER OPTION: LOVE YOUR NEIGHBOR

Ask the students to describe their neighbors—what they like or dislike about them, how they treat their neighbors, how their neighbors treat them. Then have the students list what they could learn about their neighbors. How could they obtain this information? One way would be to interview the neighbors. With the students, prepare a list of questions for the interview. The students are to visit their neighbors, explain the purpose of the visit, and interview them. The following week, when they bring in the responses, they are to share what they have learned and talk about what they learned that they didn't know before. A closure for this activity would be to have the students make a list of things they could do to improve relations with their neighbors. Have them each specify one thing they are willing to do—and do it!

Jewish Law and Modern Technology

Did you know that a *kohen* (descendant of the priestly caste) is forbidden to be in the same room or enclosure with a dead body? Several years ago an article in the *Wall Street Journal* described a dilemma confronting El Al Airlines. An Orthodox Jew had bolted from an El Al plane when he saw a coffin being loaded on it. Since El Al often carries coffins to Israel for burial, this posed a problem. What was the airline to do? Easy, it consulted the Institute for Science and Halachah, where fifteen engineers and religious scholars work to find ways to reconcile modern technology and *halachah*, the 3,500-year-old body of Jewish traditional law. After delving into the Torah and other texts, the scholars solved the airline's problem. The airline now encases coffins in cardboard containers; since cardboard is made from forest products, this gives the coffin its own "house," and therefore a *kohen* on an El Al aircraft would not be in the same enclosure with the coffin. The Institute says, "All the answers are in the Torah, you just have to know how to read it."

Our students are not religious scholars or *halachah* engineers, but they can study the Torah! They can learn to look behind the written word to find meaning in the text. Don't be afraid to use the actual text either. *The Tanakh,* published by the Jewish Publication Society, is the newest translation and easy to read. In addition, the Union of American Hebrew Congregations has published *The Torah: A Modern Commentary*, which may cost more, but is excellent and also easy to read. Copy the portion you wish to cover with the students, or write a summary of the Torah portion, especially if it is a very long one.

What Does the Torah Mean?

It is not enough simply to have the students read the Torah portion and then ask what they think it means. The questions you ask must be more directed. They must help the students to *think*, to look behind the written word. You can use *midrashim* to enhance the Torah reading, just as the sages of old did when they wrote the *midrashim*. The activity that follows is an example of how students can find meaning in the text that can apply to their lives today. It is based on an idea from Harlene Appelman, an educator in Detroit.

A SUMMARY OF SIDRAH KEDOSHIM (THE HOLINESS CODE): LEVITICUS 19:1–20, 27

Kadosh means "holy," and *kedoshim* is the plural form. Being holy means to be special and different from the other nations around us. We are not only told to worship God, but we are told to try and imitate God. "You shall be holy because I, the Lord your God, am holy." Be like God; as God is merciful and gracious, so you are to be merciful and gracious. This *sidrah* includes a good number of laws, among which are:

Respect your parents.

Do not worship idols.

Observe the Sabbath.

Be honest in all business transactions.

Leave the corners of your field for the poor.

Do not engage in tale-bearing or malice.

Pay prompt wages for reasonable hours.

Do not take advantage of the handicapped.

Judge all cases fairly.

There should be equal justice for rich and poor.

Love your neighbor as yourself.

And God reminds us to treat strangers fairly, for we were strangers in the land of Egypt.

We are to follow these laws because God took us out of the land of Egypt; because the people whom God has chosen for God's own must, like God, be holy; because God has set us apart by distinctive laws and precepts; and to keep us from adopting the religious customs of surrounding nations.

Have the students talk about:

Which of the laws listed above is the most important? Give reasons.

Is any law missing? What is it?

Of the four reasons given for obeying the laws, which is the most important, and what makes it important?

To add another dimension to the study of this portion, add the following:

Did you know that—

when we bless the wine (make Kiddush) on Shabbat, wine metaphorically represents the essence of goodness (holiness)?

the Israelites are told to show respect for the elderly?

the Torah advises us that "the wages of a laborer shall not remain with you until evening"?

"Love your neighbor as yourself" (Leviticus 19:18) is the basis of the Golden Rule expressed in a variety of ways by both Jews and non-Jews?

Have the students talk about:

How do we treat the elderly in our society?

What do you do to help the elderly?

How do you show respect for the elderly?

How does one love one's neighbor?

You can also use *midrashim*. Here is one that will help the students understand the concept of holiness:

Said the Besht: "A king dropped a gem out of his ring and gave his favorite son a clue as to its whereabouts. Thus he might show his diligence and sagacity in pleasing his father. Likewise, God has dropped sparks of holiness upon the world. Through the Torah, God gives Israel clues regarding places where sparks have fallen on earth, so that Israel may return the sparks of holiness to the Lord."

Have the students talk about:

What are the "sparks of holiness"?

How does one go about gathering them up?

How does gathering the sparks of holiness relate to the commandment "You shall be holy"?

What does it mean to be holy?

What does one do to achieve holiness?

Identify at least one activity you can do that would lead to the potential of holiness that God is asking us to achieve.

A final note: In studying the Torah, the use of summaries is fine, but it is better to read the actual text. There is more than one major concept in every Torah portion, and it is sometimes difficult to cover them all. In using the Holiness Code as an example, I concentrate on the idea of holiness. One major concept at a time is less difficult for the students to handle, and emphasizing one concept at a time seems to make more of an impact on them.

Debate the Issues: Law of the Torah

Do we pick or choose laws from the Torah to support particular interests, or are the Torah's laws a "package deal"? Using Jewish resources, students can develop strong debates on current issues—issues like animal rights, abortion, and the law of the land vs. God's law. The students do the research and debate the issues, both pro and con. As an example, here are some thoughts on animal rights:

Many Jews involved in animal rights say that their beliefs are mandated by Jewish law. The Torah, they point out, demands the prevention of cruelty to animals, and directs us to treat them with kindness and compassion. One is even obligated to feed the animals before one eats. Many *midrashim* tell how people were punished for mistreating animals. Moses and David are singled out for their kind attitude to all God's creatures. One of the reasons why Rebekah was chosen to be Isaac's wife was her kindness to animals. We find in Proverbs (12:10), "The righteous person regards the life of the beast." In the Ten Commandments, included in the Shabbat commandment, we are told to let the animals rest.

On the other hand, Noah and his descendants were given permission to eat meat, in addition to the fruit of the trees and the grain permitted to Adam and Eve. The method by which animals are killed plays a role here. Jewish law forbids injuring the animal in any way before it is killed. The laws of *kashrut* say that slitting the throat and letting the blood drain out is a humane way to kill an animal. U.S. law demands that an animal be off the ground when killed, which means that it is raised by its hind legs just before its demise, and it twists and turns before the slaughter. Animals are also used extensively for medical experiments and suffer because of this. They are also used in testing cosmetics.

The Torah clearly states that animals are not equal to human beings. It also says that animals were created for the benefit of humankind. Humans are not allowed to cause them unnecessary pain or suffering, but to use them for human need is proper.

This gives you an idea of the kind of material that is available for the students to develop in a very exciting debate. The same can be done with many of today's hottest issues.

Families in the Bible

Divide the class into small groups. Prepare a list of families mentioned in the Bible. Assign one family to each group. The students are to read about their assigned families in the Bible and any other resource materials available in the library. After they have gathered all the information, they are to create a family album which can include pictures, deeds, birth announcements, certificates for events in the family's life cycle, key family events, etc. These can be from what they have read about the biblical family or from what they imagine it experienced.

Where and How to Locate Biblical Quotations and Determine Their Themes

This activity not only teaches portions of the Torah, but shows the students how to look things up in the Bible. You can use it in studying any Bible portion you want or any biblical theme that is part of your unit. One activity would be to match up quotations from the Bible—who is talking and to whom? For example, here is a selection of quotations in which the common theme is "famous last words":

> Then he instructed them, saying to them, "I am about to be gathered to my kin. Bury me with my fathers in the cave which is in the field of Ephron the Hittite." (Jacob)

> (Genesis 49:29)

> . . . let me die with the Philistines! (Samson)

> (Judges 16:30)

Draw your sword and run me through, so that the uncircumcised may not run me through and make sport of me. (Saul)

(I Samuel 31:4)

The names are provided for your benefit; do not include them when giving the class a list of quotations. In addition to discussing the overall theme, ask the students to find out what else was happening during the same period of biblical history.

To have some fun, here are some Bible passages which refer to colors. Create a page of Jewish stars, balloons, or symbols. Place a biblical passage in the center of each symbol. When the students have identified the color, they can color the symbol accordingly.

Isaiah 37:27

Genesis 44:2

Genesis 30:33

Proverbs 20:29

Leviticus 13:30

Ezekiel 23:6

II Kings 19:26

A resource you can use to identify specific quotations and subject matter is a concordance. I have used the *Living Bible Concordance* for years. Just be sure that the quotation is given in the same translation found in the Bible your class is using.

More Bible Quotations

Compile a set of four or five biblical quotations. Write them on the blackboard. Divide the class into small groups. Each group is to identify the source of at least one quotation: Who said it? When was it said? What was taking place when it was said? What was the situation at the time?

Now have the group members make up quotations of their own based on your unit of study. Have some additional quotations ready. Put all the new quotations on the blackboard, mixing up the students' with yours. The students are to identify the events that were taking place and see if they can identify the ones their classmates created.

Another Use for Quotations

As the students read the assigned text, ask them to individually identify portions of the text that "speak" to them—passages with which they identify strongly. After they have finished reading, have them write prayers or poems based on or including their special passages. Then have them share their writings with one another.

Students Make Decisions: Bible Stories

Involve the students in the Bible's stories. Explain that you are going to tell or read a story where the main character has to make a decision. For example, Joseph has to decide how to deal with his brothers, who sold him into slavery. Stop before reading about the decision Joseph made. Ask the students to list the people, thoughts, objects, or feelings that may influence his decision. Then continue the story to see what Joseph does. Stop, and let the students discuss whether they would have made the same decision or a different one, and make sure they give their reasons.

ANOTHER OPTION

Before reading about Joseph's decision, do some brainstorming with the class, listing all his alternatives. Then let the students see what Joseph decided. Discuss what his reasons might have been.

STILL ANOTHER OPTION

Before the end of the story, stop and have the students list all the possible endings. Have them explain what decision the main character must make for each ending to be possible.

Make the TV Work for You

Youngsters are watching TV anyway, so why not use it as a teaching tool? Give your students a homework assignment they might actually like. For example: Watch *Beverly Hills 90210*; while watching the show, make notes on how many violations of the Ten Commandments take place. Bring the results to class for sharing and discussion. When the discussion takes place, make sure it covers which commandments were broken; the consequences of the violations, if any; whether most of the students noted the same violations; why some of them missed certain violations; and the social impact of a TV show like this.

ANOTHER EXAMPLE

Watch *The Simpsons*. Make a list of the different times the characters put one other down, are sarcastic, and do not care about one other's feelings. Bring the results to class and discuss them. Relate this to Leviticus 19, the Holiness Code, and to what the sages say about *leshon hara*—the evil tongue.

The Essence of Judaism

Brainstorm with the students, making a list of the ideas and concepts they regard as the essence of Judaism. Then give them the following information (it can be prepared ahead of time and copied):

The Essence of Judaism

Rabbi Simlai said: Six hundred and thirteen commands were given to Moses on Mount Sinai. The essence of these commands was distilled by David [in the Book of Psalms] into eleven.... Isaiah condensed them into six, Micah into three, Amos, one...[and also]

Habakkuk into one. (*Makkot* 23b)

What commands did David, Isaiah, Micah, Amos, and Habakkuk say are the essence of Judaism? Make a list from the following sources:

Psalms 15:1–5 (David)

Isaiah 33:15, 56:1

Micah 6:8

Amos 5:4

Habakkuk 2:4

Share your list with the class.

After the lists are shared, compare them with the lists the students made at the beginning of the activity, and talk about the similarities and differences.

The Book of Proverbs

The Bible's proverbs offer solutions to real-life problems, yet many students probably think they were written too long ago to be of any value today. This activity will let you approach the Book of Proverbs through the back door. Divide the class into small groups. You will need Bibles for each group and a collection of "Dear Abby" letters. The letters can be of your own creation or clipped from newspapers. Just keep the age of your class in mind and make sure the letters are appropriate.

Give the members of each group a set of letters with instructions to read them one at a time. After reading each letter they are to go through the Book of Proverbs to find as many proverbs as possible that offer a solution to the problem posed in the letter. The students are to record their findings and share the results upon completion.

Note: If you think the Book of Proverbs is too long for the students to browse through, choose specific portions that relate to the problems presented in the letters. Copy and give to the students.

AN ALTERNATIVE

Give out the "Dear Abby" letters and tell the students to write their own solutions to the problems. Put these aside. Now read through the Book of Proverbs and see how many different proverbs they can find that offer solutions to the problems. List these proverbs. Have the students compare their answers to the problem with what the Bible says. What are the similarities and differences?

The Talmud Comes Alive!

With this activity the class will experience the process by which the Talmud was developed. Give each student a sheet of paper divided into sections, based on the way a page of Talmud is divided. In the center section, which corresponds to the *Mishnah*, students are to write down a law or laws which they think are important. In the same column, they can illustrate the law with personal anecdotes. This corresponds to the *Gemara*. For example, if a student writes, "You are not to say things that are untrue about other people," this can be followed by a story about how a person was hurt when other people told stories that were not true. Upon completion, students are to exchange papers. In the margins surrounding the center column, the students receiving the papers comment on whether they agree or disagree with the argument in the *Mishnah* and *Gemara*. Continue passing the papers until everyone has added a commentary. Ask the students to support their arguments. Share the results.

Using Midrashim

The Jewish tradition has a wealth of literary materials that can be used in religious schools. My favorites are the multitude of *midrashim* that the sages used to teach the people and expand the meaning of the Torah. There are two kinds of *midrashim*. In the halachic *midrash*, the sages expanded the Torah and kept its laws alive. Aggadic *midrash* is a telling of a narrative, a non-legal interpretation to inform and deepen the understanding of *halachah*.

Today there is much we can learn from both kinds of *midrashim*. Although the language is different from what the kids usually read or hear, the *midrashim* provide an interesting and stimulating history lesson, replete with insights into Jewish ethics, Bible, and contemporary issues. For a short history lesson, here is an example:

> The report reached Nimrod's ears that Abraham was mocking the idols, so he ordered the boy brought before him. Nimrod turned his gaze on him and said imperiously, "Here is fire; worship it!" "My lord," answered Abraham fearlessly, "wouldn't it be better to worship water, since it can put out the fire?" Nimrod responded, "Let it be as you say: worship water!" Abraham answered, "Shall I do an injustice to the clouds which give the earth all the water?" Nimrod then said, "Very well, worship the clouds!" Abraham retorted, "But how can the clouds compare with the winds that have the power to scatter them?" "Then worship the wind!" came from Nimrod. Abraham answered, "The wind? What will the One Who directs the fire, water, clouds, and wind say to that? O you blind man! Don't you perceive the mighty Hand that guides the world?" The king was abashed and, turning away, left young Abraham in peace.

After the *midrash* has been read, do some brainstorming with the class. The questions you ask could be something like these:

What does this *midrash* tell you about the period in which it was written?

What does it tell you about the people?

How did the neighbors of the Jews worship?

What did they worship?

What was the story meant to teach?

What problem does the *midrash* solve?

Through the brainstorming the students will discover that the Jews were living in a pagan society that worshipped many gods. There was a danger that they might be persuaded to assimilate (an age-old problem). The *midrash* was written to teach them that there was a Supreme Force higher than the forces of nature worshipped by the pagans, and it also emphasized One God!

As a closure for this activity, divide the students into small groups and have them write *midrashim* that provide the same kind of lesson for today's Jews.

Reviewing Jewish History or Bible

Try this instead of a test. Have the students create mystery boxes containing 10 or 12 items related to a historical event, historical person, or a Bible portion studied during the year. None of the items is to mention the name of the person or event. The items included could look something like this:

An imaginary page from someone's diary.

An editorial about the cause of the event.

A time-line of events.

Artifacts from this period. (Draw or cut out pictures.)

A list of places where someone might have traveled.

A list of someone's accomplishments.

A list of important dates.

And so on.

Upon completion, ask the students to exchange boxes and see if they can identify one another's historical events, Bible scenes, or people.

After-Dinner Speeches

Adults aren't the only ones who enjoy after-dinner speeches, roasts, and tributes. Upon completion of a unit of study, ask the students to identify their favorite or most interesting person from the unit. Several students can form a group to work on one speech in order to prevent duplications. The speech should cover the person's major contributions, explaining why this person is their favorite or seemed the most interesting. The speech can be in the form of a tribute to the person, an after-dinner speech with jokes, or a roast. Each group chooses one member to deliver the speech to the whole class.

A Class Project: The History of Your Jewish Community

Even if someone has already researched the Jewish history of your community, this is an excellent activity. Students can find out when the first Jews arrived, what was the first thing they did, where the first synagogue was located, who the leaders of the Jewish community were, etc. They can interview the descendants of the leaders for some of the information they need. Divide the class into small groups. Give each group a specific area to research. As the groups gather their information, have class meetings to show how the work is progressing. At these meetings, problems can be discussed, solutions provided, and resources identified for further research. The end product could be a book on the history of your Jewish community to share with the congregation.

Who Is Heroic? Create a Comic Book

Save cartoons or ask the students to begin collecting comics based on the following list of values that make for Jewish heroism. This list was taken from an article in *Keeping Posted* magazine entitled "Who Is a (Jewish) Hero?"

Uses Jewish tradition, education, scholarship, and teaching.

Struggles to overcome obstacles.

Strives for perfection and excellence.

Acts courageously in spite of . . .

"One that is slow to anger is better than the mighty" (Proverbs 16:32).

Lives by the Jewish calendar.

Loves Jewish people and cares about their welfare and survival.

Serves humanity.

Strives for human dignity and values.

Ben Zoma says: "Who is mighty? One who controls oneself."

Ben Zoma says: "Who is honored? One who honors everyone."

Go over the list with the students, making sure they understand all the concepts and ideas. They can add to it if they desire. Ask them to choose partners. They are to take the comic strips, read through them, and identify the ones they will use with each Jewish value that makes for heroic achievement of some kind. Then mount each comic strip at the top of a page. Underneath put the quotation it represents. Continue until all the quotations have been placed under a comic strip. The students can design covers for their books and then share with the class.

AN ADDED DIMENSION

Ask the students to list the names of some famous Jews. After each name, they are to indicate the person's contribution to humanity or to the Jewish people.

Rank-Order: Which Achievements Are Most Heroic?

Divide the class into small groups and give each the name of a famous Jewish person. If you are studying Israel, limit the list to people identified with Israel. Each group is to research the background of its assigned individual. The members are to develop a list of reasons why the person they are researching is famous: What did the person do? How was it done? Why was it done? How did it help the Jews? And so on. Once the list has been developed, the students are to rank-order the reasons from most important to least important. They are to include an explanation for the order they have chosen.

A student from each group reports on the results of its efforts. Either you or a student should keep a record of the reasons why the members of the group felt certain of the individual's acts were especially important. Then talk about: What characteristics made these people heroic in Jewish eyes?

More Jewish Heroism: Beyond the Classroom

This activity involves parents, relatives, and even members of the congregation, since the students will be conducting a survey to discover which figures from Jewish history are regarded as having made extraordinary contributions or acted with great courage.

With the students, design a cover letter that explains the project. Create a short questionnaire limited to about three questions, with space for comments. It could look something like this:

1. Who made the greatest contribution to the history of the Jewish people?

2. What acts by this person were heroic?

3. What characteristics make this person special to you?

Include space for the responses, a set time for the questionnaire's return, and the cover letter. Send out the survey, including a self-addressed stamped envelope to use when returning it. When the responses are received, ask the students to tabulate them. Then they are to research the people named in the responses. When the research is completed, have the students prepare a poster for each person. Include a picture of the individual and important facts about the contributions this person made to Jewish history. Post the finished products in the hallway for everyone to see. In addition, have the students write an article for the temple bulletin reporting the results of the survey and telling about the "Hall of Fame" they have established.

Biographies of Famous Jewish People

List the kind of information you want the students to include in a biography of a famous Jewish person. Your list could look something like this:

Name.

Age at time of greatest achievement or contribution.

When and where born.

Where lived and description of community.

Physical description (imagined if not available).

Members of family.

What makes this person famous?

Greatest achievements or contributions.

Divide the class into small groups and assign each a different person to research. When the research is complete, the group members compile booklets that provide all the information called for on the list. After designing covers for their booklets, they share them with the class.

Last Words

If you were to walk through an old cemetery you would see words inscribed on some of the tombstones in memory of the persons buried there. These are called epitaphs, and are often in the form of couplets (two lines) or quatrains (four lines). Epitaphs are usually quite serious, sweet, or loving, but sometimes they can be funny or even caustic. Have the students research the background of a Jewish historical personality. Once they know quite a bit about this person, they are to write the kind of epitaph they envision would be on this person's tombstone. They can even draw a picture of a tombstone and place their epitaph within its borders, including the person's name. An example of what could be done:

Rabbi Leo Baeck
Here lies a man with faith so strong,
He was master of his faith his life long.

Students Prepare for a Guest

Divide the class into small groups and assign each a different Jewish personality. Tell the students to pretend that they have invited the assigned person to speak to the class. They are entirely responsible for taking care of the publicity. They also have to make all the necessary decisions about the place, date, time, and topic. Now the members of the various groups have to do some research to learn more about the persons assigned as their guests. They will need to know the speakers quite well and be able to answer any questions anyone asks about them. Once the research is completed, they are to design attractive posters, easy to read and informative, using bright colors to attract attention to the coming speaking event. Then the members of each group write a one-minute speech about their guest speaker. The speech should include biographical information and reasons why everyone will want to see and hear the guest. When all work has been completed, the groups present their posters and a member of each group delivers the speech to the class.

Evolution of Religion: An Introduction to Comparative Religion

It is important to find out what the students already know before you develop a series of lessons. When beginning to teach a course on comparative religion, I designed an activity which covered the changes religions have gone through since primitive times based on the influence of the outside world. I divided the history of the world and its religions into five time periods:

Primitive.

Period of Early Great Civilizations.

The Dark and Middle Ages.

The Renaissance.

Scientific, Technical, and Information Age.

Under each period I indicated what was going on in the world at that time, including comments on weather and lifestyle. The students' task was to discuss: What kind of religion developed in this period? What kind of religion would serve the needs of the people? How would they pray? To what would they pray? The class was divided into small groups. Each group was to determine the religious response of the people during a specific historical period.

After the members had discussed the topic, each group was given a large piece of white butcher paper, colored markers, and instructions to depict, in mural form, the religious response of the people in the assigned period. The results: walls covered with drawings, pretty accurate descriptions of the religions of the different periods, and an opportunity for the group members to share what they already knew with others. An activity of this kind can be a great help in planning future lessons, and the students enjoy sharing their knowledge.

Historical Correspondence

Teaching Jewish history? Teaching Bible? Try this activity: Have the students pretend to be historical figures living in the period covered in your unit of study. They can write letters to each other regarding problems in their time. They can even try to imitate the writing style of the period. This activity can be made more realistic by having them use quill pens and onionskin paper or imitation parchment. Here are just a few examples of the kinds of correspondence that can take place:

Moses writes his brother Aaron concerning the slavery of his people in Egypt and Aaron replies.

Yigael Yadin writes to David Ben-Gurion concerning what he has found in the excavations at Masada. David Ben-Gurion replies.

David Ben-Gurion writes to Chaim Weizmann concerning the establishment of the State of Israel. Chaim Weizmann replies.

Exploring the Past: Jewish History

When looking at where Jews came from when they immigrated to the United States, have the students create an exhibit illustrating the history of European Jewish life through maps and displays. Place a map of the world on the wall and a table in front of the map. Divide the class into small groups. As students identify the locations of different communities where Jews came from, place a flag pin in that location. Students are to find out as much as they can about the life of the Jews in the various communities. Then they are to prepare shoebox displays of samples of Jewish life, write brief descriptive information on index cards to explain the displays, and place the displays on the table. Attach a piece of yarn from each display to the flag pin of the location it represents. Invite parents to view the exhibit when it is completed.

AN ALTERNATIVE, OR IN ADDITION

Hang a map of the world in the synagogue's entry hall. Prepare small flag pins; the flag must be large enough, though, for people to write their last name on it. Have pens available on a table in front of the map. Have students staff the table and ask members of the congregation to write their name on a small flag and place the flag pin in the location of their family's origin. It will be interesting to see how diversified the backgrounds of the congregation members are.

A Different Look at "Exploring" Jewish History

Divide the class into small groups. Assign each group a period of Jewish history. Your list of different periods will vary, but it could look something like this:

Biblical era.

Hellenistic period.

Talmud/Rabbinic period.

Judeo/Islamic period.

Old European period.

Modern European period.

America.

Israel.

In their respective time periods, the members of each group are to do the following:

Identify the lifestyle of the Jews.

Identify their God beliefs.

Identify their religious practices and traditions.

Identify the outside influences.

If your class is small, take one period at a time and assign each group a specific area to research. When the research is completed, give each group a large piece of white butcher or art paper and colored markers. The members are to create a giant wall mural depicting their period. Through their drawings they are to answer all the questions. If you are just doing one period, each group creates a mural depicting the responses to the questions. Murals are placed around the room when completed, and group members explain their creative work.

How Jews Live

This activity will enable the class to look at the different ways Jews have lived over the ages (e.g., as nomads in biblical times, in the *shtetl*, in urban ghettos, on the kibbutz, in cities and suburbs, during the *Haskalah*). Divide the class into small groups. Assign each group a different period. Within that period, the members are to create a day in the life of the Jews. Include the kinds of clothes they would wear, their religious activities, what kinds of work they did, their social life, what foods they ate, how they governed themselves, the education of the children, and what their family life was like. To share the information, the groups can use any (or a combination) of the following media:

Drama.

Songs.

Art/murals.

Poetry and prose.

Create a book.

Museum Project in a Synagogue

This idea originated with the MUSE project of the Skirball Museum of Hebrew Union College–Jewish Institute of Religion in Los Angeles. I have adapted it for use in any synagogue school. A little research is necessary, but it will be worth the effort.

1. Identify the period of Jewish history you wish to cover.

2. See what artifacts are available in your synagogue for this period (e.g., Kiddush cups, *megillot*, candlesticks, seder plates, *ketubahs*, old letters). If the synagogue has some old items, see if the congregational historian knows where they came from, but if this information is not available, don't despair. You can always pretend and create your own history of the artifact to fit your specific needs.

3. Once you have a few artifacts, you will need some written documents. Resources for documents can be found in the following:

Franz Kobler, *Letters of Jews Through the Ages*

Jacob R. Marcus, *The Jew in the Medieval World: A Source Book*

Israel Abrahams, *Jewish Life in the Middle Ages*

Daniel J. Silver and Bernard Martin, *History of Judaism*

These books have quotations from actual documents or letters from individuals. They are very good for this purpose.

4. Choose a selection of letters, documents, and artifacts that will give the students enough clues about Jewish life during your chosen period. If you feel that certain clues are missing, create your own letters and documents, using quotations you find in your research to create the effect that real individuals are writing about things that are happening to them. *Another suggestion:* At an art or teacher's store you will find paper that looks old; use it to make your documents look more realistic. Find an old cardboard box, or make one look old by tearing corners, burning edges, etc.; put all your artifacts and documents in it and take it to class.

5. Now, pretend some more. Tell the students that a friend of yours who works at a museum was cleaning out the museum's basement and found this box. Since the contents were Jewish in nature, you have been asked to see if anyone can identify them, what and whom they might belong to. You have brought the box in to ask the class for help in identifying the contents.

6. Divide the class into small groups. The members of each group take one item and, after reading the document/letter or studying it, are to answer such questions as:

Who do you think wrote it?

What was the sex of the person?

How old do you think the writer was?

When do you think it was written?

How can one tell when it was written?

What does it tell you about Jewish life in this period?

Those are just some suggestions. You can, of course, think of more questions based on the contents of the box.

7. After the group members have completed their individual detective work, they share their conclusions with the other groups. With all the combined clues, see if the students can add to the story of the contents of the box.

8. A final activity would be to have the students prepare a museum of their artifacts and documents/letters. Include a display of the materials the students have discovered and identified. The museum can be set up in the library or the synagogue lobby for everyone to see.

The Impact of Historical Events on Jews

We often teach Jewish history without trying to determine the impact of a given historical event on individuals or on the Jewish people as a whole. This activity will give the students an opportunity to learn whether the event had national, religious, or cultural significance. They will rank-order historical events based on the impact on themselves personally or on the Jewish people.

The list you put together can be based on subject matter the students have already covered and could look something like this:

HISTORICAL EVENT	NATIONAL	RELIGIOUS	CULTURAL	RANKING
Fall of Masada	____	____	____	____
Giving of Torah at Sinai	____	____	____	____
Bar Kochba Revolt	____	____	____	____
Holocaust	____	____	____	____
Expulsion from Spain	____	____	____	____
Creation of State of Israel	____	____	____	____
Warsaw Ghetto Uprising	____	____	____	____
Dreyfus Case	____	____	____	____
Destruction of Second Temple	____	____	____	____
Maccabean Revolt	____	____	____	____
Exodus from Egypt	____	____	____	____
Enlightenment	____	____	____	____
Yom Kippur War	____	____	____	____

As you can see, I did not arrange the events in any specific order, and you may not even want to use all of them, but the list gives an idea of the kind of list that can be created. Have the students identify the categories in which the historical events belong and then rank-order them. Remind the students that the rank-ordering should reflect the impact of the events on them personally or on the Jewish people as a whole. Share their results with the whole class. Discuss, with the students, the different categories they used and the reasons for their ranking choices.

Quantum Leap

I really liked *Quantum Leap*; too bad it's no longer on TV, but at least it gave me an idea for teaching Jewish history. Consider: What if you were caught in the past? How would you describe your modern Jewish life to, say, Abraham? Ask the students to write about an aspect of their life as Jews in the twentieth century. Create a list of topics (e.g., Shabbat, Rosh Hashanah, Yom Kippur, a wedding). The students are to choose a period into which they make their *Quantum Leap*; the only way they can get back is to compare their current Jewish way of life to the Jewish life of the period they find themselves in.

Honoring Jewish Heroism

Discuss heroism. With the class, make a list of heroic individuals from books, TV, comic strips, Jewish history, or real life. Ask students to describe their favorites by asking such questions as:

What makes someone heroic?

What are the character traits of a heroic person?

What makes something Jewish-ly heroic?

Do heroic individuals begin that way, or do they go through some process that makes them heroic?

Do some brainstorming and list the character traits that comprise Jewish heroism.

Have students choose partners to create a person whose achievements warrant the title of Jewish heroism. They can use a real person from Jewish history or fantasize a little. Have the following supplies available: construction paper, buttons, glitter, felt, cloth, clay, yarn, dried macaroni and beans, craft sticks, etc. Students can make a small model or draw and decorate a picture of their heroic Jewish figure. They are to name the figure they make and write a short story explaining why this person was chosen as an example of Jewish heroism.

People Helping People: Jewish History

Divide the class into small groups. Assign each group a different Jewish historical figure. The members of each group are to find out as much as they can about their assigned figure. Give them a list of the information they will need:

Date of birth.

Where the person was born and lived.

What the person accomplished.

How the person's accomplishments helped others.

When they have gathered all the information, they are to create a poster conveying what they have learned, with emphasis on how the person's accomplishments helped others. Before putting the finished poster on the wall, the members of each group are to describe what their historical figure did to help other people. After everyone has shared, ask the students to compare their Jewish historical figures to people today. Whom can they identify, from today's world, who has helped people as effectively as the historical figures they have studied?

People Helping People: Famous Jewish Persons

Do some brainstorming with the class, making a list of what the students can do in their community or school to help others. Set this list aside for the time being.

Prepare a list of famous Jewish people from your unit of study. Divide the class into small groups. Each group is to choose two persons and find out as much as possible about them (e.g., the voluntary activities they engaged in, how their activities helped the Jewish people/community, what they did to help Jews, and what they did to help non-Jews). When the research is completed, the group members are to share their findings with the class.

Now go back to the list of things to do to help others. Encourage the students to come up with a class project that would enable them to help others, just as our famous Jewish figures did. Once they have chosen a project, help them to plan it to its completion.

Jewish History: A Variety of Activities

One way to get students interested and involved in Jewish history is to let them experience it through their own lives. Getting them personally involved with the past can bring history to life in the classroom. Each of these activities can be an introduction to the actual study of Jewish history. Just relate the activity to your lesson for the day.

PERSONAL SCRAPBOOK

Have students keep a scrapbook of their Jewish lives for a few weeks. Include drawings, pictures of family events, magazine and newspaper clippings on Jewish issues of interest to them, etc. Bring the scrapbook to class and exchange with a partner. Each partner is to write a biography of the other, based only on the information in the scrapbook.

NEAT AND SIMPLE

HOME ARCHAEOLOGICAL DIG

Ask students to pretend their attics or family junk drawers or closets are archaeological digs. Have them list the "artifacts" they find. Based on these finds the students can reconstruct the past history of their families.

ORAL HISTORIES

Have students interview two or three people who witnessed a specific event in the past (e.g., a fire, flood, robbery, hurricane, baseball game, Bar/Bat Mitzvah). All the interviewees should have been present at the same event. From the data gathered, the students have to determine what actually took place and write a report based on the interviews.

PICTURE HISTORY

Prior to this activity, have the students ask their parents to find a picture of a family event that took place before they were born. The students are to bring the pictures to school. Divide the class into small groups and let the students share their pictures. They are to determine what each picture is about (when it was taken, who was in it, what these people's lives were like, etc.). Make notes of what they decide about each picture. Afterwards, tell the students to ask their parents to "tell the truth" about the picture. Students make notes of what their parents tell them. During the next class they can compare the differences and similarities between their understanding of the picture and what the parents said.

History of an Object

Have the students write descriptions of the oldest Jewish object in their house. Include where it came from, how long it has been in the family, what it was used for, whether it is still used today, and why it is or isn't important to the family.

Using Receipts as Records

Household expense records, especially from the Middle Ages, are a valuable historical source. From these records, historians are able to reconstruct the daily lives of medieval families. Give the students an idea of how this was done by having them bring in store receipts, the kind that list the items purchased. When you have a sufficient supply, form small groups. Give each group a good number of receipts. The members of each group are to write a biographical sketch of the people who kept these records.

Activities Following a History Lesson

As students study the past, make it come alive by having them do activities based on the past but for today's world. Here are a few ideas:

1. Create a newspaper or a TV news show: Students become reporters and tell about interviews they have had with personalities from the period of Jewish history you are studying. Some students could even role-play the person being interviewed.

2. Pretend to be scientists and explain the noise at Mount Sinai, the separation of the Reed Sea, the walls of Jericho coming down, etc.

3. Create murals of events in history as they would look today.

A Mystery Puzzle: Jewish History

Choose an unfamiliar Jewish historical event or person from Jewish history. Prepare a series of clues and post them, one at a time, on the bulletin board. Students are to try to identify the event or person based on the clues you provide. Keep adding clues until the class identifies the event or person. When the puzzle is solved, have ready a short one-page biography of the person or description of the event for the students to read. Then divide the class into small groups. The students in each group are to develop their own mystery puzzle to try and stump their classmates. They can use their textbook or any other resource materials available in the classroom or library.

How About Some Trivia Questions?

Prepare a series of multiple-choice questions about famous Jewish people to see how much the students have learned or what they know about them. The subjects can be living, from the past, the Bible, etc. Your questions might look something like this:

1. David Ben-Gurion was: (a) president of the United States, (b) prime minister of Israel, (c) governor of Texas.

2. Ben-Gurion lived in: (a) Chicago, (b) Sede Boker, (c) Paris.

3. Ben-Gurion served during the (a) Vietnam War, (b) War of Independence, (c) Yom Kippur War.

Or you could try something like this:

1. Who was the first Jewish pitcher to win twenty games in consecutive seasons? (a) Sandy Koufax. (b) Erskin Mayer. (c) Ken Holtzman.

2. Moses Alexander was the first Jewish elected governor of a state. Which state did he govern? (a) New York. (b) Florida. (c) Idaho. (d) Rhode Island.

3. Which one of the following did not sign Israel's Declaration of Independence: (a) Abba Eban. (b) Rachel Cohen. (c) Fritz Bernstein. (d) Rabbi Wolf Gold.

A Time Machine: Decisions in Jewish History

With this activity, students learn about decision-making. They are called upon to make decisions as if they were actual participants in a historical event, examining and trying to define their own value systems while learning how choices made by individuals have shaped history. (This process is done very well in the Do-It-Yourself Jewish Adventure Series by Rabbi Kenneth Roseman, published by the Union of American Hebrew Congregations.)

This approach can be used in any historical situation where there is a "fork in the road" choice. It is of value to reexamine such situations, even if for no other reason than to discover that there are almost always alternatives when a decision is required. A few examples:

Yochanan ben Zakai and the destruction of the Second Temple.

David Ben-Gurion and the creation of the State of Israel.

The Six-Day War.

Situations during the Holocaust.

Design a "Time Machine" sheet. On the sheet leave space for the students to respond. It could look something like this:

1. Take yourself back to the time of _____ (list the time and place).

2. Briefly describe the situation.

3. Offer choices of what the students can do.

4. Student's choice is _____.

5. Reason for the choice _____.

6. What would be the consequences of this choice?

Upon completion, students share their responses with their classmates. Then talk about what actually happened, the reasons and results.

Impact of Jewish History

Divide the class into small groups. The members of each group are to choose an event in Jewish history that they think had the greatest impact. They are to create a presentation which explains the following:

Reasons for their choice.

The event in Jewish history.

What took place; who was involved; how they were involved.

What impact it had on the Jews during this period and afterwards.

The presentations can be in the form of written reports, dramatic performances, music and songs, multi-media, TV or radio news broadcasts, even comic books. Either specify a date for the project to be finished or allow time in the classroom for research and work.

Create a Novel: Jewish History

A great way to culminate a year of studying Jewish history would be to have the class write a historical novel. This is not a one-session activity. It will take anywhere from five to seven sessions to complete, but the end product is worth the effort. (And in the process, more learning will take place.)

The possibilities for historical novels are really endless, but here are a few ideas I have thought of:

Creation of the State of Israel: Israeli boy, Arab boy, and their families; or Israeli boy, Arab girl, and their families.

Before the Holocaust: Jewish boy and girl and their families; or
Jewish boy, German girl, and their families.

During the Holocaust: Jewish girl, Polish boy, and partisans; or
Jewish boy, father, and family in ghetto.

If you decide to go ahead with this project, here is a good procedure to follow:

1. Talk about historical novels. See if anyone has read any. Discuss how this kind of novel draws the reader into a particular period; how the reader becomes involved with the characters in the story: what happens to them, the problems they encounter, how they solve their problems.

2. Before the actual writing, do some brainstorming with the class to decide about the novel's time period, setting, and characters. Write all the ideas on the board, have a student record the decisions made, and make copies for the whole class.

3. To choose a time period, have the students talk about the historical conflicts they have studied that were the most interesting and what made them interesting. Which period would provide the most dramatic background and why? Discuss possible

themes and potential characters for each period under discussion. Finally, students vote on which time period to use.

4. Once the period is chosen, use the same approach to determine the setting and characters. Ask the class to think about the kinds of people who could have been living in this period, and the kinds of homes, cities, and towns they lived in.

5. Once the setting and characters have been determined, the students are ready to begin constructing the plot. Talk about the tensions that existed in this period; have students pretend they are living at this time: What do families talk about? What are children worried about? What are some of the conflicts they might encounter? Keep a record of all the suggestions, listing every possible plot line. Let the students decide which plot line they will include in the novel.

6. Fill in some of the details about the setting and characters. Choose names, decide what the characters look like, age, color of hair, eyes, weight, etc. Develop the characters' personalities, habits, likes and dislikes, etc. Research details like home furnishings, buildings, foods, and clothing.

7. The time to begin writing the novel has arrived. Divide the class into small groups of two or three. The novel can be divided into as many chapters as there are groups. Assign each group to write and illustrate one chapter. Encourage the students to work on their chapter in the manner that best suits them: they can work together or write alone and then get together to combine ideas; each could write sections of a chapter, then work on them together, etc.

8. When the first draft is completed, bring everyone together and read the story out loud. Ask everyone to listen carefully and make notes on what needs to be added, left out, changed, or redone. Make notes on factual errors, repetitions, gaps that require transitions, etc. After the oral reading, go over each chapter to make sure all the suggestions have been noted.

9. The groups then write second drafts, incorporating the suggested changes and making the story more real. Read and revise drafts as necessary until you and the students think the novel flows smoothly.

10. Final editing. Have groups exchange drafts and discuss questions and suggestions with the writers. While they are doing their final editing, ask students to begin thinking of a title for the novel.

11. Naming the novel. Do some brainstorming and list all the suggestions for the title. Don't make a decision right away, let the students think about it for a week before voting.

12. The novel is now ready to be typed, then proofread, duplicated,

and collated. Make enough copies for the whole class. Make several extra copies for the school library. You and the class can be proud of the finished product when the novel is "published"!

One final note: During the writing stage, the use of a computer would be advantageous. If your synagogue has one available, see if you can arrange for a time when your class can input its materials. Or see if a parent would be willing to do this part of the project. It will simplify the editing and changes made in the different drafts.

APPROACHES TO TEACHING THE HOLOCAUST

The Value Game

(Adapted from the original by William S. Irving and Thomas E. Linehand; published by Herder & Herder, New York, 1970.)

This game has been designed to encourage meaningful discussion. I have used it for a number of Jewish topics, including the Holocaust, situational ethics, various historical events, and youth group situations. The following was used to cover the Jewish concept of the value of human life, especially during the Holocaust.

You will need six large pieces of newsprint or posterboard. If you decide on posterboard, use different colors. Put the following statements at the top, one on each board:

Absolutely right—no reservations.

Right—many reservations.

Right—a few reservations.

Wrong—a few reservations.

Wrong—many reservations.

Absolutely wrong—no reservations.

Place the posterboards on the floor in the above order, taping them down so that they cannot be moved. Give out crayons or colored markers, pencils, and paper. The students are to use the pencils and paper to make notes on how they arrive at their decisions.

Read and explain the rules to the class: They are not allowed to ask for any additional information regarding the situations you will be reading to them. They must make a decision based on the information received. They do not take turns; as soon as they make a decision, they move to the area of their choice. One word of caution, though, there are no right or wrong answers! Their responses are based on their own value system. Before you begin playing the game, answer only three questions from the students. Then begin playing. There is to be no discussion during the reading or playing of the game. Discussion will follow after all the situations have been read.

Read the situations, one at a time. Students make their decisions and move to the board of their choice, where they write and encircle their initials and the number of the situation. They then return to their places.

Situations:

1. During the Nazi occupation of Poland, the first Jews to be removed and sent to the concentration camps were the religiously observant. Anyone with a beard or kipah was taken and deported. In response to this, an old grandmother begged her grandson to shave his beard off and put on peasant clothes to hide his Jewishness. He refused.

2. The Nazis distributed "life certificates" to the leaders of the European ghettos. There was a life-and-death barrier between those who received the certificates and those who didn't. One ghetto administrator, who was given 5,000 life certificates for 29,000 inhabitants, said, "Let no one take the documents. Either we all live or we all die."

3. The leaders of some communities accepted the life certificates and gave them to select families, but never quite enough for the entire family. One family of five, a mother, father, two children, and a grandmother, received three certificates. They decided that the mother, father, and one child would hold the certificates.

4. When the Nazis inspected a house, all the residents had to be present. If one person was not there, the others would be deported to what was certain death. Several families were living in a small house in the ghetto. They decided that the young people should leave and join the partisans outside the ghetto walls.

Once the students have reacted to each situation, go back to the beginning and talk about their reactions. Take one situation at a time and talk about:

What was the reason for your response?

How did you arrive at that decision?

What other alternatives might there have been?

How did the actions of the people under Nazi occupation correspond to the Jewish concept of the value of life?

These questions are just some examples of what you can ask to process the activity. During the discussion, other questions will surely arise; don't hesitate to make them part of the discussion. The discussion can get hot and heavy, but it is exciting to watch the students get involved.

Holocaust: What Is Prejudice?

The dictionary defines *prejudice* as "an unreasoning opinion or like or dislike of something; racial prejudice, prejudice against people of other races;

harm to someone's rights." Today, even though most people will insist that they are not prejudiced against anyone or anything, there always seems to be some prejudice hidden away. It often shows itself when something traumatic takes place, or when someone prejudges certain people because of a false assumption that all members of a certain category have certain traits.

How do children learn to be prejudiced? Let's face it: we adults teach them. For the most part, it isn't done intentionally. Just as an example: ever watch any of the talk show hosts? Like Oprah Winfrey? Watch one day and "listen" to your reaction to, say, a woman going after her sister's husband/boyfriend or homosexuals baring their souls. What do you really "hear"? The sad problems, or the "ignorance" in their language? Yes, even you may be prejudiced.

In order to make our students understand that prejudice was very much a part of the Holocaust and that it could happen again, we need to make them look within themselves and see where they are. The activities in this section will help.

DEFINING TERMS

Make up a sheet with the following terms, leaving room after each for the students to write answers:

Prejudice.

Sexism.

Racism.

Segregation.

Discrimination.

Oppression.

Explain that these terms all express or describe the inhumanity of people to other people. What do these terms mean to the class? The students are to write a definition of each term, then rank-order them from worst (1) to least bad (6). They share their responses, discussing their definitions with each response.

FOLLOW-UP

Make another set of sheets with the same six terms, but this time leave enough space for the students to draw examples of what they have seen or heard relating to each term. Their examples can be from real-life situations, movies, TV, newspapers, or magazines. Share their responses upon completion, discussing the situations as they are shared.

Looking Within

Students will explore their own ideas of what they think about other people. One way to discover what someone thinks about another person is to ask for several different descriptions of that person. Prepare sheets with at least five lines per item, so that the students can list at least five different ideas about each group. Here are some items that could be included on your list (remember to put in five lines after each of them):

I am _____

Men are _____

Women are _____

Asian people are _____

Black people are _____

Mexican people are _____

Italian people are _____

Jewish people are _____

Arab people are _____

Homosexuals are _____

Students fill in the responses for each item and then share. In discussing the results, talk about how they feel about what they have written: What prejudices are obvious? What prejudices are hidden?

DINNER STORY

(This activity is adapted from *Deciding for Myself: A Values Clarification Series*, published by Winston Press, 1974.)

Prepare copies of this story for the students:

One night Mr. A and Ms. B go out to eat. The restaurant is very crowded. They have to wait a long time before being seated at a table with a family, Mr. and Mrs. C and their child, little c. Little c looks at Mr. A and Ms. B and loudly proclaims, "These two people are different colors. They don't belong together."

"Shut up," blurts out Mr. C. And he cracks little c on the head. Mrs. C chides Mr. C, saying, "I wish you wouldn't be so hard on the child, dear." Mr. C snorts, "Isn't that just like a woman! I'm the head of this family, and I'll do what I want." At this point, Ms B throws her napkin on the table and angrily exclaims, "You didn't need to hit the child, you sexist pig." "Mind your own business," snaps Mrs. C to Ms. B.

Mr. A rises and glowers at the C family. "We don't have to take this kind of abuse," he says. He calls the manager over and demands that the C family be thrown out of the restaurant. But the manager, knowing the C family are regular customers, insists that Mr. A and Ms. B leave instead. After they've gone, the manager turns to Mr. C and says, "I try to keep people like that out, but you know how it is these days." "Sure thing," replies Mr. C. "Here's five dollars for your trouble."

The students are to make a list of the characters in the story and rank-order them from 1 (most negative) to 5 (least negative). They are to write the reasons for each ranking next to the character's name. Students share their rankings and the reasons for their choices. Also talk about: What would they have done in a similar situation?

Give the students a chance to decide how they would act in certain situations. What decision would they make in situations that might take place with family, friends, or relatives? Here are a few examples (put on paper with space for students to write their responses):

> You are with your parents and a few of their friends. One of your parents' friends tells a joke that makes fun of a certain ethnic group. What would you do?
>
> One of your friends makes a derogatory remark about a black football player. What would you do?
>
> A friend is planning a birthday party and is going to invite everyone in the class except for two black students and a Mexican-American student. What would you do?
>
> In the school cafeteria, members of the different ethnic groups sit in their own little cliques. What would you do?
>
> A group of students want to form a club at school where members of different ethnic groups can come together to better understand each other. What would you do?

After completing their responses, the students share and discuss why they made their respective choices.

Closures for Activities on Prejudice

Prepare a sheet with the following incomplete sentences. Ask the students to complete them with the first words that come to mind.

> I learned that I _____.
>
> I think that racism is _____.
>
> I think that sexism is _____.
>
> My prejudices are _____.
>
> One thing I will do to overcome my prejudice is _____.

The responses may be very personal. I would only ask for sharing by those who wish to do so, and only of statements they wish to share.

Recognizing Discrimination, Racism, Sexism, Stereotyping, Religion: Viewing TV

The kids like to watch TV, so why not put it to good use? This is one activity where you do not need to assign any specific show, just ask them to be aware of what they are watching. They are to look for any signs of discrimination, stereotyping, racism, sexism, religious prejudice—and not just against Jews. Ask them to keep a record for one week of what they watch and what they see.

Remind them that what they see may be subtle, although in some cases it may be blatant. Tell them to be sure to watch the commercials as well.

Have them watch for little things, like why do Jewish grandparents always have "Jewish" accents? (I'm a grandmother and I have no accent!) My pet peeves are commercials that show children putting their parents down! These are little things, and unless you look for them, you won't see them.

When the students bring in the results of their week of watching, have them share with their classmates. Let them identify one or two instances they feel very strongly about and write a letter to the station, calling the manager's attention to what a show or a commercial is doing. Not long ago, there was a program on one of our local radio stations called "Wednesday Weirdness." It happened to be a station I always listen to, and one Wednesday the "weirdness" was about a Jewish music group from New York, and the cast talked about how weird the group was for teaching Bible through its weird music. It just so happens that I knew the group members, and they were anything but weird. I faxed a letter to the station complaining about what it had done. Immediately, I received a phone call from the station; its representative apologized, and the program was not repeated. So, you see, you can speak up, and there are people who will listen!

Bring History to Life: The Holocaust

Instead of simply teaching the facts about the Holocaust, be more creative. To introduce the Holocaust and provide background information, invite a Holocaust survivor; but if one isn't available, try being inventive. For instance, why not invent a character of your own who survived the Holocaust? You certainly know your students better than a stranger, and you could tailor your presentation to them. To play this character convincingly, you must have authentic knowledge. Gather information from books and movies about personal experiences during the Holocaust, and also about World War II and Jewish life in prewar Europe. Give your character a name (e.g., Grandma or Grandpa), and have a few props to go along with your persona, like a cane and glasses for Grandpa, an old shawl and glasses for Grandma. One of the props could be a Jewish ritual object of some kind that can be used as part of your story/presentation.

The day you are ready, leave the room for a minute. Upon returning, take on the voice of an elderly person. Pretend you are talking to your grandchildren, even give them names. Tell your grandchildren all about World War II, then go into the personal story of your character: what happened to your parents and siblings, your experiences in the camp (include the name of the camp). While telling your story, incorporate the use of the ritual object; for example, if you are using Shabbat candlesticks, you might say that your parents were taken on Shabbat, never to be seen again, and the candlesticks are a last memento of your home life together.

When you have finished your story, leave the room for a minute and remove your character's persona. Come back into the room and explain to the students that the character you played was a composite that you created to introduce them to the Holocaust. Ask them to write their reactions to the character's story and share their writings with their classmates.

Holocaust: A Simulation

Section off a corner of the room for students who are not "citizens." As a convenient means of separating a "minority," these can be students who were born in other states. Prepare six-pointed yellow stars for the non-citizens; check with the school office to see how many stars you will need. They will have a record of those who were born in the state and those who were not.

PROCEDURE

Get the attention of the class by saying that you have an important announcement to make. Read the Citizenship Laws of the State in a very slow, terse manner.

1. Identify students not born in the state (or your city).

2. Separate them from the citizens. Place them in the sectioned-off area, which simulates a ghetto.

3. Hand out yellow stars to these students.

4. If any of these students, who are now classified as "subjects" rather than "citizens," have positions of responsibility, take these responsibilities away from them and give them to citizens.

5. Tell the subjects they are to remain in their places and can only come out during (give some specific times they may come out).

Do this role-play for a few minutes—no longer than ten; five is usually enough. Respond to the reactions of the students, confirming the Laws of the State.

STOP THE ACTION!

With the students talk about what has happened.

How did the non-citizens feel about being segregated?

What was their immediate reaction to the situation?

How did the citizens feel?

What were the concerns of both groups?

Be sure to let the students vent their feelings.

Now hand out copies of the Third Reich Citizenship Laws and the Wannsee Protocol. Read them with the students. Compare the Citizenship Laws of the State and the Third Reich Citizenship Laws. What are the differences and similarities?

How do they think Jews felt during this period?

What were the reactions of the Jews?

Were they similar to the students' reactions? In what way?

Have any other people been treated in this manner?

Follow this up with an activity on discrimination.

CITIZENSHIP LAWS OF THE STATE

Paragraph I

1. A state subject is anyone who belongs to the protective association of our state and who is therefore obligated to it.

2. State citizenship is acquired according to the regulations of the state and the state citizenship law.

Paragraph II

1. Only those born in the state or of kindred blood are citizens. Anyone not born in the state or of pure blood is a subject and not a citizen.

2. Only a citizen is the exclusive bearer of full political rights.

Paragraph III

The Minister of the Interior shall promulgate the necessary legal and administrative regulations for the execution and supplementation of this law.

PROTOCOL

1. All subjects (not born in the state or of pure blood) are to be dismissed from positions of responsibility.

2. All subjects (not born in the state or of pure blood) are to wear either on the left forearm or embroidered on the left side of the chest a yellow six-pointed star.

3. All subjects (not born in the state or of pure blood) are subject to restrictions and strict curfews within the confines of specific settlements within the cities.

4. All material possessions and financial wealth of the subjects are to be confiscated and become the property of the state.

THIRD REICH CITIZENSHIP LAWS

The Reich Citizenship Law

(The Reichstag unanimously passed the following law, which was made public on September 15, 1935.)

Paragraph I

1. A state subject is anyone who belongs to the protective association of the German Reich and who therefore is especially obligated to it.

2. State citizenship is acquired according to the regulations of the Reich and the state citizenship law.

Paragraph II

1. Only the state citizen of German or kindred blood is a Reich citizen. Anyone not of pure blood is considered a subject but not a citizen.

2. The Reich citizen is the exclusive bearer of full political rights.

Paragraph III

1. The Reich Minister of the Interior, in agreement with the Deputy of the Fuhrer, shall promulgate the necessary legal and administrative regulations for the execution and supplementation of this law.

THE WANNSEE PROTOCOL

(The following decrees were added to the above citizen laws between the years 1938 and 1942.)

1. All Jews are to be dismissed from positions of responsibility in guilds and trades. (1938)

2. Jews who do not hold jobs essential for the economy will be deported to a city in the east in the course of the next few months. The property of the Jews to be deported will be confiscated for the German Reich. Each Jew may keep 100 Reichsmarks and 110 pounds (50 kg.) of luggage. (1941)

3. All Jews are to be expelled from all professions. (1942)

4. All material possessions and financial wealth are to be confiscated and are to become the property of the Third Reich. (1942)

5. All Jews are to wear either on the left forearm or embroidered on the left side of their chest a *Judenstern* (six-pointed star) and will be subject to restrictions and strict curfews within the confines of the Jewish settlements in the cities and the province. (1938)

6. All Jews are to be deported in order to prepare for the Final Solution.

7. As a further possibility of solving the question, the evacuation of the Jews to the east can now be substituted for emigration, after obtaining permission from the Fuhrer to that effect. However, these actions are merely to be considered as alternative possibilities, even though they will permit us to make all those practical experiences which are of great importance for the future Final Solution of the Jewish question.

   The Jews should, in the course of the Final Solution, be taken in a suitable manner to the east for use as labor. In big labor gangs, separated by sex, the Jews capable of work will be brought to these areas for road building, during which task undoubtedly a large number will fall through natural diminution. The remnant that is finally able to survive all this—since this is undoubtedly the part with the strongest resistance—must be treated accordingly, since these people, representing a natural selection, are to be regarded as the germ cell of a new Jewish development, in case they should succeed and go free (as history has proved). In the course of the execution of the Final Solution, Europe will be combed from west to east.

Reading between the Lines: Current Events

The news is often one-sided, and as a result we have to read it very careful-ly. There are many instances of one-sided reporting, especially about Israel, and unless your knowledge of Israeli history is very strong you will not be able to read between and behind the lines. In this section, though, are a few activities which can help students to develop this ability.

FACT OR FICTION?

Talk about: How true is everything printed in the press or reported on TV? What influence do reporters have on their audiences? How do they use this influence? In what way can their personal opinions influence us? What kinds of words do they use to make a strong impression on readers or view-ers?

1. Use two articles on the same subject of interest to Jews, one from a secular newspaper and the other from a Jewish newspa-per or magazine.
2. Have students compare the two articles.
3. Make a list of the similarities and differences.
4. If a historical event is mentioned, have the students research it. In fact, when it comes to the history of Israel and what is taking place there, it is essential that they know some of the history of the period before the establishment of the state—back to the Balfour Declaration.
5. After their research, the students are to write an article or letter to the editor, clarifying the facts and setting them straight.

A Writer's Prejudice: Does It Show?

Have the class read the following article, which, let's pretend, was in the local newspaper:

PEARL JAM CONCERT

On Monday evening, October 22, 45,000 screaming adolescents pushed their way into the Astrohall for this noisy concert. After each loud rendition of their so-called music, the sweaty adolescents broke out into boisterous applause, screamed their brains out, and acted like a pack of obstreperous, loud-mouthed animals. The food service reported that the young monsters swilled down 60,000 cans of soft drinks, gobbled up some 50,000 hot dogs slopped in mus-tard, and munched their way through 55,000 deafening bags of potato chips. The management considered the pig-out event to be a box-office smash hit.

With the class, talk about:

1. How does the writer of this article feel about young people? About the concert?

2. What words give you clues to how the writer feels? Underline or highlight words that describe what the writer thinks about young people.

3. Rewrite the story, stating the basic facts without revealing any prejudice.

This, of course, is an article I created as an example. Instead of using it, be on the lookout for newspaper articles that clearly reflect the prejudices of the writer. Make copies of the articles for the class. Follow up this activity by asking the students to identify articles in newspapers and magazines which show the prejudice of the writer and see how many they can collect over a specific period of time. This will help the students to see that there are two sides to every story, and that the reporter's side may not be the right one.

Distinguish Fact from Opinion: Current Events

This activity is another way to help students learn to look behind the written word. Can your students distinguish fact from opinion in a news article? Do they know what information may not be provided? Can they identify bias in a news article? Ask them to collect several news articles on the same subject. Or you bring in at least three articles on the same subject, copy them, and give them out. The students are to compare the articles, looking for such things as:

Does one article have more information than the others?

Does one use a different approach?

How are the articles similar? Different?

Which article is the most objective?

Which article is the most biased?

How factual are the articles?

What information is missing?

Have them make lists of what they have found and share with their classmates.

A News Tree: Current Events

Devote a bulletin board to this activity, or take a large posterboard and attach it to the wall. Draw a large tree with leafless branches. Tell the students to gather news stories about Jews, Israel, and other events that affect the Jewish community. For each article, the students are to write two questions:

1. A content question—a factual or opinion question about the article's content.

2. A question about the impact on the Jewish community.

Mount each article and its questions on cards, and post them on the different branches of the tree. As the tree begins to fill up, spend one session using the "News Tree" with its articles for your lesson on current events.

First-Person Accounts: Current Events

Copy some news articles of Jewish interest and give a different one to each student. After reading their article, the students write their own first-person account in which they imagine themselves participating in the same events. Encourage them to add missing facts and imagine the outcomes. Share their stories with the class.

It's in the Bag: A Current Events Bulletin Board

Prepare the background by covering the bulletin board with colorful art paper. Cut pictures out of magazines or newspapers of Jews in the news, events in Israel, environmental issues, social issues, etc. Mount the pictures on colored paper. Place them on the bulletin board and give each picture a heading which covers the subject matter. Below each picture place a small lunch bag, open so that articles can be put inside. During the week, the students are to find additional articles or pictures about the different subject areas, and at the next class session are to put them in the appropriate lunch bags. About every other week, take the articles from the bags, go over the news, and discuss what impact the news has on the Jewish people or the community.

Resolving Conflicts: Current Events

Bring in a selection of newspaper and magazine articles about conflicts that must be resolved (e.g., Israel, prayer in the public schools, environmental concerns, social issues). Divide the class into small groups. Give each group a different set of articles. The students read the articles, then, assuming the roles of the different individuals or organizations involved, prepare their side of the story, their part in the conflict, including a list of reasons why they think their side is right.

After each group tells its side of the story, see if the students can come up with ways to resolve the conflict. What compromises are possible? How can they reach consensus? For example: Prayer in school. There are those who think there is nothing wrong with silent prayer, nondenominational prayer, etc. Others say that any kind of prayer will infringe on individual rights. This presents quite a problem. Adults can't seem to solve it; maybe the kids can.

A Scavenger Hunt: Current Events

Divide the class into dyads, and give a newspaper to each pair of students. Also give them a "Scavenger Hunt" list of articles you want them to find in the papers. Your list could look something like this:

Israel.

A good deed.

Someone in need.

Violence.

War.

Peace.

Truth in advertising.

Advice.

Editorial on _____ (name a subject).

Give each dyad a newspaper, the list, and scissors. The students are to search the paper to find and cut out all the articles on the list. Share their findings with the class.

Students Write Articles: Current Events

Gather some newspaper and magazine pictures. Make two copies of the pictures. Put one set aside for use later on. Remove the captions from the second set, mount the pictures on construction paper, and put them on the bulletin board. Divide the class into small groups and assign each a different picture. The group members are to write a collective news report based on what they see in the picture. Upon completion, the groups share their reports. Compare their reports with the actual news, as indicated by the captions on the first set of pictures. How close did they get to the real thing?

Political Cartoons: Current Events

Divide the class into small groups. Ask the students to collect political cartoons from newspaper and magazine editorial pages. To avoid duplications, assign specific newspapers and magazines to each group. Set a time limit for the collection of cartoons—about one or two weeks to ensure a good assortment.

Ask the members of each group to divide their cartoons into categories (e.g., social issues of Jewish concern, current events, world events, national events, community events). On the bulletin board, arrange the cartoons from each group by categories. With the students "read" the cartoons. The members of each group choose one or two which they regard as particularly interesting and discuss its implications. What is the cartoon's message? What does it say? What issue is covered by the cartoon? What does Judaism have to say about it?

Here is where the students will need to do some research. They are to find out everything they can about what Judaism has to say on the issue, how Judaism would handle the situation. When their research is completed, they share their findings. Based on what they have learned, they are to write a group letter to the editor, offering solutions or alternatives to the cartoon.

JEWISH HOLIDAYS

Building on What Students Know

By this time the students have been exposed to many different approaches to the Jewish holidays. This activity lets them take a look at a holiday from a deeper perspective and challenges them to think. They will be doing some brainstorming. By asking for clarification, you will induce them to justify their thoughts, and will also be able to explain facts about specific holidays. By making lists the students can go from a simple recollection of a holiday and what they already know to deeper levels of insight and association.

Divide the class into small groups. The members of each group are to make a list of things pertaining to a specific holiday, but give them a series of topics to choose from. The topics you offer could include the following:

Things to believe.

Things that are easy to forget.

Things that cause warmth.

Things that fade.

Things that are difficult to share.

Things that glow.

Things you do not want to share.

Silent things that are loud.

This will give you an idea of what kinds of lists the students can make; add to the choices as you wish. Have the members of the groups brainstorm with each other, then bring the groups together for sharing. Ask for clarification of any of the things as necessary. Then talk about: What they discovered about the holiday. What they learned about the holiday that they didn't know before.

Teach Them What They Don't Know

Students often complain that the holidays are all they learn about in religious school. This is probably true, even though the holidays are usually taught on different levels to different age groups. It is wise to find out how much the kids know about any holiday before you teach anything about it.

Here is a simple activity to find out how much they already know.

List the various elements of the holiday. Begin by asking the kids to identify the holiday by the different subjects you present. From your list, name the elements one at a time until the students guess the holiday. Aspects of the holiday with which they are not familiar are the ones you will need to cover in your lesson.

A College Holiday Kit

Review the holiday to be sure the students know enough to do the project. The project will take more than one session, but the product makes it worthwhile.

1. Role-play: Ask the students to imagine that you are the owner of a Jewish manufacturing company; give it a name. The students are your employees. Your company manufactures religious articles and has been asked to design a "Holiday College Kit" for Shabbat and other Jewish holidays.

2. Brainstorm: Develop a list of Jewish holidays to be included in the kit. Identify those holidays college students will come home for, and those for which they will stay in school. This information can come from the students' own experiences with brothers, sisters, cousins, etc., or they can interview people who have children in college.

3. Develop ideas: As designers the students must decide what to include in the kit. Remind them that the finished product will be sent through the mail, and this will have to be taken into consideration. Divide the class into small groups. The members of each group are to brainstorm ideas for the kit, including a list of its contents, then draw up a design and a list of the materials needed.

4. Share the results: The members of each group are to make a presentation of their design. Then the class must do one of the following:

   a. Choose the design it considers to be the best.

   b. Choose the design it considers to be the most cost efficient.

   c. Take the best ideas from all the designs and make a composite kit.

5. Make a model: Have the class make an actual model of the Holiday College Kit, with each group making a different part of it. Invite a member of the sisterhood and brotherhood college committee to the class. Offer this design as a project for outreach to the college students from your congregation. The sisterhood and brotherhood could provide the funds, and the students can make up the Holiday College Kits.

Holiday Letters

This activity will not only review the holiday, but will enhance the self-esteem of the older students. Inform the K–2 grade teachers in your school that your students will answer letters written or dictated by the children in their classes. The children can ask questions about the holiday, how they can celebrate it, what fun things they can do, etc. Plan ahead so your students can do research on the holiday to make their responses fun and knowledgeable. Once the letters from the lower grades are received, divide your class into small groups. The group members develop games and activities the children can do, and create riddles, puzzles, poems, songs, short stories, etc., to share with them. Take this a step further and have them design stationery to use for this activity.

How Jewish Holidays Have Evolved

Most Jewish holidays have changed from what they were in biblical times. Divide the class into small groups. Assign each group a different holiday. The group members are to first find the passages in the Bible which tell the Israelites how and when to celebrate the holiday. Then continue their research to see how the holiday celebration has evolved since the beginning. For example: Pesach was originally two different celebrations, and it was not until the period of the First Temple that the two were combined into one holiday. Students begin at the beginning and bring the holiday to the present day. Upon completion of their research, they can create a giant mural presenting the information they have gathered.

High Holy Days

Emphasis is usually on the younger child when creating materials for the High Holy Days. Here are some ideas for the older student. The text is from Herbert Danby, *The Mishnah* (Oxford University Press, 1977).

Mishnah Rosh Hashanah 1:1–2

...on the 1st of Tishri is the New Year for [the reckoning of] the years [of foreign kings], of the Years of Release and Jubilee Years, for the planting [of trees] and for vegetables; ...on New Year's Day all that come into the world pass before Him [God] like legions of soldiers, for it is written, *He that fashioneth the hearts of them all, that considereth all their works...*

This text suggests that we live in three different spheres: nature, political, and religious.

Have the class read the text and do the following:

List examples of their daily activities that fall into each area.

Specify which activities are distinct to each area.

Specify which activities overlap.

209

Ask the students to divide their papers into six sections, three across and two down. Across the top, head the three sections, *Nature, Political,* and *Religious.* Taking their lists of daily activities, on the top half, under each heading, list the ways in which their lives are affected by that area. On the bottom half, list ways in which *they* affect each area. Share their responses, and talk about: How are we subject to these forces? How do we affect these forces, if at all?

ROSH HASHANAH 17B

This passage from the Babylonian Talmud describes the stages of repentance and response. They are:

Charity: a private act.

Raising one's voice: a public affirmation.

Changing one's name: taking on a new sense of identity.

Changing one's way of behaving.

In small groups, have the students compile lists of issues in the community that need attention. Ask them to brainstorm to identify as many approaches as possible to one of the problems. Then ask them to rank-order the approaches from least important to most important. The rank-order is to be in terms of the effect the action would have on them and the community. Share the results with the class.

The class then rank-orders the issues and actions from least important to most important, finally choosing one issue and action it thinks is the most important. Have students develop a plan of action and organization to complete the project they have chosen.

Another activity based on the same reading: Have the students, working individually, compile lists of personal issues which they think need attention. Ask them to list as many actions as they can think of that address one of the issues. Have them rank-order their lists and set times when the actions can be accomplished. Ask the students to report the results of their actions when the tasks are completed.

CHANGING ONE'S NAME

You can also explore the idea of changing one's name. Ask students to make name charts. Divide a sheet of paper into three columns, and in the first column have them list all the names and nicknames they are called by. In the second column, have them list the names of the people who call them by each name. Finally, in the third column, have them list what each name reveals about them. Sharing of lists of names by those who wish. Talk about: What have they learned about the relationship of their different names to their different actions? How about their names in relation to the people who use them?

Pesach: Elijah

There is an aspect of Pesach that is often overlooked, in part because there is almost never enough time to include it. We rarely look at Elijah, although Jewish folklore abounds with legends about him as a mysterious stranger who miraculously and unexpectedly appears. He aids the poor in times of hardship, but more frequently serves as a tutor in Torah. Elijah is invited to the *berit* ceremony and asked to view the ongoing continuity of Jewish life because he worries about the Jewish people and its survival. But we are most familiar with Elijah during Pesach, when we place a glass of wine for him on the table. At the end of the seder a special prayer is said while the door is opened for Elijah to enter. Jewish tradition states that Elijah's greatest mission shall come when the Messiah appears on earth to usher in the long-promised era of permanent peace and tranquility. It is Elijah the Prophet who will precede the Messiah, or the Messianic Age. Elijah will announce its arrival and, with it, the arrival of freedom and peace for all people. Additional information and material on Elijah can be found in I Kings 17–19, Malachi 3:23–24, and the *Encyclopaedia Judaica* or the *Jewish Encyclopedia*.

SOME ACTIVITIES

Have the students research who Elijah was, what he did, what his mission was—obtaining as much information as they can. Once their research is completed, they can choose to do any one of the following:

1. Make a chart of Elijah's positive and negative traits.
2. Trace Elijah's travels on a map of ancient Israel.
3. Identify the traits of leadership and dedication displayed by Elijah and compare him to someone living today.
4. (For several students working together) Prepare a dramatization of Elijah's encounter with the prophets of Baal on Mount Carmel.
5. Compare Elijah's mission to the mission of Jews today. How are they similar? Different?
6. (For several students) Prepare a newspaper ad or TV commercial to sell the idea of hope for the future which Elijah's spirit brings during the seder.
7. (For the whole class) Prepare a class newspaper—a special edition containing articles about Elijah. Include puzzles, hidden pictures, etc.
8. (For the whole class) Organize a debate on the pros and cons of the Messianic Age.

Pesach: A Look into the Past

Ask students to recall their first seder: What do they remember? What happened? Who was there? What did they eat? Whom did they sit next to? Who asked the Four Questions? What do they recall as the highlight of

211

their first seder—like who found the *afikoman*? Have them write down their memories and share with the class.

Prepare the following Torah portions for the class, or use a Torah text: Exodus 12:43–46, 12:6–10, 12:14–15, 13:14–16; Leviticus 23:5–6; Numbers 28:16–17. These passages describe how Passover was to be celebrated. Have the students read the material, then talk about:

Who is to take part in the celebration?

How is the meat to be cooked?

When is it to be eaten?

How much of the meat is to be eaten?

What is to be eaten with the meat?

How long do we eat unleavened bread?

When is the celebration to take place?

What are the reasons for this celebration?

How does all this compare to how we celebrate Passover today?

What are the differences and similarities?

These are just a few suggested questions; add others if you wish.
As a closure for this activity, do one of the following:

1. Remind the students of the Ten Plagues mentioned at the seder. Ask them to list Ten Plagues found in today's world.

2. The Four Questions: Ask the students to write four more questions they would like answered, with their answers to them.

Purim

Even though the students are a little older now, there are still aspects of Purim they could investigate. For example:

1. Explore the hidden nature of God's presence. (God is not mentioned in the Purim story, and Esther's name means "I will hide.")

2. What is the definition of a miracle? Discuss the meaning of miracles in today's world. Talk about what they think are miracles today.

3. Provide your definition of a miracle and have the students discuss their views of miracles (e.g., a surprising and out-of-the ordinary event—ask for examples; an event that leads to peace and justice—ask for examples; when people can't help themselves, an event takes place that helps them—ask for examples).

4. Prepare *mishloach manot*—packages of food for needy families. Get parents to help students deliver them to a food pantry.

The custom of *mishloach manot*, also known as *shalach manot* (sending gifts), is often overlooked because we are always so busy having fun on Purim. It is customary to deliver *two* portions of food to at least *one* friend.

An additional mitzvah is *matanot la'evyonim* (gifts to the needy). This is the custom of giving to at least *two* needy persons on Purim. *Tzedakah* is a typically Jewish way of sharing our most joyous occasions with those who are in need.

ISRAEL

The Peace Process

Negotiating peace is difficult. It will not be easy for the students to fully understand the Middle Eastern negotiating process, but you can help by having them take a look at their own everyday lives.

Talk about the disputes that arise within a family. Either as a class or individually, have them list the disputes that have arisen in their own families. Then discuss ways the disputes could be or have been settled peacefully. What are some of the peaceful ways they have settled disputes? What was easy to do? What was difficult? Then talk about disputes in school. What kinds of disputes are encountered? How are they settled peacefully? Not all family or school disputes are easily solved or settled, but looking at what takes place in their everyday lives will give the students an idea of the problems being encountered by Israel.

Peace: Cause and Effect

Peace isn't the easiest thing to imagine in this day and age. There may not be any major conflicts right now, but there sure are a lot of "small wars" in different parts of the world. Do some brainstorming with the students, listing all the current conflicts and even potential conflicts, including minor skirmishes that could develop into major conflicts.

Look at the list and see if the students know anything about the causes of the conflicts. List the causes next to the countries named. Help the class with this if necessary. Or assign the conflicts the students do not know about as research projects for small groups. When all the causes of the different conflicts are identified, take a look at them. Let the students relate the causes to their own lives (e.g., some of the causes are ignorance, prejudice, covetousness of other people's property, power struggles, discrimination, hatred of those who are different).

It has been said that real peace will not be achieved until people accept one other's differentness and acknowledge their unity with all living creatures. Discuss how, in their own lives, the students can eliminate the causes of conflicts. List things they can do to eliminate conflict and seek peace in their everyday lives. Encourage them to choose one idea and develop it into a class project.

Archaeologists: Israel

This dig is good enough to eat! The activity in this section was originally created by Leslie Perfect-Ricklin and Suzanne Perfect-Miller, both professors of education.

Take the kids on an archaeological dig in Israel! Plan what you want the site to look like, and what you want the students to find and learn. Then make two double recipes of cake and bake each double recipe in an aluminum foil roasting pan. (Two cakes are needed.) Bake either yellow or chocolate, but for ancient Israel, I would use a yellow cake to represent the desert. You can use cake mixes, but they are usually too light to be good for "digging."

Leave one cake in the pan, arrange, and insert the "artifacts." For artifacts, try to find miniature facsimiles of actual items, and be sure they are as historically correct as possible. Most miniature and doll house shops have some inexpensive artifacts. Wrap each artifact in aluminum foil and set inside the bottom cake. When all the artifacts have been buried in the bottom cake, spread with frosting. Remove the second cake from the pan and place on top of the first cake. Frost it with part light-green and yellow frosting. You can decorate the top of the "dig" with trees, ponds, stone walls, etc. Candy "pebbles" are good for stone walls, chocolate chips also work. For fencing or twigs, use pretzels; ponds or streams can be made with blue cellophane or light-blue construction paper. Once your cake "dig" is made you will also need string, plastic spoons and forks as tools, toothpick markers, a grid, small paper plates, and an artifact sheet for each participant.

Tell the students they are going to become archaeologists for the day and give them information about the site and time period. Have them view the site and ask questions like: Who lived there? How might they have lived? The students are to record their questions and answers. Now they are to study this settlement and dig for artifacts. They have to organize the dig so that any historical evidence they find can be recorded accurately. Really play it up, emphasizing how careful they must be not to break any artifacts or destroy any evidence of the history of the period.

Use a large sheet of paper to divide the site into a grid pattern. The size of the grids will depend on the number of students in the class: one grid square for each student. Have the class elect two leaders who will organize the dig. Using the string, they copy the numbered grid pattern onto the cake. Toothpicks with numbered flags can mark each square. Cut the cake and give each "archaeologist" a numbered piece on a paper plate along with tools for digging (spoon and fork).

Remind the archaeologists to dig slowly. As they discover an artifact, they are to record its location in the proper place on the paper grid. As they work, and eat, they also fill out the artifact worksheet. Upon completion of the dig, students review their pre-dig comments with the post-dig findings and share their worksheet information.

Your Artifact Worksheet could look something like this:

1. Describe your artifact: measurements, weight, material, etc.
2. Where did you find it?
3. In what time period do you think this artifact was used?
4. Who used it? And under what circumstances?
5. What does this artifact tell you about this period and its religion?
6. Is there a modern version of this artifact in use today?
7. Where could you find out more about this artifact?
8. How do all the artifacts relate to each other?

Elections in Israel

Consider: What does it take to be a leader in the Jewish community? Do some brainstorming, making a list of the character traits and abilities the class would expect in a leader. The list could look something like this, but is not limited to these traits:

Intelligence and wisdom.

Kindness, politeness, and generosity.

Ability to make wise decisions.

Compassion and tolerance.

Wisdom to compromise.

Ability to work with people.

High Jewish ideals.

Commitment to the Jewish people.

Commitment to the Jewish way of life.

A good listener.

Consider: What other requirements are needed to be a leader? Do some brainstorming, listing the additional requirements. You could include the following:

Age.

Education (Jewish and secular).

Active in community.

Financial support.

Gender.

State of health.

Now, let's have a simulated Israeli election. Get a current copy of *Israel Facts* from the Israeli consulate. This will have a brief description of the country's many political parties. Divide the class into small groups, each designated to represent a specific Israeli party and develop a political campaign based on its purpose and platform. As the students prepare their campaigns, they must deal with the current issues and problems concerning voters in Israel. Students in each group can role-play the party leaders and prepare campaign speeches, keeping in mind the list of character traits and requirements. The campaign can include posters, ads, slogans, speeches, etc., as in a real political campaign. After the election, the students process the activity. How did they choose a candidate? What did they base their votes on? How did their choices reflect current issues facing Israeli voters? What did they learn about Israel and its problems?

Note: As you cover the history of Israel, or Jewish history in general, take a look at the people involved. Compare their character traits and requirements to those on the lists the students made. What are the differences and similarities?

Can We All Be Experts?

Prepare a list of famous Jewish people identified with the State of Israel. Either assign each student one person to learn as much as possible about, or have the students choose the person they want to study. What did the person do? What made the person famous? How did the person help the State of Israel? Once the research is completed, the students take turns at being experts on the person they have studied. As they do so, their classmates try to stump them with questions they can't answer. Whoever asks the question that stumps the expert then becomes the next expert. Continue until everyone has had a chance to be the expert.

A Book of Memories: Jerusalem

Through the ages Jews have remembered Jerusalem in their prayers, literature, and songs. Divide the class into small groups. Assign them to research Jewish literature and list the different ways Jerusalem has been remembered. When the research is completed, the members of the various groups share their findings and make a composite list of memories of Jerusalem.

Assign each group the same number of memories to be used in creating a portion of a Book of Memories. The students design a different page for each memory. They can use art, poetry, prose, pictures, etc., to convey the message of "remember Jerusalem." As a class, they design a cover for the book and compile all the pages together. The Book of Memories can be displayed in the synagogue lobby for everyone to see.

News of the Day: Bringing the Past Alive

Students can develop a TV news program based on a historical event that took place in Israel, like the establishment of the state. After researching the materials, they present the information in the form of a TV news program. They can even include the weather, human interest stories, sports analysis, etc., to make the news program more complete.

Keeping Track: Current Events in Israel

We are living in an exciting period. The peace process is difficult, but gradually the situation in the Middle East is improving. This activity is designed to make students aware of the historic events that are taking place.

Prepare a large map of Israel and its neighbors, and hang it on the wall. Identify each country. Have students, during the week, collect news articles related in some way to the peace process. Take five or ten minutes at the beginning of class to share the articles. Have colored index cards ready and ask students to write one-line descriptions of what has taken place. Place the cards on the map in the area or country involved. The articles themselves can be mounted and put alongside the map, with colored yarn attached to the article and going to the appropriate card. For example: There was an article about the Chief Rabbi of Israel going to visit the Pope in Rome, raising the possibility of the Vatican recognizing the State of Israel, after all these years. A card reading "Rabbi to visit Pope" could be placed in Italy, with the article to the side and the yarn going to the card in Italy.

What Do We Really See? Current Events

Many times, people give conflicting reports when they are interviewed about events they have witnessed. Reporters in the Middle East and Israel are supposed to be more than casual observers, but how much do they really see? Do they just see what they want to see and leave many details out of their reports? This activity will show your class that news reports aren't always as accurate as they might be.

Call on a parent, a friend, or a member of the congregation to help—preferably someone the class does not know. Ask this person to enter the classroom unannounced at a prearranged time, dressed in colorful and rather outlandish clothes (e.g., a cowboy or straw hat, red kerchief, large dangle earrings [whether a man or woman], colorful shirt, maybe a false nose, mustache or beard, glasses) and blowing a horn, beating a drum, or playing some other musical instrument. Play the role of teacher to the fullest: be shocked at the interruption, asking "What do you want? You are interrupting the class!" Be amazed! Play the part as though you didn't know it was all prearranged.

What does the stranger do? The visit must be very brief. The stranger may be mute, but should do a few little things while in the room, such as picking up a book and putting it into a shirt or carrying bag, taking something from the desk, or pulling out another scarf or hat to put on. Just be brief.

When the stranger leaves, ask the students: What happened? Who was that person? What did this person look like? How long was this person in the classroom? What did this person want? What did this person do? Ask the students to write down as much as they can remember about the incident, right now, before they forget. After they have made notes on what they saw, each student writes a "news report" about the incident.

The students may realize that the whole incident was a set-up. No matter! The written accounts of what took place are what is important. How different will they be? Upon completion, have the students share their written news reports. How accurate were their descriptions of the incident? Discuss the whole activity.

Ask students, during the next week, to gather news articles they think are inaccurate or misinformed. Look for headlines that slant the reader's reaction; for instance, an article is headed something like "Palestinian Woman Shot," yet if you read all the way to the end you find out that she was trying to stab an Israeli policeman! The articles the students bring in can be shared and their accuracy or lack thereof discussed. Students can even write letters to editors in response to blatant bias in reporting.

JEWISH IDENTITY

Survival of Judaism

This may seem like a silly activity, but it will lead into a good discussion on the survival of Judaism, Jewish identity, and what Judaic concepts are most important to the students.

Tell the story of the "blue erg" (or any silly name you can think of). To really have some fun with this, find an artist to render a drawing of the blue erg or make one yourself. Distribute copies to the class. The erg is half human and half animal. The blue erg is the last of its kind. Some people want to destroy it because it is so ugly. Some would buy tickets to see it. There are zoos that would love to exhibit it. Others want to feature it in horror films, while some want it for medical research. But, lo and behold, the blue erg has been given to you! What will you do with it? And why? With the students, go over all the possible options and discuss any choices the students may make. What are the reasons for their choices?

Now tell the class to put aside the blue erg for a while. Ask them to substitute Judaism for the blue erg. Prepare a sheet with information something like this on it:

This is Judaism. It has been a living religion for over 5,000 years. It is the last of its kind. Some people want to destroy it because it is too difficult and different. Some study it to understand. Some love to publicly confirm their Judaism. Some deny it, while others are only practicing secular Jews. Judaism has been given to you! What will you do with it? And why?

Give a sheet to each student. Allow time for everyone to respond to the questions in writing.

Upon completion, encourage students to share their responses. With the students, discuss: What if they were really the last remaining Jews? Would they be satisfied with the solutions they gave in their responses? What are their reasons for being satisfied or dissatisfied? Have there been moments in their lives when they felt all alone, the last of their kind? How did they feel? What did they do about it? What are they willing to do to be sure that Judaism survives?

NEAT AND SIMPLE

Being Jewish!

From time to time it is good to encourage the students to think about who they are as Jews. Set aside a block of time for them to write about themselves. Ask them to select one thing about being Jewish that they regard as so important that they would not be willing to give it up. They can write stories, slogans, cartoons, advertising brochures, radio announcements, or TV news reports, design posters, or use any other creative means to convey their message. Display the completed unsigned projects on the bulletin board and let the class try to identify the author of each piece. Then talk about their choices and the reasons for them.

Creating a Jewish Community

The first exercise I ever designed was adapted from a NASA Moon Project experiment back in the early 1970s. It is still valid today, but in a different form. Prepare a sheet with the following supplies listed:

Torah	$1,000.00
Bible	$5.00 each
Candlesticks	$20.00 a pair
Candles	$3.75 per hundred
Shofar	$75.00
Menorah (seven-branch)	$85.00
Chanukiot	$125.00
Ner Tamid	$200.00
Sleeping bags	$40.00 each
Wall tent (six-person)	$175.00
Vinyl boat (three-person)	$250.00
Jewish calendar	$10.00
Siddur	$7.50 each
Haggadah	$7.50 each
Talmud	$65.00

Hebrew books	$5.00 each
Guide to Jewish living	$10.00 each
Kosher wine	$50.00 a case

In the back room, the following is yours for the asking:

10 empty 50-gallon oil drums

1 keg of rusty nails

500 yards heavy-duty canvas

10 nylon parachutes

60 feet of heavy-duty rope

10,000 reams white copy paper

1 antiquated mimeo machine

3 antiquated portable typewriters

250 packages mimeo stencils

Divide the class into small groups. To the students: You are to establish a new community far beyond the planet Earth. The planet has the same atmosphere as Earth, and there is adequate plant and animal life. There are also farms already established to supply food. You will be the first Jewish community on the planet. Your challenge is to set an example for future Jewish settlements.

Explain that they will have a $2,500 budget to purchase the needed supplies for the trip. Pass out the list of supplies. Remind the students of their budget line. Give them time to decide what supplies they will need to establish a Jewish community. From time to time remind them that they are creating a *Jewish* community and are to be an example for future settlements. Upon completion, have the members of each group explain how they approached the problem, how they arrived at their choices, and the reasons for the choices.

With the students, talk about the results: What kind of Jewish community would they be creating? What do they think was the most important item they needed to create a Jewish community? What was at the top of their list as the most important? What was the reason for this choice? (Hopefully, their top choice will be the Torah, but you must be accepting of their efforts even if you do not agree with their choices. You can offer your own list, though, which would show the Torah as the first and top choice.)

A Life-Cycle Event

Even older students need to be reminded about the Jewish life cycle, but do it in a different way. Ask them to pretend that either they or some members of their family are anticipating the birth of a child. They are to write a letter to the newborn baby. Before writing it, they should consider questions like the following:

What would I like to tell this child about being a Jew?

What it is like to live as a Jew here and now?

What do I know about Judaism which is important for the new
baby to know?

What are some of the hopes, fears, doubts, and joys I will encounter
as a Jew?

When they finish their letters, share with the whole class.

The Tree of Life

The Torah has been compared to a tree: "It is a tree of life to those who
hold fast to it" (Proverbs 3:18). A tree is deeply rooted, giving strength, support, and shelter. This symbol could be extended to each of us individually,
as we interpret our own Jewishness through the symbol of a tree. The
strength of its supporting root structure will determine its longevity, the
sweetness of its fruit will determine its beauty, worth, and value to others.
This activity allows the students to examine their own Jewish identities and
how they can be strengthened.

For everyone in class you will need an outline of a tree with supporting
roots and a number of empty branches, a pen or pencil, and colored markers.

Give each student the outline of a tree. Tell the students to draw symbols
or write words at the roots that express their Jewish roots. For example:

Family: parents, grandparents, siblings, etc.

Home and holiday celebrations.

Lifestyle.

Jewish education.

Special Jewish activities.

In the branches, they can draw symbols or write words that represent
such things as:

Jewish accomplishments: *Berit Milah*, Consecration, Bar/Bat
Mitzvah.

Jewish experiences: worship, camp, Israel, etc.

Jewish skills: Hebrew, education, holiday celebrations, etc.

Have the students share their completed trees. Compare the similarities
and differences between the trees. Talk about: What the students think
they can do to *strengthen* their Jewish roots. List everything they can do,
then ask them to choose *one* thing they can do and create a time-line of
how and when it could be accomplished.

Discrimination: Jewish Identity

You think this topic doesn't have a place in a Jewish classroom? Think
again. Maybe someone has shouted at you: "Dirty Jew, get off my sidewalk!" You may not have had to wear a yellow Star of David, but have you
had pennies pitched at you? Or have kids left the table in the lunchroom
when you sat down? Have people ever looked at you strangely and finally
asked: "Where are your horns?" I am not exaggerating; all these things

have happened to Jews today, and many are still happening. The same kinds of things, maybe structured a little differently, are being done to blacks, Asians, and Mexicans. And our kids are doing it! Here we have been discriminated against over the years, and we turn around and do the very same thing to others. It is important to work with our students to help them understand the harm discrimination causes and what they can do to eliminate it. The following activity is not new. I remember doing something like this years ago, and it does work. The secret to its success is careful processing after the activity is completed.

When the students are settled in the classroom, make an announcement something like this:

> Anyone wearing red today does not have to attend worship services. Anyone with brown hair will not be permitted to leave the room for *any* reason. Anyone wearing sneakers (Nikes, Reeboks, etc.), must move to the back of the room.

After the class gets over its initial shock at the announcement, the students will probably tell you that you are being unfair, or that they don't believe you. Give them all a chance to vent their feelings about your announcement! After everyone has spoken, write the word *discrimination* on the board. Tell the students to write a definition of it. If they say they don't know the definition, tell them to write what they think it means. Do not define the word for them.

Now tell the class to imagine that the government has ordered them to put yellow Stars of David on all their clothing. Anyone caught without a star will be arrested and sent to a boot camp. Have the students write down how they would feel about this decree and the reasons for their feelings. Share their responses.

After the sharing, ask for their definitions of *discrimination*. If no one has the right answer, give them the definition from the *Oxford American Dictionary*: "to make a distinction; to give unfair treatment, especially because of prejudice; to be biased."

> Give examples of discrimination today. List examples, and ask the following:
>
> Have you ever been discriminated against? What was happening at the time?
>
> How did you feel when you were discriminated against?
>
> What was your reaction to being a victim of discrimination?
>
> Have you ever discriminated against anyone? What was happening at the time? Why did you discriminate? How do you think the victim felt?
>
> Have you ever watched when someone was discriminated against? What was happening at the time?
>
> What was your reaction to what you saw? Did you do anything?
>
> What were your reasons for doing nothing or doing something?

What are the causes of discrimination? List them.

How can discrimination be avoided?

Have the students write answers to the following questions:

Based on the examples and causes of discrimination, what are you
willing to do to help eliminate discrimination against others?

What are you willing to do if you see others being discriminated
against?

What will be your reaction when you are the one being discriminated against?

Have the students share their responses with their classmates and talk
about the evils of discrimination and how important it is to eliminate it.

SYMBOLS, RITUALS, AND CONCEPTS

The Jewish Calendar

Even older students can learn something about the
Jewish calendar that they didn't know before. On the
day the class meets closest to the first day of a Jewish
month, have the students identify all the Jewish events
that will take place during the new month. If they say
that nothing exciting takes place during any particular month, think again: there is always Shabbat!

Now they can do a mitzvah! Ask the class to create a series of activities that will tell others what takes
place during the month. First, identify the target age
group; then create puzzles, write songs and stories,
create a mural, write a play, or develop a newspaper
for the month. When the students finish their creative
work, they can share it with the younger children.

Comparative Religion

The way to begin the study of comparative religion is with one's own religion. List the features of a religion. For example:

God idea.

Religious practice/tradition.

Life-cycle events.

Holiday observances.

Rituals and symbols.

Historical background.

Social justice/mission.

World to come.

Ask the students to describe all of these features as found in Judaism, distinguishing between the Reform, Conservative, and Orthodox approaches. Once you are sure they know the basic tenets of their own religion, move on to other religions.

With the students, decide which religions they would like to understand better and know more about. Make a list of the religions to be studied. If possible, schedule field trips to visit houses of worship of the selected religions. Be sure to arrange beforehand for a member of the clergy or some other knowledgeable person to host/guide the class during the visit. If fields trips are not possible, invite speakers from the selected religions to visit your class. Space the visits at appropriate intervals that allow for learning about the religion beforehand and discussing what the speaker says afterwards.

Prepare for each visit by giving the class an overview of the religion. Based on your established list of features of a religion, have the students prepare a list of questions they want answered. These should be sent to the speaker before the visit.

Keep a record of the visits on a chart hung on the wall, or give the students their own small charts for keeping their own records. The chart could look something like this:

Subject	Judaism	Catholicism	Methodism	Baptism	etc.
God idea					
Life-cycle events					
etc.					

Under *Subject* list the various areas the class has created for comparison of the different religions. Under each religion, the students are to write how and what the religion practices or believes in relation to the subject at the left-hand side of the line. This chart will become a visual guide for the comparative religion course.

Prayer: An Issue of Concern

In times of crisis or when an issue of major concern faces them, it would be good for the students to be able to decide how they feel about the issue or situation. This activity is designed to help them identify their concerns and what they must consider if they are to be involved. It is a simulation. Simulations can be valuable learning experiences, but they can also be dangerous if not properly processed. When I used simulations, I always made sure first that the students knew it was time to "Let's Pretend."

For example, tell the class to pretend that the government has issued a decree: "All Jews throughout the country are forbidden to assemble in synagogues for the purpose of prayer." Let the students voice their immediate reactions to this decree. Questions will probably be asked, but the only information you have is the statement. Ask them: What are you going to do?

Make a list of all their suggestions. Let them choose one idea, or a combination of several, and make plans to carry it out. Let's say they want to involve the whole Jewish community in a mass demonstration against the proclamation. Discuss what would be involved in organizing such an effort. Divide the class into small groups. Give them time to make some plans, something like this:

Posters: Design posters that will bring people out and get them involved.

Radio and TV advertising: Create an ad campaign.

Letter writing: Prepare appropriate letters for people to sign.

Petitions: Organize a campaign to obtain signatures.

Bring the students together to share their ideas. Consider what will work. Then (this is the processing part of the activity) talk about:

What made you so interested in the project?

If you don't really go to pray anyway, what made you so interested?

Whom were you doing this for?

What rights were you trying to protect?

Whose rights were you trying to protect? Why?

What does this project have to do with freedom of speech? With freedom of religion?

Who else might be involved in this project besides Jews?

Why would anyone else, other than Jews, wish to be involved?

What good do you hope to accomplish with this project?

And, finally, to what historical period could this project be compared?

A suggestion: this activity could also be done with the issue of prayer in the public schools. The decree from the government could be: "The only place prayer is permitted is in school!"

Jewish Humor

There is a wealth of materials that tell the story of the Jewish people through laughter and humor. Some of the resources for these are William Novak and Moshe Waldoks, *The Big Book of Jewish Humor* (Harper & Row, 1981); Henry D. Spalding, *Encyclopedia of Jewish Humor* (Jonathan David, 1973); Nathan Ausubel, *Treasury of Jewish Folklore*. With a little research, the class could easily create and produce its own Jewish comedy radio or TV show.

As a class, determine the theme for the show (e.g., East European Jewry, Purim laughter, Holocaust stories, the wise men of Chelm, how we laugh at ourselves). Divide the class into small groups. Each group collects stories, riddles, jokes, and dialogue for the show. Then the group members choose the ones they like best. The whole class comes together and goes through all the humorous stories, etc., and decides which ones to use. Divide the stories, etc., into three acts. Have each group write the script, identify props, and choose the performers for one act. The whole class comes together again, this time to go over each act, watching the time. Keeping the show to not more than 30 minutes, the students complete the organization of the whole script. Then, rehearse! Whether your production is a TV or radio show, tape the results.

The Chosen People

The chosen people concept is often confusing. Over the years it has caused quite a bit of trouble. This activity will enable the class to examine what it means to be a chosen people.

Pass out a copy of "A Covenant in Shechem" to everyone in the class.

A Covenant in Shechem

Said Joshua to the Israelites: "Now therefore fear the Lord, and serve God in sincerity and in truth; and put away the gods which your ancestors served beyond the river, and in Egypt; and serve you the Lord. But if it seems evil to you to serve the Lord, choose you this day whom you will serve; whether the gods which your ancestors served that were beyond the river, or the gods of the Amorites, in whose land you dwell. But as for me and my house, we will serve the Lord."

And the Israelites answered and said: "Far be it from us that we should forsake the Lord, to serve other gods; for the Lord our God brought us and our ancestors out of the land of Egypt, from the house of bondage..."

Yet Joshua warned them of the dangers connected with the choice they were making. The Lord does not tolerate idol worship. Our Lord is a jealous God. Still the people insisted: "Nay, but we will serve the Lord."

Then Joshua said unto the Israelites: "You are witnesses against yourselves that you have chosen the Lord, to serve God." And they said, "We are witnesses." "Now therefore put away the strange gods which are among you, and incline your heart unto the Lord, the God of Israel." And the people said to Joshua: "The Lord our God will we serve, and unto God's voice will we hearken."

Make a big thing out of choosing two or three students to read the story. Make it a privilege to be chosen! Once you have chosen the readers, ignore the rest of the class. Have the chosen ones read the story, which is from the Book of Joshua. After the reading, praise the chosen readers, then go over the story, asking such questions as:

Whom did Joshua choose to serve?

What did Joshua ask the people to do?

How did the people answer?

What were the people witnesses to?

Who did the choosing?

What did the people choose to do?

Now, go back to the beginning, when you chose certain students to read. Ask the students who were chosen: How did it feel to be chosen? Display three feelings cards with the words *honored*, *special*, and *different* respectively. Ask the chosen students which card (only one!) best describes their feelings about being chosen. When they have responded, ask: What made you feel _____?

Now, ask the students who were *not* chosen how they felt about not being chosen. Display three feelings cards with the words *unwanted*, *rejected*, and *jealous*. Ask the students who weren't chosen which word best describes how they felt. Ask what made them feel _____.

Compare their reactions to how non-Jews have reacted over the years to the concept of the chosen people. You might want to gather together some of the biblical quotations which talk about this concept, such as Exodus 19:4–6, 8; Isaiah 42:1, 4–6. A Catholic bishop, Rev. Edward H. Flannery, once said, "It was Judaism that brought the concept of a God-given universal moral law into the world; willingly or not the Jew carries the burden of God in history and for this the Jew has never been forgiven." Share this quotation with the class. Talk about its meaning. What moral code is it referring to? What do they think about Bishop Flannery's idea that the Jews have suffered because of this moral code? Today, what animosity do the students encounter? How do they handle it? What do they do? How has this activity helped them to better handle any animosity?

We Are One!

Through this activity the students learn to work together. They discover that individuals can work together as a group to achieve a goal. For each group of students you will need a large piece of red construction paper, a large piece of black construction paper, scissors, and glue or tape.

Divide the class into small groups. Each group is to make a checkerboard. A total of 20 minutes will be allowed for this: 10 minutes for the group members to plan a strategy for creating the checkerboard, during which they may not touch any of the materials, and 10 minutes to actually create the checkerboard, touching the materials, but not talking. Emphasize that during the planning stage they are allowed to talk all they want but may not touch anything. And during the creation stage, they may touch the materials but may not talk. Keep time strictly during both stages. After the activity, discuss the results and what the students have learned from it about communal effort.

Problem-Solving: Jewish Ethics

There are several different options when giving students a situation or problem to solve. Here are a few:

1. A situation in Jewish history posing a problem which the students have to solve. Usually research will be necessary.

2. A potential personal situation in which the students might find themselves. This could also be a situation which the students write up for their classmates to solve.

3. A situation involving medical ethics, morality, business ethics, etc.

Divide the class into small groups and have the members brainstorm ways to solve a problem or deal with a situation that you have presented. If the situation or problem is historical, they can do some research in the Bible, responsa literature, etc., to find answers. The following sections present a few examples of situations and problems suitable for this activity.

MEDICAL ETHICS

On the "L.A. Law" TV show, a case was brought to court by the parents of a young woman who was being kept alive by means of machines that fed her food and liquids. She could not talk, was not aware of what was happening around her, and was irreversibly brain-damaged. Although she could breath on her own, she was unable to respond to her parents, doctors, or anyone else who visited her. She had been "lost" to her parents for over a year. The parents want permission to "pull the plug," but the hospital administration refuses. If you were the judge and had to decide this case, what would you do?

SPANISH INQUISITION

In the fourteenth and fifteenth centuries the Jews of Spain were persecuted, and many were forced to convert to Christianity. Ultimately, those who did not convert were driven into exile. Large numbers of Spanish Jews pretended to convert but secretly practiced Judaism. They became known as Marranos or secret Jews. If you were a secret Jew, how would you celebrate Passover? How would you know when it was Passover if you had no Jewish calendar? How would you arrange your Passover celebration so as not to be discovered and arrested?

CAUGHT CHEATING!

Present the following situation: There is going to be a very important history exam tomorrow. Sam has been studying very hard all week because he wants to get a good grade. The exam is so important that it will be proctored by several teachers. Max, one of Sam's best friends, comes up to him and tells him he was busy working to earn enough money to buy the new bike he wants and hasn't had time to study. Max asks Sam to let him see his paper during the exam. If you were Sam, would you want to take the risk of being caught cheating, even for one of your best friends? What would you do?

Another Approach to Jewish Ethics

Prepare a set of cards detailing situations, both everyday and extraordinary, that require decision-making. Prepare a sheet listing the Jewish responses to these situations, based on *midrashim*, the Torah, the Talmud, *Pirke Avot*, Proverbs, and similar sources. Read one of the situations aloud. Have the students do some brainstorming, making a list of all the possible responses and their consequences. Following the discussion, hand out the Jewish-perspective sheets and talk about what Judaism has to say about the situation. Compare the Jewish perspective to the students' solutions. What are the similarities and differences?

TV and Jewish Ethics

What can we learn from TV? Without our knowing it, many TV shows may be giving the wrong (or right) message to our young people. Even though many parents (one hopes) control what their children watch, TV shows often convey elements of prejudice, bias, sexism, racism, discrimination, and violence. Why not make use of this medium and give your students an assignment to watch TV (they will love you!)? Pick a few shows after you have done some previewing to identify the ones you would like them to watch. "Beverly Hills 90210," reruns of "MASH" (great show!), "Star Trek: The Next Generation," "Roseanne," "Fresh Prince of Bel-Air," and "The Simpsons" are just some examples.

Prepare a TV Watching Sheet that includes the name of the show and a particular character to observe, or have the students do a general evaluation of the show. List some questions for the students to consider. For example:

1. What hidden agenda or secret purposes does this character have?

2. List any power-plays any of the characters engage in (e.g., "Don't you think you ought to _____?" or, "Of course, you are going to _____.").

3. List any put-downs by any character and whom they are directed at.

4. Which characters are hiding things (e.g., what they think or feel)?

5. To what extent does any character seem to threaten others? Or, is any character threatened by others?

6. What nonverbal communication is observed?

7. Do any of the characters have a potential for prejudice, bias, racism, sexism, or discrimination?

Add any other observations which you want the students to make. When the students bring their results to class for discussion, relate their findings to what Judaism has to say on the different subjects they observed.

Honesty Is the Best Policy: Jewish Ethics

It is kind of scary, but there is a trend among both children and adults to lie, cheat, and generally not be honest in their everyday lives. A recent survey showed that college students found nothing wrong with plagiarizing in order to pass a certification test, inflating business-expense reports, lying to achieve an objective, and exaggerating an insurance damage report. How would your students act in these cases? What would they do? Situation ethics may be out, but this is still a good introduction to what Jewish tradition says about lying, cheating, and dishonesty. Here are some situations you can use:

1. In order to be admitted to the college of your choice, you are required to write an essay on "The Value of Education." You find a well-written article by a scholar that covers everything you think the school wants from you. You can either write your own essay or use the article and say you wrote it. What would you do?

2. You are working for a big company and are sent on a business trip. You will be reimbursed for all of your expenses. You can keep an accurate record of your expenses, with receipts, or, whenever you get a receipt for something, you can ask that another $10 be added to the total. What would you do?

3. You bang up your car and take it to the repair shop for an estimate of repairs for the insurance company. You can either turn in the estimate as given or ask the repair shop to pad it so you can cheat the insurance company. What would you do?

Ask the students to write their responses to each situation. Upon completion, have them share their responses. Keep in mind that you may not like what you hear. Without being judgmental, discuss their responses. Either have a Bible for each student or provide copies of passages from the Bible that relate to the situations: Leviticus 19:11, 13, 15, 16, 35–36; Deuteronomy 25:13–16. Remember, "The first question a person is asked in the world to come is, 'Have you been honorable in business?'" (*Shabbat* 31b). In business *kedushah* (holiness) means honesty; on the baseball or football field, it is fair play. Ask the students how these quotations relate to their responses? As a closure to this activity, try an incomplete sentence, such as: In the future, I will try to be _____.

ALTERNATIVE

Ask the students to research what the Jewish tradition has to say about lying, cheating, and dishonesty. Give them the situations after they finish their research; based on Jewish tradition, what would they do? In addition, have them interview family members and congregants to see what they would do in the given situations. The students share what they have discovered with the class.

The Jewish God Idea

Over the eons of time, the Jewish God has been constant: One God. The God idea has changed, though, from one period to the next. *Finding God* by Syme and Sonsino (UAHC Press) is an excellent resource for the following small-group activities:

1. The group members are to list all the different ideas of God they can find in Jewish resources. They are to identify the period for each God idea and discover what life was like for Jews in that period. When the research has been completed, share their findings with the class. Talk about the different ideas of God and what influence the outside world had on Jews and their ideas of God. Ask the students to identify one, two, or several God ideas with which they feel comfortable. Share with the class.

2. Give each student a siddur (prayer book). Each group is to go through the worship services and list the different God concepts found in the prayers. Identify the God concepts from the list developed in the preceding activity. Share the students' findings with the class.

3. As a closure, have students find or write prayers that fit their personal God concepts.

The Names of God

We think of God in human terms because we are human beings with human limitations. Abraham Heschel once wrote that we only have human language with which to describe God and it isn't really enough. Our names for God are stated in human terms, but the rabbis and sages of old were aware of this problem and wrote a *midrash* to explain the different names of God.

> Rabbi Abba b. Memel said: God said to Moses, "Thou desirest to know My name, I am called according to My deeds. When I judge My creatures, I am called Elohim; when I wage war against the wicked, I am called Sabaoth; when I suspend judgment for a person's sins, I am called El Shaddai (God Almighty); but when I have compassion for My world, I am called Yahweh, for Yahweh means the attribute of mercy, as it is said, `Yahweh, Yahweh (Lord, Lord), merciful and gracious' (Exodus 34:6). This is the meaning of the words, `I am that I am,' namely, I am called according to My deeds."
> (*Exodus Rabbah, Shemot* 111:6)

The following activity teaches that even though God has different names, God is One. You will need enough copies of the *midrash* for everyone in class, paper and pencils, prayer books, newsprint or a blackboard, and colored markers or chalk.

1. Divide the class into small groups. Instruct the students to go through the prayer book and list all the different names of God they can find.

2. Have the students share their lists with the class, making one composite list of all the names.

3. Have the students make a list of all *their own* names. Give some examples of names or designations that apply to you (e.g., wife/husband, mother/father, sister/brother, etc.).

4. Have the students share their lists, then make a list of all your own names. Talk about all the names you have and all the names each student has, emphasizing that despite all the different names, you are still one person.

5. Hand out copies of the *midrash* and have a student read it aloud. Discuss the meaning of the *midrash*: What is it telling us about the different names of God? What relationship do your different names have to your deeds and activities? How can we relate God's names to God's deeds and activities?

Talk with the students about their ideas of God—be accepting! Let them share their ideas of God. As a closure—and this is an excellent closure for any lesson that covers the different ideas of God—hand out large pieces of white drawing paper and crayons or colored markers. Have the students draw pictures of God's name, which they should feel free to embellish. As the students finish, take their individual works of art and tape them together to make one long work of art. Ask a student to take one end and have all the other students gather together in a small group. You take the other end and wrap it around the whole group. Tell the students something like: "We are wrapped up in a number of different ideas of God"; or, "God is all around us"; or, "Just as God is One, even with all the different ideas of God, we are still one people with One God."

Language Game: Hebrew Rakevet (Train)

To make a Hebrew train, use a 28 x 30 piece of posterboard.

1. Cut twenty-two 4 x 3 3/4 pieces of different-colored construction paper for train cars.

2. Fold each piece to make an envelope.

3. Cut out a red engine, yellow caboose, and 46 wheels.

4. Glue the engine, train cars, caboose, and wheels to the posterboard.

5. Write a Hebrew letter on each car.

6. Laminate; cut open pockets carefully with an Exacto knife.

7. Cut twenty-two 2.5 x 2 cards from tagboard.

8. Glue pictures of Jewish symbols, holidays, etc., to the cards.

9. Laminate the cards.

To play: each student, in turn, matches a picture card to the train car marked with the same letter of the Hebrew alphabet as the first letter of the item depicted on the card.

Yiddish Culture

The culture of Yiddish-speaking Jewry is now almost lost, but our young people can learn about the life of the East European Jews before the Holocaust through the many songs and stories that are a legacy from the past. We have a large resource of Yiddish music, stories, and poetry that can tell us a lot about their lives. Some of these materials will be found in Ruth Rubin, *The Voice of a People*; Nathan Ausubel, *Treasury of Jewish Folklore*; Irving Howe and Eliezer Greenberg, *Treasury of Yiddish Poetry*; and Irving Howe, *World of Our Fathers*. Yiddish music can be obtained from Tara Publications, 29 Derby Avenue, Cedarhurst, NY 11516.

EXAMPLE

One of the more familiar songs is "Oif'n Pripechik" ("In the Oven"). The words, in English and Yiddish, are found in the *Treasury of Jewish Folklore*. Distribute copies of the song. Play the music and ask the students to listen closely and follow the words as they listen. Talk about: the mood of the music; what are they hearing? You might want to play it again. Then give the students drawing paper and colored markers or crayons, and based on what they heard and read in the words, have them draw illustrations to the lyrics. Upon completion, ask them to describe their illustrations and give the reasons for the style of their drawings.

EXAMPLE

Read the Yiddish story "Gimpel the Fool," which gives a good example of Jewish family life in the shtetl. Prepare a list of questions looking something like this:

Trace your family tree back as far as you can go.

What business is your father in?

What business was your grandfather in?

What business was your great-grandfather in?

Can you trace a business, within your family, that was handed down from one generation to another?

Do you live in the same house your parents did as children?

Is it the same house your grandparents lived in?

What does your father teach you?

What does your mother teach you?

What are the similarities and differences between Abba's wife and your mother?

Who has the final say in your house—your father or your mother? Or is it equal?

What is the difference between the way your family makes decisions
and the way decisions are made in the story?

What preparations does your mother make for the Sabbath?

What preparations do you make?

These are just a few of the questions you can ask. As the students respond, remind them that some questions will be difficult to answer, especially when it comes to grandparents and great-grandparents, but that's okay. As they share their answers they will be comparing their lives today with the family life of the shtetl.

Yiddish: Is It Really a Lost Language?

Believe it or not, Yiddish, through selected words and idioms, is very much a part of English. Our language has definitely been influenced by Yiddish. Just look through Leo Rosten's *The Joys of Yiddish* and you will see what I mean. That is, if you haven't already recognized its use by people (many of whom are not even Jewish) every day. There is no reason why our kids shouldn't know something about this influence and take pride in it.

Divide your class into small groups. Have the group members identify as many English words and phrases as they can that are derived from Yiddish. They can use dictionaries and word-origin books, or ask friends and relatives for ideas. Perhaps someone in your congregation who speaks Yiddish would be willing to work with them. As the groups identify words and idioms, keep a running list posted on the blackboard, bulletin board, or on sheets of paper mounted on the wall.

Group members can design posters using themes based on the Yiddish phrases they have identified (e.g., "You should live so long"; "Go fight city hall"; "You should live to a hundred and twenty"; "It shouldn't happen to me"). Of course the tone of voice is used in Yiddish too (e.g., "Did you write your mother?" Answer: "Did I write my mother?" scornfully, for "Of course I did!"). Yiddish words the students might encounter include *shmooze, klutz, klezmer, chutzpah,* etc.

For a closure, have a Yiddish party and invite parents to participate. Ask parents or the sisterhood to make a few of the traditional foods, such as mandelbrot, even knishes, as snacks. Let the kids show off their new knowledge. Or they could prepare a Yiddish dictionary with all the words and idioms they have discovered. Design a cover, copy, and compile into a book which they can take home to share with their parents.

Into the Future: Prayer—Holidays—Bible

Before beginning the activities in this section the class must have a good background in Jewish history, Bible, and prayer. These activities are designed to enrich and enhance what the class has already learned about its Jewish heritage.

We always seem to use activities that look into the past. We even try to imagine how Moses, Abraham, and other historical figures would react if they came into our sanctuary today, but what have we done to prepare for the future? What do our kids think about the future? With all the changes that have taken place in just the last 20 or even 10 years, what will the future bring?

Brainstorm with the class, listing all the changes the students can think of that have taken place in the last 10–20 years. (There are so many that it amazes me; in the field of information gathering alone, it's wild.) Look at the world itself and there is more: the changes in the political status of Germany, Russia, Israel, etc. Be sure to include any changes in Judaism, including the impact the changes in the world may have had on Jewish life.

Distribute drawing paper and crayons or colored markers. Ask the students to draw a series of pictures as they see themselves when they are, say, 35 years old. How will they dress? What will they look like? What kinds of jobs will they have? How will they celebrate Shabbat? Rosh Hashanah? Yom Kippur? Other Jewish holidays? What kinds of persons will they marry, etc.? Upon completion, share their drawings and talk about the changes they anticipate in the future. Be specific and lead the discussion into the changes they envision for Judaism.

A Time in the Future

Prepare a list of things that you think might take place in the future. Your list could look something like this:

Rabbis come down off the bimah to pray with their congregations.

Religious school becomes a learning experience enjoyed by kids and parents.

Everyone learns prayer book Hebrew and knows the meaning of all the prayers.

Parents attend religious school with their children.

The worship service is totally participatory, including singing.

Intermarriage becomes a thing of the past.

Shabbat services are as well attended as High Holy Day services.

Congregations care for the needy and homeless whether they are Jews or not.

Anti-Semitism disappears along with hate, prejudice, and discrimination.

Jewish family abuse and violence become a thing of the past as people learn to respect one another.

The elderly are treated with a lot of TLC (tender loving care).

Put your list on a sheet with two columns, one headed *Student* and the other *Adult*. Let the students fill in their column by indicating the year this might take place or writing "never" or "possible" on the appropriate lines. Discuss their responses, especially the reasons why they responded "never" or "possible." Also talk about what would have to happen within Judaism for these changes to take place.

Either let the students take their sheets home or give them clean ones. (A clean one would mean that the adult would not be influenced by the student's ideas.) They are to ask their parents or relatives to respond to the statements. It would be helpful if the adults include the reasons for their responses. (I would design a new sheet specifically for adults with space for including reasons.) Have the students bring the completed sheets back the following week. Share and discuss the adult responses.

News of the Future

Have the class watch a few TV evening news shows during the week. Ask them to make notes on the major stories, the human interest stories, the final story, what the commercials were advertising, etc. Bring the notes to class.

Divide the class into small groups. Assign them to write the script for a day 50 years into the future. Give each group a specific news area (e.g., news, religion, human interest, feature story on a famous Jewish person, weather, etc., and don't forget the commercials). If you wish, be specific about the different stories (e.g., Israel and Egypt [or Syria, Iraq, etc.] 50 years from today; a feature story: Prime Minister of Israel visits _____ [name the country]; weather: major hurricane or earthquake; human interest: a unique elderly Jew).

To make the news program more realistic, once the scripts are completed, rehearse and edit them so that the whole program is not more than 30 minutes, including commercials. When ready, videotape it! Then show it to other classes in the school.

Into the Future: The Worship Service

Ask the students to write a Jewish worship service for the year 2046. Prepare a sheet that lists the order of an Erev Shabbat service. Be sure the students know the meaning of each prayer in the service.

Divide the class into small groups, each to be responsible for a portion of the service. Now comes the fun part: Tell the students to write their own creative prayers, but without changing the ancient meaning of the original prayers. Their prayers must be gender-free (no he/she). If a man's name is used, a corresponding woman's name must be used. Don't let them get hung up on questions about God. Let them use their own ideas of God, whatever they may be at the moment. The main thing is to encourage creativity. Have fun!

Using Midrashim to Teach Jewish Values

In Leviticus 19:14 we find: "You shall not insult the deaf, or place a stumbling block before the blind. You shall fear your God: I am the Lord." Discuss with the class the meaning of "the deaf" and "the blind." Who are the deaf and who are the blind? How do we "insult" the deaf? Give an example, like talking about other people behind their backs. What "stumbling blocks" do we place before the blind? Give an example, like providing the wrong information when someone asks for directions.

Divide the class into small groups. Each group is to design a skit not more than 3 minutes long which shows the different ways words can hurt someone: ways we insult the deaf or place stumbling blocks before the blind. You can make suggestions, but it is best if the students create the skits based on their own personal experiences. What you are looking for, though, is such subjects as putting someone down, taking up a salesperson's time with no intention of buying, pretending to like someone, giving the wrong information, falsely claiming that someone did something, etc.

Let the group members perform their skits. Watch the reactions of the class, making notes on what you see and hear. After all the groups have performed, talk about: What were the different ways words hurt? How did you react when something like this happened to you? What does wronging with words have to do with the quotation from Leviticus? Most of your questions will come from the reactions you noticed as the skits were taking place.

After the skits and the discussion, distribute copies of the following *midrashim* to the class:

R. Meir said: One must not buy vessels with money borrowed for the purpose of buying fruit, or vice versa, because by so doing the borrower steals the mind of the lender.

(*Tosefta, Megillah* 1:5)

As there is wronging or overreaching in buying and selling, so there is wronging in words. Do not ask the price of something if you have no intention of buying it. Do not say to a person who has repented [and changed his or her way of life], "Remember your former deeds." If a person is a descendant of proselytes, do not say to this person, "Remember the deeds of your ancestors," for it [the Torah] says, "A proselyte you shall not vex or oppress."

A man asked his neighbor, "Could you please lend me a pound of wheat?" "I have no wheat," replied the other. "Or barley, then?" said the man. "I have none," repeated the miser. "Maybe you can give me a few dates?" the man persisted. "Sorry, I don't have any," said the miser, closing the door.

What used to happen is that the house of a miser who acted this way would be stricken with the symptoms of leprosy, and the *kohen*, summoned for an inspection, would rule that all the miser's belongings had to be cleared out. They were put in the street, in full view of everyone. "Didn't he claim he had nothing?" said the neighbors, upon seeing the barley, wheat, and dates. "Why he brought the curse of leprosy on himself by pretending that he was poor when he was really blessed!"

Note: According to tradition, the leprosy described in the Torah is not the same as the disease we know as leprosy today. The treatment commanded in the Torah does not conform to any rule of medicine. The leprosy of the Torah was caused by sins. In the *Gemara* and *Tanchuma* leprosy is caused by such sins as idolatry, blasphemy, theft, *leshon hara* (slander), false testimony, distorted judgment, murder, miserliness, arrogance, robbing, conceit, illegally entering another's domain, and causing quarrels.

Read these *midrashim* with the class one at a time and discuss how each of them relates to the Leviticus quotation. For example:

R. Meir: Give some examples of money being obtained for one purpose and used for another. When this happens, in what way is the mind of the lender being stolen? Would you define this as a "stumbling block" or an "insult to the deaf"?

Wronging in words: Who are you hurting when you ask the price of something you have no intention of buying? How is the other person hurt? Have you ever done any of the things mentioned in this *midrash*, or have any of them been done to you? How did it happen? How did you feel?

The miser and leprosy: Give some examples of a stingy person. Have you ever been stingy? Why? How do you think the miser felt when all his belongings were placed outside for everyone to see? How would you feel if this happened to you? How do we define biblical leprosy today?

With each *midrash* specify which part of the Leviticus quotation it refers to. One final question for the class might be: How can we avoid hurting other people with words or otherwise? And as a closure, ask each student to complete the following sentence with the first words that come to mind: In the future, I will be _____.

Control Your Impulse (to Anger)

"Who is heroic? The person whose desires are controlled" (*Tamid* 32a). A person who desires something and can't obtain it is prone to anger. The anger comes in many forms, of which violence is one. The activities in this section emphasize the Jewish concept that one should control the impulse to anger.

Give out blank sheets of paper and ask the students to divide them into three columns. In the first column, they are to list all the things that make them angry. In the second column, opposite each item, they are to write the reason it makes them angry. In the third column, they are to write what they can do to control their anger in this area. Have them choose partners and share their responses. Give them time to share. Then ask for some general sharing by those who wish; but don't push, this is personal.

Distribute copies of the following *midrashim* after the preceding exercise:

The Castininer Rabbi made it a rule for himself never to express his displeasure with anyone on the same day when he was offended by that person. On the morrow he would say to the person, "I was displeased with you yesterday."

238

Rabbi Wolf Zitomirer said: "Angry people fill their mouths with live coals and sharp, hard needles. For each angry word we utter, we deserve to be banished from holiness in shame and disgrace, and to suffer grievously until our soul is purified from its blemishes. We must all be masters of our mouths."

With the class, talk about: By not expressing his anger immediately, how was the Castininer Rabbi controlling his impulse? How can we be "masters of our mouths"? When a person makes you angry, what can you do to control your impulse to anger? Give some examples of when you have controlled your anger. What was happening? What made you angry? Would it have been possible to wait till the next day? What would be the advantage of waiting? How can you handle your anger? How can you handle your anger positively?

TRUE TO LIFE

Prepare a sheet with the following statements taken from Rabbi Nachman of Bratzlav's commentary on anger. Use as many or as few as you like. After each statement is read, ask the students to give examples from today's world that show how the statement is true.

Break your anger by compassion for the one with whom you are angry.

Anger and cruelty arise from deficiency of understanding.

Those who subdue their anger achieve a good name.

Anger causes a person to be far from truth.

Angry people cannot attain the goals to which they aspire.

Those who restrain their anger will not see their enemies rule over them.

One who is not in the habit of complaining about people is well-beloved.

Falsehood and jealousy cause anger.

Anger shortens the days of one's life.

The person without anger is able to humble the arrogant.

If you are angry it is a sign that all your good works are for the purpose of obtaining honors.

Charity prevents anger.

Who is heroic? The person who conquers all desires.

Prepare the following *midrash* for the students to be read after the above activity:

A heathen once made a wager with another that he would anger the gentle Hillel. So he went to the house of Hillel, who, next to the king, was most exalted of the Israelites. Rudely the man called out, "Where is Hillel? Where is Hillel?"

Hillel was in the act of dressing for the Sabbath. Without noticing the stranger's rudeness, he put on his cloak and, with his usual mildness, asked him what was his pleasure. "I want to know," said the man, "why the Babylonians have round heads." "An important question, truly," answered Hillel. "The reason is, because they have no experienced midwives."

The man went away, and came again in an hour, vociferating as before. The sage again said to him, "What do you want, my son?" "I want to know," said the man, "why the Tarmudians have weak eyes." Hillel answered, "Because they live in a sandy country; the sand flying in their eyes causes soreness."

The man, perceiving Hillel's good nature, went away disappointed. But resolving to make another effort, he came again to the sage. "What is your pleasure now?" said the latter mildly. "I want to know," rejoined the former, "why Africans have broad feet." "Because," said Hillel, "they live in a marshy land." "I'm willing to ask you many more questions," said the man, "but fear you will be angry." "Fear nothing," said the meek instructor of Israel, "ask as many questions as it pleases you, and I will answer them if I can."

The man returned again and demanded, "Teach me the Torah while I stand on one foot." Hillel said, "Do not unto others what you would not have them do unto you." Truly astonished and fearing to lose his money, the heathen decided to insult Hillel to his face; therefore he said, "Are you the Hillel who is considered the prince of the Israelites?" Hillel answered in the affirmative. "Well, then," said the man, "if so, may Israel not produce many like you." "And why?" asked the sweet-natured Hillel with a smile. "Because it will teach you to be more prudent and not make such foolish wagers. Besides, it is much better that you lose your money than that Hillel should lose his patience."

Read this *midrash* with the students and talk about: their lists of causes, reasons, and actions to control their impulses to anger; how Hillel was able to control his anger (patience); by controlling one's anger, what does one achieve? (Refer back to Nachman of Bratzlav's statements.)

FREE AS A BIRD

Ask the students to imagine that they are as free as birds, free to do whatever they wish, free to go wherever they want. Have them each draw a box in the center of a blank sheet of paper. Inside the boxes they are to write one-word names of all the things they would do if they were as free as birds to do what they wanted. (Allow a few minutes.)

Outside the boxes, they are to write one-word names of what keeps them from doing what they wish they were free to do, what is holding them back. (Allow a few minutes.)

Now have them draw a circle around these names (and the box). Outside the circle, write the words that express how they feel when they can't do what they would like to be free to do. Next to each feeling word, write down what actions their feelings cause them to take. (Allow a few minutes.)

Have the students choose partners and share their responses. Ask for general sharing by the entire group. As a class, talk about:

How would being free to do as you wish enable you to control your anger?

What can you do to control your anger when you cannot do as you wish?

How can others help you to control your anger?

Pirke Avot 4:1 says: "Who is heroic? The person who keeps desire under control." How can you control your desires?

What effort will you make to control your impulse to anger?

A good closure to this series of activities would be to create a "Control Your Impulse" contract, where the students agree to work toward controlling their impulses to anger.

Jewish Communities around the World

Divide the class into small groups and assign each a continent. To make maps of the continents for the groups, hang a large piece of white butcher paper on the wall and project a transparency of a map of the world on it with an overhead projector. When the first group of students have traced their continent, remove the paper and hang a new piece on the wall. Continue until each group has a map, making sure to keep the projector in the same position until all the continents have been traced.

Distribute a list of questions for the groups to answer. Your list could look something like this:

Which countries have Jews living in them?

In which cities are the most Jews located?

How do the Jews in these communities make their livelihoods?

What kinds of Jews are they (Orthodox, Reform, Conservative, etc.)?

How involved are they in the general community (politics, social welfare, etc.)?

How prominent are the Jews in the general community?

Some countries will be easy to research, others a little more difficult. The students may have to contact an organization in their assigned country to obtain the information desired. A good book to use for this purpose would be *The Jewish Travel Guide* (Sepher Hermon Press, 1265 46th Street, Brooklyn, NY 11219).

When the groups complete their research, have scissors, glue, and lots of old magazines, newspapers, and workbooks available. Cover one wall of your classroom with blue paper to represent the oceans, or use the wall in the school hallway so that everyone can watch the project develop. Have the students cut out or draw pictures that represent some of the information they have learned about the various communities. They arrange and

241

glue the pictures in their proper locations, identify sites and cities of Jewish interest, and print index cards with pertinent information, etc., on their continent. When each continent is completed, attach to the blue paper, being sure that it is located in the right place. A final touch would be to identify the bodies of water.

Our Jewish Community

Are your students familiar with the Jewish agencies and organizations in your city? This activity is a way for them to learn more about their "Jewish city," and the roles of the various agencies and organizations in your community.

Divide the class into small groups. Have a city map available for each group. Let the students do the easy things first (e.g., locate their homes, the synagogue, the Jewish community center). Use colored peel-and-stick circles to identify each location.

Next, locate the Jewish agencies in your city. Assign each group to find out where specific agencies are housed, what purposes they have, and how they go about performing their functions. As the students gather information, they are to indicate the locations of the agencies on their maps, along with what they have learned about the agencies.

ALTERNATIVE

Have a Jewish Organization Fair. This could be an event for the entire school and congregation. Identify all the Jewish agencies in your city and invite them to participate. Give each agency its own booth, so that students can go from one to another in small groups, gathering information. If the congregation is invited to participate, the adults will also be able to learn more about the different agencies. (This was done years ago in Cleveland and was very successful.)

Another Option: Your Jewish Community

Mount a large map of your community on the bulletin board. If you cannot find a map large enough, use an overhead projector to project a map on a wall covered with white butcher paper. When you have the size you want, trace the outline of the map and identify key locations, streets, etc.

Brainstorm with the class, listing the different elements of the Jewish community they will need to identify (e.g., synagogues, Jewish schools, Jewish community center, Federation, Anti-Defamation League, home for the aged, Jewish Family Service, and any other Jewish institutions you wish to cover). Have students work together to create symbols for the many different agencies. Write the key to the symbols at the bottom of the map, then identify the location of each place. Label with symbols.

Have students choose partners. Assign each pair a Jewish communal agency to research, including an interview with someone who works in the agency. For the interview, the students can ask such questions as: What is it like to work for a Jewish agency? What is the most difficult part of your job? What are your daily duties? What part of the community do you serve? As they gather the information, they are to write it up in an attractive manner and place it next to the corresponding symbol. A picture of the person interviewed would add a more personal touch to the display.

A final activity after completing the bulletin board could be to consider: What worker seems to have the most impact on the Jewish community? And, if you had to choose from the list of jobs, which would you choose, and why?

Jewish Community Bulletin Board

Prepare your bulletin board space. You will need a large map of your community, push pins, white paper for background, labels in different sizes, yarn in different colors, colored markers, and pictures of all the Jewish institutions in your community or a Polaroid camera to take the pictures. On one side of the bulletin board put the map, on the other side, pictures or cards from the Jewish institutions in your community. They can be placed in a cluster.

Divide the class into small groups. Assign a Jewish institution to each group. The group members are to identify its location, and find out its purpose and role in the community. They are to write the information they have gathered on labels, then place labels next to the picture of the appropriate institution. With a push pin, attach a piece of yarn to the picture of the institution, and extend the yarn over to where the institution is located on the map of the community.

Take this lesson a step further by asking the students what kinds of agencies, if any, are missing. What communal needs are not being met? Where could a new agency be located? Describe what it would do and add this information to the bulletin board with special identification as a potential new agency.

What Would You Do? Anti-Semitism or Jews in the Diaspora

Prepare an outlandish story something like this:

A weird-looking thing that resembles a spaceship has landed on the beach near the city's bathing park. An odd-looking creature, very obviously non-human, has been seen coming and going from the location. The things it does indicate that the creature is intelligent. Though it seems ferocious and surely is different-looking, there is no evidence that it has done anything bad. The leaders of the community have to decide what to do about the intruder. The options open to them are:

1. Investigate the creature.
2. Exterminate the creature.
3. Warn the creature to leave.
4. Welcome the creature.

5. Confine the creature to a specific place.

Make signs for each option, placing one in each corner of the room and one in the very center. Ask the students to think about the choices, select the one they prefer, and move to the area near the appropriate option sign. When this occurs the class will be divided into five groups. Give the group members time to talk about why they chose that option and to select a group spokesperson. The spokespersons are to explain their groups' positions to the rest of the class. Everyone must be free to express an opinion; if any of the students are swayed by the logic of another group's position, they may move to that group, but they must explain why they have changed their minds.

Compare this activity, their decisions and responses, to the situations in the life of the Jews as they moved from the land of Israel into the Diaspora and began to encounter anti-Semitism.

We Are One: Kelal Yisrael

Even teenagers are not too old to play with Tinker-Toys, as in this activity. Divide the class into small groups. Give each group a set of Tinker-Toys. Tell the students they can take the Tinker-Toys out of the box but cannot touch them. Their assignment is to come up with a plan for building the tallest self-supporting structure they can, talking all they want, drawing diagrams, etc., but without touching the Tinker-Toys. Give them 10–15 minutes for this planning stage. Tell them that when they actually begin to build the structure, no talking will be allowed, so it is important to do all the planning now. Have them put all the toys back in the box when the planning stage is over. Now give them 2 minutes to do the construction, but without talking. Get ready, get set, go—and time them. Stop when the 2 minutes are up.

Give everyone in the class an opportunity to express admiration for the various structures. Talk about: What happened during the planning and building stages? Were they individuals, or were they a group working together to achieve a goal? I have done this activity many times, and the results are always the same. The students realize that by working together they can accomplish their task, just as Jews, when given a task, work together as one.

ALTERNATIVE

The same activity can be used to teach Bible. It is a good launching device for the story of Jacob as he prepares to meet Esau after so many years of separation. After doing the exercise the kids are anxious to get to the Bible to see the relationship between what they did and the Bible story. It works!

Mitzvot: Taking on Some Responsibility

At the time of their Bar/Bat Mitzvahs, students often declare, "Today I am a man/woman!" What isn't added, though, is that they are now of age to be responsible for observing the mitzvot (commandments). The total number of mitzvot in the Torah is 613, which goes well beyond the Ten Commandments already known to most students. Why not let them take a look at some of the other mitzvot?

The Reform movement has defined most mitzvot as good deeds, which implies that they are a matter of choice, whereas tradition defines the mitzvot as obligatory. You will find a complete list of the 613 mitzvot in the *Encyclopaedia Judaica*. From these you will probably identify about 75 to which the students could relate. Prepare a list of the mitzvot you want to use, numbering them. Prepare another sheet divided into four columns, headed *Gemilut Chasadim* (Deeds of Loving-Kindness), *Tzedakah* (Righteousness), *Rituals/Ceremonies*, and *Prayer/Holiness*. Make copies of the mitzvah list and the four-column sheet for everyone in class.

Divide the class into small groups to read through the numbered list of mitzvot. As the students read, they are to classify the mitzvot by placing the number of each mitzvah in the appropriate column on the other sheet. Give them some examples before they begin; as they work, answer any questions they have about the meaning of any of the mitzvot. Have the groups share their findings and give reasons for placing the mitzvot in the various categories.

Now have the students choose at least four mitzvot each to do on a regular basis for a fixed time period set by you. Talk about the choices they have made and the reasons for the choices. Post a chart on which they can keep a record of their performance of the mitzvot. After the set period is over, talk about what was easy to do and what was difficult, how they felt when doing the mitzvot, what their sense of responsibility was, etc.

Jewish Mysticism: Create a Good Society

Mysticism is a fascinating subject. Although tradition says that one should not study the Kabbalah until the age of 40, there is still quite a bit that youngsters can learn from this aspect of Judaism. Ezekiel is often regarded as a biblical forerunner of Jewish mysticism, as reflected in his vision of the throne of God. Merkabah mysticism, the mystical school that may have begun in Ezekiel's time, provides a good basis for a lesson.

Divide the class into small groups. Have them research the meaning of Merkabah mysticism and the ten steps of the Sefirot. Upon completion of their research, ask each group to create a mystical society. They are to write membership rules and regulations, and in addition create a name for it. Then they are to plan a campaign to "sell" their society. Write campaign slogans, TV and radio ads, advertising posters, and compose a song based on the society's rules. Each group, when finished, is to sell its society to the whole class.

Teaching Prayer

This section provides ideas on how to teach several prayers from the worship service. The ideas are not in the order of the service, but can be used as needed for classroom activities.

PRAYER IS...

This is a simple introduction to the idea of prayer in Jewish life—an opportunity for students to think about what prayer means to them. You will need strips of colored paper, colored markers, and tape.

Talk about prayer and our attitudes toward it. Prayer means different things to different people. Give an example of what it means to you (e.g., commitment). Then ask the students to each fill out a strip of paper, using only one word to complete the statement "Prayer is ____." After the students share their responses with their classmates, collect the paper strips and tape them to the wall to make a "quilt" collage of the responses.

BARECHU

Barechu is the ancient call to worship, urging us to praise God. This activity will help the class to understand what praising God means.

Prepare a "Praise Sheet," leaving room after each statement for the students to write their lists. Here is an example:

List all the things you think are worthy of being praised—things you
    do, things other people do, or something you see, hear, or feel.

List those things for which you receive praise.

List those things for which you would praise God.

Introduce this activity by talking about praise (e.g., what we praise, what we find worthy of praise), giving a few examples. Pass out the sheets and ask the students to complete them. Allow time for them to think before writing their responses. When they finish, have them share their lists, one section at a time. Then share the final section, comparing the differences and similarities between it and the other lists. Upon completion, talk about the background of the *Barechu* prayer; its purpose as a call to worship, urging us to praise God as God is to be praised.

AHAVAH RABAH/AHAVAT OLAM

These two prayers immediately precede the *Shema*. *Ahavah Rabah* is used in the morning service, and *Ahavat Olam*, in the evening service. For this activity you will need a Torah scroll, rolled to the weekly portion, and prayer books for everyone in class. Have the students sit around you in a circle.

Take the Torah scroll and hold it for a minute while you talk to the class about God's gift of Torah: how God showed love by giving the Torah and commandments to the people of Israel, and our reverence for the Torah, its heritage and tradition. Tell the students that you will pass the scroll to the person sitting next to you, who will hold it for a moment, then pass it to the next person, and so on through the whole class. Before passing the scroll on, each person is to silently reflect for a moment about what the Torah means, both personally and to the Jewish people, and about how it feels to hold the sacred scroll.

After the Torah scroll has made the complete circle, tell the class that it will be passed around again. This time, however, the students are, in turn, to tell what the Torah says to them individually, what role it plays in their lives and in Jewish life generally, and how they feel about holding a heritage over 3,000 years old. Set the example by beginning with your own statement, then pass the scroll on to the next person. A student who does not wish to speak can just hold the scroll briefly and then pass it on; do not push anyone to speak.

Follow this by reading the Torah portion for the week. Ask everyone to join in reciting the blessings, and as the Torah is undressed, give a brief explanation of how Torah scrolls are written by a scribe, and about the columns, parchment, and use of the *yad*. As the weekly portion is read, discuss its ramifications for the lives of the students. Include *midrashim* for difficult parts of the portion to help the students attain a deeper understanding. After reading the Torah portion, roll up the scroll, replace its cover, and put it away.

Then read *Ahavah Rabah* and *Ahavat Olam*. Go over the meaning of the prayers in relation to the Torah service the class has just experienced. *Ahavah Rabah* praises God for giving the Torah with "abounding love." *Ahavat Olam* praises God for giving the Torah with "everlasting love."

KAVANAH

Words are our only medium for prayer. Words have different meanings, but in themselves mean nothing. They only have meanings because people attribute meanings to them. Introduce this activity with the following old Chasidic tale, providing a copy for each student:

A simple man came to the synagogue for Yom Kippur. During most of the service, he just sat and listened, for he did not know very much. He could not read the Hebrew of the prayer book. All around him the members of the congregation were standing in prayer, each person speaking with God in a whisper. And the simple man wished to speak with God too. He wished to tell God what a magnificent world God had made. He wished to thank God for the blessings of health and life, but he could not find the right words. When he thought his heart would break with shame and sadness, he said, "O God, I cannot speak a beautiful prayer for You because I am a simple man and have forgotten what I was taught as a child. I am not good with words. But You, O Lord, You know

247

how to do everything. So I will give You the alef-bet, and You can make a beautiful prayer for Yourself." Then he recited, "Alef...Bet...Gimel...Dalet..." And the rabbi who told this story added, "Of all the prayers spoken that day, this one was the dearest to God."

With the students, discuss the story and the meaning the man gave to the Hebrew alphabet by saying it with all his heart. Then talk about the "music of our voice"—the meanings we give words by the way we say them. Have the students give examples of the music of their voice. Have them, either individually or together, say their names

Lovingly.

Angrily.

As a question.

As though they want something.

Ask the students to choose partners. The members of each pair are to take turns saying their partner's name as you direct them. Upon completion, talk about:

Which tone of voice was the nicest?

Which one was the most annoying, the one they didn't like?

Which one did they like the best?

What made them like it the best?

Relate this activity to the concept of *kavanah*. Prayer has no meaning unless it is said with feeling, unless you really mean it. *Kavanah* is the spirit in which we recite the words of a prayer.

THE SHEMA

The first prayer most youngsters learn is the *Shema*. Make copies of the *Shema* as it appears in the Torah. If anyone in class cannot read the Hebrew, include a transliteration. Give copies to everyone. Talk about: When did you first learn this prayer? What does it mean to you? What does it mean to the Jewish people? Ask the students to complete the following sentences with the first words that come to mind:

When I say the *Shema* I _____.

The *Shema* is important to me because _____.

The *Shema* teaches me that _____.

When I say the *Shema* I feel _____.

These statements can be read one at a time or put on a sheet of paper for written responses. Upon completion, ask the students to share.

Ask the students to say the *Shema* silently whenever they feel like it. Then ask them to say the *Shema* out loud whenever they want—they do not have to wait for anyone else. Finally, ask them to watch you. Raise your hand over your head and tell them that when your hand comes down, they are all to say the *Shema* together.

Ask the students which way of saying the *Shema* made them feel as one with their fellow students. Having done this exercise many times, I know the answer. But you can also discuss how they felt when they said it silently and how they felt when they said it out loud. (Just as we talk about God as One when we say the *Shema* together, so are the Jewish people one. We gain strength as one, just as we gain strength in communal prayer.) Now, go back to the *Shema* as it is printed in the Torah. Have them look carefully at how it is printed. Point out the larger Hebrew letters which end the first word and the last word. These letters together make the Hebrew word *ed*, which means "witness," to emphasize that the Jew who pronounces the *Shema* is a witness to the Holy One. Discuss with the students what this means to them. In what way are they witnesses?

Concepts in Prayer

Many young people have no idea that different concepts and values are found in the various prayers that comprise the worship service. You will need a prayer book for each student. Divide the class into groups of three. Prepare a set of index cards for each group with the following concepts/values on each card:

Am Yisrael

Family

Freedom

Friendship

Justice

Knowledge/wisdom

Nature

Peace

Truth

Tell the students to go through the prayer book and find the prayers that express each concept/value. If they do not find a prayer that matches any concept/value, they are to write one.

Upon completion, have them share their findings, along with the prayers they have written. Briefly discuss the meaning of the Hebrew word *tefilah* (prayer), explaining that prayer is a way of relating to ourselves and judging ourselves. Through prayer we consider who we are and what we can become. Discuss: What do we usually turn to prayer for (e.g., personal comfort, strength, fellowship, self-expression, self-assessment, identity)?

Jewish Symbols: Ritual Articles

An archaeological dig: do we really need to have a dig to examine an object or artifact that might have been found in a tell? I don't think so. The students can use their creative imaginations. For example: "Let's pretend it is the year 2040..." The students are members of an archaeological team recording data on the artifacts of an ancient culture.

Divide the class into small groups. Each group "discovers" an artifact—which you can assign. The artifact could be a *yad*, Torah breastplate, menorah, Kiddush cup, *ketubah*, bagel (petrified, of course), *challah*, etc. As scholars, they are asked to identify the uses of the object: what it is, what it means, how it was used, how it happened not to deteriorate. Among other things they should consider the age of the object, the period it came from, the place where it was found, the day, date, and century of the "excavation," what other objects it was associated with, what kind of person created it, whether it was revered in any way, etc.

Each group is to research and discover as much as possible about its object and write a report for the sponsoring organization. Yes, even name the organization, something like "The Intelligence Service of Jewish Antiquities."

Create a Synagogue Guidebook

This is an excellent closure for a study unit on the synagogue. Bring in a selection of guidebooks so that the students can familiarize themselves with the type of information provided by a guidebook. Their task will be to design a guidebook for their synagogue. As a class, they are to decide on a format. Do some brainstorming, making a list of all the unique features of the synagogue. Include some of its history as well. Organize the list into sections and decide on the order in which the guidebook will present information. Divide the class into small groups, assign a section of the synagogue to each group, and have the students develop their assigned portion of the guidebook, writing the text and illustrating it. When the groups finish, compile the sections in the proper order. The class can give the completed book to the president of the congregation.

The World around Us: Social Problems, Current Events

Are today's young people sufficiently aware of what is taking place in the world around them? For this activity you will need a piece of butcher paper 15–20 feet long, colored markers, magazines and newspapers, scissors, and glue.

Discuss some of the social problems prevalent in society today. Ask the students to do some brainstorming, listing all the social problems they can. Have them go through the magazines and newspapers, cutting out pictures and articles that represent the social problems. Roll out the butcher paper and have the students make a mural of the social problems they have identified. They can draw pictures or write about any problem for which there is no picture or article. Place the words *Social Problems* at the top of the butcher paper, leaving room on the mural for potential solutions and what Judaism says about such problems. Upon completion of this part of the mural, mount it on the wall.

Taking one problem at a time, have the students do some research to see what Judaism has to say about it. How does the Jewish tradition tackle the problem? Post their findings on the mural under the appropriate heading. Do some more brainstorming with the students, listing ways this problem can be solved. Try to have them propose solutions in which they could eventually become involved. Let them decide which is the best solution or combination of solutions. Talk about ways they can be personally involved. As a closure, have the students choose a project aimed at helping to solve one of the social problems.

Note: Do not expect to go through the entire mural in one session. Ask the students to discuss the problems with their parents and get ideas from them about solutions. They can even interview people in the field of social work to see what the community is doing to solve the problems. This lesson may take several sessions, depending on how long your list is, but it certainly will help the students to become more aware of their world and what they can do about it, not only as human beings, but as Jews.

Preserving the World: Our Environment

Ask the students to pretend they are going to live together in a house served by a small generator that can make only enough power for three electrical appliances. Divide the class into small groups. The members of each group are to decide which three appliances they would choose. Upon completion, list each group's choices on the board, then have the whole class choose three from the group lists. Talk about the choices: What makes these appliances so important? What other alternatives are there for cooking, lighting, entertainment, etc.? Finally, how does conserving energy help to preserve our environment? Relate this phase of the discussion to the Jewish tradition of *tikun olam*.

Another Form of Tzedakah

Teaching the art of giving is not always easy. Nowadays *tzedakah* has come to mean giving a monetary donation. Yet we need to teach young people that giving of oneself is the greatest gift of all. Try this activity when you want to change the emphasis from giving money to giving of oneself. Put the following poem, "The Gift" by Greta B. Lipson, on the blackboard or on newsprint, large enough for everyone to see:

> The most precious gift,
> I am told,
> is all the love
> the heart can hold.
> I give it to you,

You give it to me—
There's enough for the world,
and the gift is free.
Will you take my love—
More precious than gold?
It's the finest gift
That the heart can hold.

Discuss the meaning of *tzedakah* in relation to the poem. What does the poem say is the true meaning of giving? What are the differences between material gifts, things purchased with money, and the gift of ourselves? Which gift has more meaning? Which provides more pleasure, is more satisfying? What kind of gift is more lasting, more enduring: the one purchased or the gift of self? Have the students list all the different ways they can give of themselves. From their lists, ask them to choose one or two gifts (of time, money, labor, etc.) they can give and to whom they will give them. Have them share the results of their gifts along with their feelings about giving.

A VARIETY OF IDEAS FOR ANY TOPIC

NEAT AND SIMPLE

Write a Drawing

Something different: when giving a reading assignment, ask the students to do their reports in the form of a picture. It might be easier to make some notes on the reading, then, based on a theme they choose, draw a picture that represents what they have read.

Making Murals

Just because the kids are older doesn't mean they don't like to be creative. Divide the class into small groups. Give each group a different reading assignment on your unit of study. Once they have read the assignment, they are to create a mural to convey its major message. Have the drawing materials ready for them (butcher paper or posterboards, colored markers or crayons) and space to work. Note: there will always be those who say they can't draw. Remind them that we are not looking for great masterpieces; the important thing is the message they convey. Have the members of each group share their work, describing the drawing and what it means. Mount the murals on the wall.

Book Reports

Writing book reports can be a bore! (And a chore!) Encourage students to read, but when you give a reading assignment, let them demonstrate what they have learned in other ways than by writing a book report. Here are just a few ideas:

Create a collage.

Write a poem.

Prepare a dramatic skit.

Prepare a slide presentation.

Write an original short story about a favorite character.

Create a picture book.

Prepare a lesson to teach the subject matter.

Design a scavenger hunt through the book for other students.

Write a letter to the author stating what was liked or disliked about the book, giving an opinion of the characters, discussing ways the book could have been different, and anything else that seems important.

Stretching Their Minds

Don't ever forget that our kids are smart! In the classroom we need to challenge them to think and stretch their minds, and not spoonfeed them! Working in small groups they can make lists. Reading and discussing one another's lists will be almost as stimulating as making the lists. Here are a few ideas:

List all the parts of the Passover seder.

List all the parts of the Shabbat evening worship service.

List all the Jewish holidays.

List at least 10 cities in Israel.

List all the books in the Bible.

List at least 12 Jewish symbols.

An added dimension would be to add to each item on the list, as appropriate, its meaning, location, summary of content, etc.

Descriptions

Bring in a good number of *large* pictures, books, and objects related to your unit of study. Place the pictures, books, and objects around the room. You will also need a lot of newspapers and magazines, glue, plain paper, and scissors.

Ask the students to each select one of the items on display, keeping their choices to themselves. Pass out the old newspapers, magazines, and other materials. The students are to find at least 20 words which describe the object they chose, on the basis of which their classmates will be able to try and guess what it is. The words are to be cut out of the newspapers/magazines and glued on the plain paper. Give a specific time to complete this by, then have the students exchange papers and try to identify what is described on the papers they receive.

Talk about: Why did you choose that particular item? How did you decide how to describe it?

Attention!

Sprinkle a little fun into the day's activities and catch the attention of the students. Chose one to five words and write them on the board. Tell the class that sometime during the morning you will be using these words. Whoever hears you say one of them is to stand up. The first person to stand up will win a privilege or prize (something simple). Select words from such areas as:

Words you want the students to learn.

Hebrew words to learn for the day.

Words important to the lesson.

Names of people you want the students to know.

Turnabout Is Fair Play

Instead of you asking the questions, have the students ask them, and see if they can stump the teacher. Give the students a reading assignment. Tell them to prepare questions to ask you. The goal will be to try and stump you with a question you cannot answer.

IN THE BAG

Place an object in a paper bag. Tell the students something about the object, but not what it is. They are to ask questions that can be answered yes or no. See if they can identify the object in less than 15 questions.

WHAT'S WRONG?

Prepare a picture of a scene from which something is missing or of an object that has something missing or broken. Students are to develop a list of questions they would ask to find out what is wrong. Then have them prepare a list of possible solutions: how it can be repaired, how what's missing or wrong could be found or replaced.

Writing in Code

Write a paragraph that includes a topic you intend to be the major part of your lesson. Write it out first to be sure you are including everything you want to say—keep it short! Then type it out using the following code (or any other code you design): 1 = a, 2 = r, 3 = e, 4 = o. Use the numbers in place of these letters. Here is a sample:

The well-known baseball player Pete Rose was sent to jail for cheating on his income taxes. The question which has been raised by many has been: Can Pete Rose still be considered for the Baseball Hall of Fame if he is a convicted felon? We now know that he cannot be voted in.

Th3 w3ll-kn4wn b1s3b1ll pl1y32 p3t3 24s3 w1s s3nt t4 j1il f42 ch31ting 4n his inc4m3 t1x3s. Th3 qu3sti4n which h1s b33n r1is3d by m1ny h1s b33n: C1n P3t3 24s3 still b3 c4nsid323d f42 th3 b1s3b1ll h1ll 4f f1m3 if h3 is 1 c4nvict3d f3l4n? W2 n4w kn4w th1t h2 c1nn4t b2 v4t2d in.

After the students decipher the message, have them discuss the question.

Before a Lesson: What Do They Already Know?

Students know more than we think, and often we don't give them credit for it. Here are a few activities that you can do before a lesson or reading assignment to see what they know.

CHOSEN TOPIC

Announce what the subject matter will be. Divide the class into small groups and give each a few index cards. Tell the students to develop a list which tells what they already know about the subject matter. Allow 3 minutes. Have students read their lists and write them on the blackboard. Discuss the information they know and how it relates to the material you will be covering. As the students read the material, have them make a list of new information they have gained from the reading, i.e., what they didn't know before. Share these new lists.

ANOTHER OPTION

Give out paper and have the students divide it into three sections. Head one section *K* (Know), the second, *W* (questions they Want answered), and the third, *L* (new information Learned). Announce what the subject will be. Do some brainstorming, and have the students list in the first column whatever they already know about the subject. In the second column, have them list questions they want answered. Have them read the assignment and then list in the third column what they have learned that they didn't know before. If any questions from the second column haven't been answered from what they have read, take some time to go over them and find the answers.

Create a Story: Bulletin Board

Cover your bulletin board space with white paper. Draw lines on it to make the board look like a student's writing paper. Bring in small pictures of items related to your unit of study. On the bulletin board, mount the pictures in various places on the lines. Spread them out so there is room for the students to put the sentences they will write to create the story.

Have the students choose partners, and give each pair several sentence strips. They are to write sentences which incorporate the pictures. The sentences must make sense and tell a brief story. The groups will have to work together to create a story theme which goes with the pictures, then create their story. It would be best for the students to write out their sentences on plain paper, working together to create the story line, then transfer them to the sentence strips.

Make a Book

On the board write a list of words related to your unit of study. Give out plain white paper, one sheet per student for each word. Students are to place one word on the top of each piece of paper. Below it, they are to write a short sentence which describes what it means. Under the sentence, they are to draw a picture which shows that they understand the meaning of the word and its impact on the Jewish heritage. The completed pages can be placed in a folder after the students have shared their work. Add to the "book" as your unit continues.

Creative Writing: Making Use of Old Filmstrips

Some schools have old filmstrips with outdated scripts. Choose a filmstrip related to your unit of study. Providing no script or commentary, ask the class to watch it carefully and think of ideas for a script to go with each scene. As the students watch, they can jot their ideas down. After the first showing, have the students share their ideas. Do some brainstorming to determine which ideas would be the most effective. The students may want to watch the filmstrip again before they finalize their script. They can then make any additions, changes, or corrections as necessary. Be sure to thank them for their efforts, for now you have a new and creative script to go with an old filmstrip, and the kids have performed a mitzvah while they were learning!

Comic Strips

Students can create their own comic books! Ask them to bring in their favorite comic strips from the Sunday paper, or you can bring some in for the class. White out the captions with correction fluid. Make copies of the comics, distribute, and ask the students to create new captions to go with them. The new captions can cover a Jewish concept or tell a story based on what the class has learned.

Complete the Story

This activity is a good lesson closure. Prepare sheets with the beginning and ending words of a paragraph. Leave enough space between beginning and end for no more than five sentences, drawing lines on the page so that the students will know how much to write. It could look something like this:

The sun turned the Dome golden _____

_____

_____

_____

_____all the faiths that claim Jerusalem as theirs.

Alphabet Poetry

This activity is also a good closure for a unit of study. Divide the class into small groups. Prepare a list of topics from your unit. One-word topics lend themselves well to this kind of poetry (e.g., Israel, Jerusalem, Holocaust, peace, *Shema*).

Use the traditional arrangement of the ABCs for a framework where the writer can choose the topic, select words that capture its essence, and arrange them in alphabetical order. The groups will need dictionaries, and the students will have to do a lot of brainstorming. Encourage them to search for strong, colorful words to describe the subject. This will be a free verse activity to encourage creativity. Remember, though, that the verse must make sense, and do not specify any number of words per line. Here is an example of what can be done with Jerusalem:

> Ageless, big, charismatic,
>
> dynastic, everlasting, famous,
>
> gentle, hallmark, idyllic, Jewish,
>
> keystone, laudable, magnetic, noble, old,
>
> peaceful, quaint, radiates, schmaltzy,
>
> tenacious, unique, vibrant, wonderful,
>
> exceptional, yellow, zestful. (Yes, you can take poetic license with spelling!)

Commercials

Our students know a lot about TV and are well aware of the commercials. Some commercials are cute and humorous, some serious, even educational, while others are just plain dumb, offensive, and even irritating. Probably the most popular commercials, though, are those which are humorous and entertaining. Commercials, of course, are made to sell a product or service. Well, we have something to sell, too! This activity can be used as a closure for a unit of study.

Begin with a short discussion of commercials. Let the students talk about their favorites, and the ones they consider most dumb or most offensive. It is important for them to identify the ones they don't like so they will be aware of what won't sell as well as what will.

Divide the class into small groups. The members of each group are to decide what Jewish product or service they want to sell. To avoid duplications, have someone from each group write its topic on the board. Working together, the group members create their own commercials, which can include any of the following: singing, dancing, art, poetry, straight talk, or any combination thereof. Each person in the group must have a part in the presentation. Remind the students that commercials are short, sweet, and to the point, so the ones they produce should be no longer than 60 seconds (which would cost a bundle!).

Successive Stories

This is also a closure which involves creativity and total class participation. It can be used to see if the students understand the concept of historical events.

In successive stories, also called progressive stories, the teacher begins the narration; at a logical changing point, one of the students takes over, and the progression continues through the whole class. One good way would be to follow the usual seating order, or have the students sit around you in a circle. Set a specific time limit for each student, about 30–40 seconds. The story can take any turn the narrator wants it to, but additions to the story must make sense and be part of the subject matter. Narrators can add characters if they wish, but have to keep the old ones in mind.

Incomplete Sentences

After completing a unit of study, prepare paper strips with incomplete sentences related to it. The incomplete sentences should be thought-provoking; a good way to achieve this is for there to be more than one possible completion: e.g., "The Holocaust happened because _____." Prepare at least one or two incomplete sentences for every two students in the class. Working in pairs, the students select one or two strips from a box. Each pair of students is to come up with two ways to complete the sentences. The students share their responses and discuss the different completed sentences to determine which was the most viable.

HELPFUL HINTS

CLASSROOM MANAGEMENT

Cooperative Learning

Years ago, working with large groups of students, I learned that much more could be accomplished with small groups. I divided the large group into small groups of four to eight, the size depending on the task to be completed and the total number of students. Each group included a good mix of high achievers and low achievers. (The low achievers were not low achievers in the usual sense of the term, but students who didn't want to be there or who were goof-offs.) In the small-group situation, the high achievers presented a challenge to the low achievers to participate and do their part. The low achievers wanted to look good in the eyes of their peers. Those who were in the middle, I found, followed the example of the others and did their parts as well. Each group was given a specific task, with instructions that everyone must be involved. At times I spelled out the specific task that each person was to do. The results: students worked together, their work was creative, and they took responsibility for their own learning. Problems? Yes, there were times that I goofed on group assignments, and there were personality conflicts. In these instances I challenged the students to work out their differences.

Today, cooperative learning is used extensively in the classroom. If you decide to use this technique, here are a few tips to keep in mind:

1. Every group needs a leader. All group members should be assigned roles and be responsible for specific tasks. It is important to rotate the different roles so that everyone has a chance at each of them.

2. Every member of the group should be responsible for learning a specific topic and then teaching it to the others. This makes each member a peer tutor responsible for a portion of the work.

3. For review: Each group chooses a spokesperson; you ask review questions and the group members discuss the best possible answer. The spokesperson delivers the answer the whole group has decided upon.

4. Let each group choose a name for itself and design an attractive poster to hang in the area of the room in which it will be working. The members can design a logo that goes with the name and include it in the poster.

5. In organizing groups, begin with your most difficult students and form the groups around them. Depending on the situation, "most difficult" could mean: doesn't want to be there; isn't interested in anything being done; knows it all; usually isn't cooperative; is more socially inclined; etc.

6. Groups are not etched in stone. They can be changed after a few sessions if you see that they are not working out.

7. Try having the kids provide their own grouping suggestions or preferences (Ask: Whom do you want to sit next to? Whom do you not want to sit next to? Whom can you work with? Whom can you not work with? etc.). Take some time, outside of school, to read over their requests; make up your groups based on the lists and your sense of the class and its group dynamics.

8. Reaching consensus is an important aspect of group dynamics. Here is a simple exercise to help students learn how to reach consensus. After the groups are formed, have the members design group posters following these rules explicitly:

   Everyone must have a say about the design.

   Everyone must agree to every decision.

   Anyone who objects to a decision should not be pressured to agree.

9. Groups need rules. To begin, do some brainstorming with the whole class about the problems that may be encountered while working in groups. One frequently voiced objection is: "I don't want just a few members doing all the work." A rule will be necessary to handle this problem.

10. If you wish, have each group develop its own set of rules and then share them with the whole class. Write all the rules down in categories on the board. Eliminate or condense overlapping, combine some, and reach consensus with the whole class as to the final version of the rules for all the groups.

Additional Pointers on Cooperative Learning Groups

The use of small groups has been refined in the years since I began teaching. In my discussions of teaching ideas, I always recommend dividing the class into small groups. Learning groups are not just for the upper grades, they can also be used in the lower grade levels. The next section offers some more tips on working with small groups.

FORMING GROUPS

Carefully structured groups are the key to successful cooperative learning. Keep the following in mind when dividing your class into groups:

1. In the lower grade levels, start with pairs or trios. Try groups of four in the middle and upper grades.

2. Aim for mixed-ability groups. Remember to mix high and low achievers. Make sure there are boys and girls in each group.

ASSIGNING ROLES

Role assignments encourage children to do their fair share and feel a part of the group effort. Regularly rotating the role assignments helps keep the kids from falling into their natural behaviors (e.g., being the leader, being the shy one). Instead, everyone gets a chance to experience each kind of role. With defined roles, each group's success hinges on the participation of all its members.

Roles will vary according to the task the children are assigned, but common roles and responsibilities include:

Recorder: Writes down the group's different ideas.

Spokesperson: Shares the group's ideas with the class and answers questions provided by the group.

Timekeeper: Helps the group budget the time allotted for the task.

Materials manager: Collects the materials needed for the task.

Reader: Reads the directions to the group.

Checker: Confirms that everyone in the group agrees with and supports the answers or products.

Encourager: Encourages active participation by all group members and praises all contributions.

Or the group roles could look something like this:

Leader: Gives direction and sees that everyone follows through on assignments.

Reader: Does research and provides necessary information to complete the task.

Task manager: Sees that all members do their parts in completing the task.

Presenter: When the task is completed, makes presentation to the class.

You can assign roles in different ways. Some teachers ask group members to count off from one to four and then distribute the roles randomly. Other teachers use a wall chart, posting cards with students' names on them beside each task and rotating the cards every few weeks.

BEFORE YOU BEGIN

Arrange your classroom furniture so that each group will have a shared work space. This may simply mean assigning each group to a table of its own, or it may involve moving several desks together to form an island.

Decide on a signal to get everyone's full attention and let the class know when it is getting too noisy. (In my opinion, noise usually indicates that everyone is fully involved in the activity, but you will have to be the judge.) Suitable signals include ringing a bell and flashing the lights.

ASSESSING YOUR SUCCESS

There are several ways to assess how well cooperative learning is working in your classroom.

1. Use a checklist to monitor how well the groups are functioning. Are the members taking turns? Being tolerant? Persevering to complete a task?

2. Ask the group members to use markers of different colors when completing written work with the group. This will enable you to assess individual knowledge levels and whether or not the task has been shared equally.

3. Use a checklist to have the students assess how well they are getting along. Include such questions as: Did all the group members perform their assigned roles? Did everyone contribute ideas? Older children can circle *always*, *sometimes*, or *never*. Younger ones can draw a smiling face or a frowning face.

BUILDING GROUP SKILLS

As you begin to use cooperative learning groups, you will find the following activities helpful in building the youngsters' "people skills":

Name the group: Invite the groups to choose names for themselves. Ask that every member contribute ideas and agree on the final choice. Insist that the names be positive. Afterward, ask the groups to create a cheer or song to introduce the group's name and members to the class.

Create a group symbol: Discuss the idea of having a symbol to represent each group. Give the group members 5 minutes to create a group symbol which everyone agrees upon.

Create a collage: Have the group members interview each other to learn something new they didn't know before. Then have them create a collage to introduce the group and its members to the rest of the class.

Here are a few examples of what you can do with your class when working in cooperative learning groups:

Bible: The Essence of Judaism

This activity is for groups of four.

> Rabbi Simlai said: "Six hundred and thirteen commands were given to Moses on Mount Sinai. The essence of these commands was distilled by David [in the Book of Psalms] into eleven....Isaiah condensed them into six, Micah into three, Amos into one....[and also] Habakkuk into one." (*Makkot* 23b)

For your information, the biblical passages referred to can be found in Psalms 15:1–5, Isaiah 33:15, Micah 6:8, Amos 5:4, and Habakkuk 2:4.

Give the following instructions:

1. Take one of the above-mentioned passages from Psalms, Isaiah, Micah, Amos, or Habakkuk and list what it treats as the essence of Judaism.

2. Compare your list with those made by the other members of your group and see what ideas they have in common.

3. Make a personal list of the ideas or traits that you regard as the essence of Judaism today.

4. Share your list with the other group members. By reaching consensus, make up a composite list.

5. Finally, with the other group members, prepare a presentation to the class to share what you have learned and what you consider to be the essence of Judaism.

Tzedakah and the Synagogue

1. Each group of four students receives $1,000. Let's pretend that it is "bonus" money from your synagogue's fund-raising event. (Don't we wish!)

2. Assign each group a specific area in the synagogue where this money can be spent (e.g., adult education, religious school, caring community, synagogue building).

3. The members of each group are to research the needs of the assigned area, dividing the research among themselves, with specific tasks assigned to each student (e.g., interviewing the rabbi, members of various synagogue committees, and members of the congregation). They might also investigate what is new in the field that the synagogue does not have.

4. The group is to identify the benefits to the school/congregation based on what the members have discovered from their research.

5. Each group prepares a presentation outlining what the members

wish to spend the funds on, the reasons for this expenditure, and the benefits to be derived.

Israel

The study of Israel lends itself very well to cooperative learning. Each group can be given a specific subject area to research (e.g., government, agriculture, geography, religions, historical sites, cities). Within each specific area there are several sub-areas that can be divided among the group members. For example:

Government: political parties, Knesset, national organizations

Agriculture: crops, kibbutzim, moshavim, locations, exports

Geography: Galilee, Negev, Golan Heights, Judean Desert

Religions: Judaism (divided into different denominations), Christianity, Islam, Druse

Historical sites: Western Wall, Tel Dan, Masada, Megiddo

Cities: Jerusalem, Haifa, Tel Aviv, Safed (assign one city to each group; within the group, divide the city into separate subject areas, e.g., geography, population, historical sites, religion, government)

After the group members complete their research and gather all the necessary information, have them prepare a presentation to share what they have learned with the rest of the class. Let them use any medium they feel comfortable with, including such formats as newspapers, TV shows, radio shows, posters, murals, travel brochures, etc.

READING ASSIGNMENTS

Haven't Had Time to Plan a Lesson?

If you are unable to prepare a lesson in advance, divide the class into small groups and give a reading assignment. Give each group a different task based on the reading. Here are some examples:

1. Create a 3-minute skit which covers the highlights of the text.

2. Choose an important Jewish concept from the text and create a poster that conveys its message.

3. Write a short biography of an important person in the text.

4. Develop a radio or TV news broadcast based on information from the text.

Reading or Book Reports

Instead of assigning a book report or any kind of research reading or report activity, try giving your class some of the activities listed below. These activities are suitable for use with readings of many kinds, including chapters from your textbook and portions from the Torah. When asking for a product from your students, open the options to as many possibilities as you can.

1. Imagine that you are a Broadway dramatist. What story scenes would you create for a play, and what story scenes would you eliminate? Be sure to include the reasons for your choices.

2. Create a Twenty Questions game to play with the class based upon what you have learned from the assignment.

3. Create a comic strip based on the reading assignment.

4. Tell how the story would be changed if one of the main characters was eliminated.

5. Create a board game of the story's plot and explain how it relates to the story.

6. Build three or more shoebox settings of the story. Explain the impact of each setting on the story.

7. Make magazine collages of the main characters. Explain each character's relationship to the story.

8. Create a crossword puzzle or word search of the story elements. Explain your choice of words.

9. Describe the boring sections of the reading assignment.

10. List 10 words that are important to the story. Tell why they are so important.

11. Write a one-page summary of the story. On another page, write what you wanted to add to the page but couldn't. Explain why you left that information out.

12. Write a short chapter to follow the last chapter in order to change the story's ending or as an epilogue.

13. Assume the role of one of the main characters and tell the story from that character's point of view.

14. Create a mobile of the story. Utilize parts of the mobile to represent characters, settings, conflict, and the resolution of the conflict.

15. Come up with three endings that differ from the original.

16. Imagine that the story has been made into a movie. Design and write an ad about it for a newspaper.

17. Do a mock TV broadcast about one or more of the major incidents in the reading assignment.

18. Write a seven-day diary that one of the main characters might have written.

19. Imagine you could interview the book's author. List five questions you would ask and give the responses you would expect.

Making Reading Assignments More Fun

Whether the reading is a short story, a chapter in a history text, or a portion of the Bible, here are some activities that can enhance the assignment. Choose whatever best fits the reading materials.

Have the students—

List similarities between Jewish life then and today.

Choose two characters, list their differences and similarities, and describe their feelings.

Describe what they would do to help the person caught in the situation in the story.

Make a list of words used to describe the situation, setting, mood, characters, etc. Write their own descriptions of the situation.

Describe what they would have done if they were in the same situation.

Describe or draw a picture of a gift for the main character and the reasons for giving it.

Rewrite the title of the chapter or story, giving reasons for the choice.

Write a letter from one character to another that will make the other character feel better or explain the first character's attitude toward the situation in the story.

Keep an imaginary daily diary for one character which explains the incidents in the story and the character's reactions.

Make a list of questions to use in interviewing the main character, or any character.

Give details about a character to be added and what impact this new character would have on the story.

Develop a character's history *before* the story takes place, including incidents in the character's life that might have had an impact on actions in the story.

Create a play based on the material and act it out.

Tape their favorite part of the story with sound effects.

Develop a time line based on events in the story.

Create a TV commercial to sell the story's main idea.

Develop a comic book based on the material.

Use a roll of white shelf paper to draw a series of pictures which tell the major events in the story.

Make puppets based on the story and use them to tell about a major incident in the story.

Become news reporters and design the front page of a newspaper account of something that happens in the story.

Become movie critics and review the material as if it were a movie.

Develop a word-search puzzle with words from the story.

On white butcher paper, create a mural which tells about the story.

Create a children's book based on the story, with illustrations, for younger readers.

Design a collage with pictures from magazines to tell the story.

Plan a group trip to the location of the story, designing travel brochures, etc.

Keep a list of the most interesting new words in the story.

Make illustrations of the most interesting aspects of the story.

List what has been learned from the story.

Write a poem about the story.

Write an ad promoting the story.

ANOTHER APPROACH

When giving a reading assignment, include specific activities based on the text. For example:

List the feelings described in the reading material. Describe what happened when you had similar feelings. Pretend you are a character in the story; write a letter to a relative or friend, explaining how you dealt with these feelings.

List the reasons why some characters in the story are liked and others disliked. List the important and unimportant reasons why people like you.

Pretend you are one of the characters, even dressing the part. Act out the role, explaining who you are and what you do in the story.

Rewrite favorite parts of the story as a short play. Get some classmates to take part and direct them as they act it out.

Design a cover for the material. At the bottom of your cover, explain the reason for your choice of design.

Before reading the assignment, draw a picture of what evil looks like. Describe, in writing, the forms evil might take. After reading the assignment, discuss the form evil takes in the story, as well as the differences and similarities between good and evil in the story.

Before reading the assignment, predict the outcome. (There are no right or wrong answers here, but the students must be able to justify their answers.) After reading the material, discuss the outcome and compare it to your prediction.

In addition to these activities, here are some questions for discussion:

Was there a character in the story much like you? In what way?

Was there a character who was not like you? In what way?

Did anything happen in the story that you would like to have happen to you? What are your reasons?

Was there a subject in the story you would like to know more about? What was it? Why do you want to know more about it? Where would you go to research it?

Bloom's Taxonomy

Use the following ideas when giving reading assignments. They dovetail with Bloom's taxonomy of asking questions to encourage creative thinking skills. The ideas can be written on index cards, using different colors or colored dots to designate the different categories. There are enough ideas here for each student to follow a different approach. This will make it possible for the students to share ideas about the reading material. If the students all have different reading assignments, give them several tasks to perform. Be sure that the tasks go from the simple to the more thought-provoking.

Actions taken: These tell you something about the incident. Describe an action taken and explain why it was taken.

Change: Incidents that take place often cause change. Describe what change has taken place.

Where and when: Identify the place and time of your story and how you determined this information.

Main idea: In one sentence describe the whole story: who, what, when, where, and why.

Order of the story: What was the sequence of events? Make a list, in the proper order, of at least five things that happened in the story.

What will happen: Read part of the story, then make a list of what you think will take place. Also list the clues that helped you with your guesses. Finish reading. How many right guesses did you make?

Between the lines: Draw a picture of your favorite character or of the most exciting/important incident. Read between the lines and tell as much as you can about the kind of person the character is or about the effects of the incident.

Before you read: Read the title, look at the pictures, make a list of what you think the material is about. When finished reading, think about how the story could continue after the ending. Write a short paragraph as an epilogue.

What do you think? Give your reasons for liking or disliking the main character. Were you satisfied with the way the story ended? How would you have ended it? What changes would you make in it?

Right or wrong: List some of the facts in the story. Next to each fact, write what you think about it.

What happens next? (1) Describe an incident in the story, explaining why it occurred and its effect on the story/Jewish people. (2) List the things or ideas that are important to the main character. Next to each, tell what the character does about it and what event or person influenced the character to think this way.

Purpose of the author: Briefly state why the author wrote this material, explaining how you arrived at this conclusion.

And here is one more idea about how to utilize reading assignments:

Divide the class into small groups. Give each group at least five questions on the reading material. After reading the assignment, the members of each group discuss their answers, arrive at a consensus, and decide on the best way to present their information (e.g., poster, song, poetry, radio or TV news broadcast, drama).

IDEAS FOR CLASSROOM MANAGEMENT

Disruptive Students

A student who is disruptive should be taken aside and "privately" asked:

What are you doing?

Is it helping you?

Is it against the rules?

How will you change it?

Have the student write a plan for change, then set times to review the student's progress.

When it comes to discipline, involve the students in decision-making. Let a student who is a behavior problem make a list of possible alternative behaviors.

Classroom Rules

If you do not have classroom rules, try some, but only if the students have a hand in developing them. To begin, write on the board two rules you want, e.g., *Be respectful* and *Be a good listener*. Explain that rules are needed to create a positive learning atmosphere. These are the two you want; point to them. Then brainstorm with the class to identify the rules the students want. Vote for the final list, not more than ten, including your two. Post the list in a prominent place.

Staff-Support Groups: Breakfast Time

Even supplementary schools that meet just once a week need to have teachers get together on a regular basis. During this meeting time, problems can be discussed, teaching successes can be shared, the rabbi can offer a study session, and the staff has an opportunity to shmooze. Remember, when one teacher has a problem, sometimes others can offer solutions; and what works for one, can work for all with a bit of adaptation.

Everyone's time is precious, but once-a-month "breakfast" meetings before religious school, lasting from 45 minutes to an hour, can do wonders for morale, strengthening and uniting the members of the teaching staff. In large schools, teachers can be divided into teams that take turns providing the food, keeping it simple, or perhaps the sisterhood/brotherhood could take it on as a project. Increase interest (and attendance) by having a raffle or drawing for a prize at each meeting.

Students Control Their Actions

Give the students a chance to take control of their own actions. Designate one chair in your room as a "select" chair. Tell the students they can "select" to sit in it if they feel they are losing control and are about to break a rule. Do some brainstorming with the class to identify situations where someone might need to sit in the chair to calm down and decide how to handle a situation. This is similar to a "time-out" chair, but here the student *chooses* to sit in the chair.

The "Grumpy" Seat

Designate a chair in the room as the "grumpy" seat, to be used whenever a child feels sad, blue, or grumpy. Sitting in the special chair may help the child to feel better. It is also wise to privately find out the reasons for the child's mood and make an effort to ease the pain, no matter what it is. The chair should be available at all times, and a child should be allowed to remain in it as long as necessary to feel better.

The Peaceful Classroom

Designate a table or space in your classroom as a place where children know they will be heard and understood. Create simple rules like:

Everyone, including the teacher, must touch the table/space before speaking.

No one can come to the table/space and say what has already been said.

When a conflict arises, the teacher is the moderator. Children involved in the conflict come to the peace table/space and tell what happened in their own words. Anyone in the class can add to the presentation of the problem. After all points of view have been covered, ail the children in the class have the opportunity to offer suggestions about how to solve the problem. The teacher, as moderator, need accept only real solutions. Thus, if a child says, "They should be nice to each other," the teacher might say, "How could they do that?" The teacher restates the alternatives, but never tells the children what to do. They must solve the problem on their own. The children are to be praised as "peace-makers" when the problem is solved.

Classroom Tips

Visual Appeal

Bring in props, pictures, models, artifacts, souvenirs, and mock-ups to enhance your lesson.

Interest

During lessons keep interest high by varying the tone of your voice, maintaining eye contact, and focusing on facts and ideas that students care about.

Simplicity

During lessons emphasize basic concepts and state them in easy-to-understand terms.

Involvement

Get kids involved in the lesson by asking questions that encourage thinking and participation. They like to talk about themselves, so make your questions personal.

Time

Gear your lesson to the attention span of the class. Watch for such signals as fidgeting, stretching, and talking. All these are indications that it's time to move on to a new idea or teaching approach.

Spontaneity

Be flexible! When questions arise or the class gets excited about a particular point in the lesson, be flexible enough to grasp the moment. At the same time, be flexible enough to change the topic, or lesson plan, if the class shows a lack of interest in the subject matter.

Student Responsibility

Encourage students to take some responsibility for their own learning. Instead of making the usual demand that they complete a specific task by a certain time, give them some choices. With the students, develop a list of topics from your unit of study that they would like to investigate. Then do some brainstorming with them to come up with a list of intriguing and developmentally appropriate activities. Let the students choose a topic and activity. Together with them, decide how much time the project/task will need. The students now have ownership of the project and are responsible for its completion.

Classroom Responsibilities

Students of all ages need opportunities to be involved in implementing classroom responsibilities. For example:

1. Instead of just collecting for Keren Ami, let the students form a committee to research and identify potential recipients. They could even present their findings and recommendations to the entire school.

2. Form a committee to search out materials and information needed for a class project.

3. Let the class help plan field trips.

4. Organize clean-up of the room after class.

This is just the beginning of a list of things that children can do in the classroom. As they work together, these activities will help to build a sense of community.

Getting to Know Your Students

Develop a class "Yellow Pages" book. Prepare a simple questionnaire to give the students an opportunity to tell you something about their capabilities. Include such things as sports, games, crafts, and hobbies; can they sing, act, or dance? Categorize the information from the questionnaires into a Yellow Pages format, even cross-referencing. When it is complete, you will know more about the ability of your students, and they will have a resource when they need an artist, a musician, or whatever, for a specific project.

Ideas to Enhance Your Classroom

1. Giving a test? Give the students the answers and let them provide the questions.

2. Gather together a collection of puzzles, mazes, brainteasers, crossword puzzles, connect-the-dots, hidden pictures, anagrams, word searches, etc. Let the students work in pairs to solve them, and you can circulate around the room offering hints and support.

3. Having trouble hanging things up? Place a strip of self-adhesive Velcro fastening tape on the wall. Put small pieces of the corresponding Velcro tape on your posters and notices, and attach to the strip on the wall.

4. Keep track of teaching tips and new ideas by organizing them under specific topic headings, e.g., *Classroom management and organization, Games, Holidays*, etc. Write, paste, staple the ideas on looseleaf pages and keep in a binder. To protect them, insert them inside clear plastic pages, available at any office supply store. The clear plastic will show both sides of the page.

5. Store items like posters, maps, bulletin board displays, games, etc., for future use by organizing them in categories. Put items

in the same category in a plastic trash bag. The size used will, of course, depend on the size of the items being stored (very large items may require bags of their own). Label the bag and place on a wire hanger, securing it with clothespins. Hang in a closet for future use.

6. Need a circle? Just collect various sizes of plastic lids. Punch a hole in the center of each and slip it on a ring or ribbon. You will have circles handy for any time you need them.

7. Saving posters: If you can't laminate your poster, make it last longer by putting strips of masking tape *all around* the back of it—down both sides, top, bottom, and in the center. Make circles of masking tape and place these on the masking tape instead of on the poster when hanging.

8. Make individual chalkboards for your students. Just laminate a 12 x 14 piece of tagboard. This makes a very good substitute for a chalkboard and can be used over and over again. It can be written on with watercolor markers and erased easily with a damp cloth.

Working with Your Students

1. Challenge them. Encourage them to reach a little to learn. Young people are smarter than many adults think and quite capable of being creative, just give them the opportunity.

2. Make it relevant. The word *relevant* is often misused, but to really reach our young people we must synthesize the heritage of Judaism with their lives.

3. Be creative! Use as many different teaching techniques as you can to stimulate thinking.

Variety Is the "Spice" of the Classroom

When planning a lesson, consider the following factors:

The age of your students.

Their immediate needs.

A variety of learning styles.

Classroom atmosphere.

Your own teaching style.

Activities in the classroom should be varied and should appeal to the different learning styles of the students. You want to catch their attention *and* keep it throughout the lesson. If you use the same approach for each lesson, it soon becomes old hat, and the students will quickly lose interest. Use a broad range of techniques and methods to make each lesson an adventure! A lesson is usually composed of at least five different parts:

1. The opening (also known as the launching device, focusing, or set induction). Activity that helps students focus on the instructional objective. Whether a single word, a puzzle, staged props, a short movie, a riddle, etc., it should be quick, eye-catching, and thought-provoking.

2. The learning experience. Activity designed to enrich the students' Jewish competency. It could be a poem, Bible reading, midrash, music, movie, game, etc., that centers on the lesson of the day.

3. Sharing. Time for students to work in small groups, where learning can be enhanced by *doing*. This can include research, creative work, arts and crafts, etc.

4. Reviewing. Reinforcing and evaluating the learning experience. It can often be combined with the sharing time.

5. Closure. The end of the lesson, leaving the students thinking about the lesson completed.

Awards

Don't wait till the end of school to give out awards. Certificates and awards for academic accomplishments are very important and can be used all year long. They draw attention to the progress students are making and encourage others to praise and compliment them. Even very simple awards go a long way to help students feel good about themselves and the time they spend in religious school. Hebrew Grams and Simchah Grams are good formats for awards. Prepare them in advance, with blank spaces for the child's name, your signature, and a brief message. They can look something like this:

SIMCHAH GRAM

To _____

for _____

Teacher _____

Date _____

Or:

I am glad to announce that _____

has learned _____

Teacher _____

Date _____

In one corner place a gold seal and/or a red or blue ribbon to make it really look official.

Letters of Encouragement

Everyone likes to receive mail. You can give your kids some happy moments by just sending them letters of encouragement several times a year. These can be prepared ahead of time, leaving blank spaces for the child's name, what the child has accomplished, and your signature. Your letter could look something like this:

Dear _____
I just wanted you to know how proud I am of you. You have done such a grand job and are working hard. I am especially happy because you _____
Signed_____

Rules for Brainstorming

1. Defer all judgments. Students must feel free to speak up and encourage one another. See that they don't say things like "That's dumb" or "You can't do that."

2. List all ideas. Accept everything the students offer and write it on the board or newsprint, regardless of how far out it might be.

3. Encourage free-wheeling. Let the students call out anything that comes to mind.

4. Learn to spark or piggy-back on ideas. Expand on ideas already offered.

5. Aim for quantity, not quality. Daring to have an idea recorded is essential to the process. Encourage students to keep their ideas coming, including ideas that may seem impractical or fantasy-based.

6. Listen carefully. Careful listening allows for more piggy-backing and helps to create a cooperative atmosphere in the classroom.

7. Ask open-ended questions. Good questions motivate students to think creatively.

Teacher's Unique Opportunity

You may think that because you only have the children for a few hours a week, you don't really have much influence on them. The time you spend with them is actually very valuable. Just think for a moment: what you do or say can have a powerful effect! You can make the synagogue a place the children enjoy. Through you, the synagogue can become a safe haven where they feel good about themselves, a place where they want to be.

When you provide a supportive, encouraging climate in the classroom, you are giving the children a very positive experience. Here are some things you can do in your classroom to ensure that this takes place:

Show unconditional acceptance.

Follow the interest of the children instead of imposing your own ideas.

Encourage and challenge the children to try out their own ideas.

Be more concerned about the child than the subject.

Allow time for thinking, discovery, experimentation, playing with ideas.

Have a sense of humor.

Plan for individual differences.

Encourage learners to make their own judgments.

Provide a climate free from excessive competition, anxiety, or coercion.

Use a variety of teaching and learning methods.

Praise and affirm the child's self-worth.

Make the Religious School Classroom a Special Place

Children feel special when they are recognized in a positive manner and on special occasions. Here are some little things that will make your students feel special:

1. Prepare simple "sick day bags" for children who miss a day of school. Of course, you never really know whether a child is absent because of illness or for some other reason, but to be remembered by the teacher makes a child feel special. Use paper lunch bags and fill them with a few puzzles, riddles, paper games, pages to color, short stories to read, etc. Also include a "We missed you" card. Mail to the child. These bags can be prepared in advance and ready to use when needed.

2. Celebrate birthdays. Mark everyone's birthday on your calendar. At the class meeting nearest to the date, give the birthday child a special birthday hat (prepared in advance) to wear and tape a sign saying "Our Birthday Boy" or "Our Birthday Girl" to the child's chair. Have the whole class make a group birthday card: Just fold a piece of construction paper in half, and on the cover print an inscription, such as "Friends make birthdays special." Leave space to write the child's name. Invite everyone in the class to help decorate the cover and sign the card.

   And don't forget those with summer birthdays or whose birthdays fall on days when they are not in religious school. Have an "Unbirthday Party" to recognize these children!

3. Friendly tree. Encourage children to do or say something nice about their peers. If you can actually use a branch of a tree for this project, that's great; otherwise, draw a leafless tree on butcher paper and title it "The Friendly Tree." Cut out Jewish symbols from construction paper and print a friendly action on each, such as *Say something nice to someone, Smile at someone, Tell someone that he or she looks nice, Write a friendly note, Share something, Help a classmate*, etc. Punch a hole at the top of each symbol. Pair the children, and have each pair choose a symbol and perform the friendly action.

After performing the friendly action, the pair of children hang their symbol on the tree.

Expressing Feelings

Sometimes children find it difficult to express how they feel. This is usually because they don't know the right words to describe their feelings. Give them an opportunity to identify their feelings and understand what they are feeling. When you have completed a unit of study that involves feelings, give them a chance to learn how they feel. Compile a small booklet, using 8.5 x 14 paper folded in half, for everyone in the class; in addition, you will need magazines, glue, scissors, and crayons.

Have the children make and decorate covers for their "Picture Dictionaries of Feelings." At the top of each page, either you write or have them write words that describe feelings and moods, like *happy, sad, afraid, silly, angry, caring, serious, hopeful, joyful*, etc. Talk about what each word means, giving examples of what might evoke such feelings. Let the children share experiences that evoked such feelings. Then have them illustrate each emotion, either drawing original illustrations or cutting out pictures from magazines. The pages do not all have to be completed in one class session. Do a few each class, or when certain feelings are present during or after a study session.

Positive Self-Esteem

Helping children feel good about themselves is a step toward self-discipline and good classroom management. Children who feel good about themselves are ready to make friends and ready to work. It is well worth your time to devote a few minutes of the first few sessions to doing some self-esteem exercises. For example: Let each child take a turn in front of the class for two minutes. The others ask questions to find out more about the child. After the two minutes, everyone in the class writes a short paragraph which includes the information gathered and *only* positive statements about the child. Collect these sheets and staple them together. Give to the child to take home. Let each child have a turn in front of the class during the early weeks of school until everyone has had a turn.

Put Yourself in Your Students' Shoes

How would you feel if someone said the following things to you? Rank them on a numerical scale, with 1 indicating *upset*, 2, *sad*, 3, *OK*, 4, *happy*, and 5, *delighted!* Then think about why you might feel that way.

That's a nice job. You get 100%.

Don't ask questions! Just do what you're told.

I don't understand. Will you help?

This paper is a mess. Why are you so sloppy?

Copy this paper over. I know you are proud of your work when it is neat.

I can't talk to you right now, so go away. I'm busy.

I'm working right now, but if you wait a few minutes I'll be able to talk with you.

Stop and think for a minute! You have just put yourself in your students' shoes. Which statements made you feel good, and which ones bothered you? Children will react the very same way. Keep that in mind when you are working in the classroom.

Communication

Don't be afraid to use illustrations, including stick-person characters, arrows, and asterisks, on the instructions and assignments you give to the class. Illustrations draw attention to your message and increase readership as well as understanding. Media professionals say that people like graphics of this kind and regard them as friendly.

Teaching Music

How do you go about teaching music when your school lacks a music teacher and you can't sing? Here is a simple approach for teaching Jewish songs just by using tapes or CDs. Choose the song you wish the children to learn. For the first one keep it simple. Use a machine that has good volume so that the children can hear the music and words clearly. Tell the children to listen carefully to the song. Play the music once.

Spend a few minutes discussing what the song is about. Then play it again, this time asking the children to hum along—and you hum along too. Stop the music! *Say the words slowly, having the children repeat them after you.* Do this a few times until the children begin to know the words. If they can read, put the words on the board or on paper for them to follow along with you.

Now play the music again. This time have the children sing along with the music. Be sure to sing with the children, even if you can't carry a tune. Children like to see their teacher participating.

Asking the Right Questions

The use of thinking skills in teaching is an extremely valuable tool. Asking the right questions at the right time raises the level of learning that can take place. There are six levels of thinking, according to Bloom's taxonomy. They are listed here, beginning with the lowest.

Knowledge: Learning from information.

Clues: define, list, label, state, recall, name, who, what, where, when.

Comprehension: Understanding the information.

Clues: interpret, discuss, describe, explain, identify, report, illustrate.

Application: Using the information.

Clues: show, use, apply, practice, illustrate, demonstrate, classify.

Analysis: Examining specific parts of the information.

Clues: decode, classify, order, distinguish, compare, analyze.

Synthesis: Doing something new and different with the information.

Clues: create, improve, compose, design, change, reconstruct.

Evaluation: Judging the information.

Clues: judge, select, rank, evaluate, critique.

Using Leviticus 19 as a basis, here is an example of the level of questions to be asked:

Knowledge: Define the statement in Leviticus 19 from which this portion of the Bible derives its name (i.e., Holiness Code).

Comprehension: Explain the meaning of the statement "You shall be holy, for I the Lord your God am holy."

Application: Show how we can use God's characteristics to achieve holiness.

Analysis: Arrange the laws found in Leviticus in order of different categories (e.g., business, personal relationships).

Synthesis: Create rules for a community that is holy. What would such a community expect of its members? Create a publicity campaign to sell your community.

Evaluation: In today's world, how would it be possible to create a holy community?

Additional words that will lead students to think are: recognize, remember, compare, reorder, solve, which, what is, choose, reason, deduce, detect, support, predict, produce, write, design, develop, decide, assess, identify.

How We Remember

People generally remember—

10% of what they read.

20% of what they hear.

30% of what they see.

50% of what they see and hear.

70% of what they say as they talk.

90% of what they say as they do!

Keep this in mind when planning lessons and teaching!

Fidgety Kids

Some children are fidgeters. They find it difficult to sit still during story time or while watching a film. Give them a ball of clay when you want them to listen to a story. They can pinch, poke, and squeeze the clay as they listen. At the end of the story, collect the clay balls in a pan.

Dependent Kids

Some children are dependent. They often waste time with this behavior. When a dependent kid asks an unnecessary question, redirect the question right back to the questioner. For example:

Student: I don't understand this.
Teacher: Show me the part you don't understand.

or

Student: I don't get this.
Teacher: Show me exactly where you are stuck.

or

Student: Where is my pencil?
Teacher: Where do you think it might be?

Rewards

Rewards do not have to cost money. Here are some rewarding ways to motivate a whole class, an individual, or a group that has won a game:

WHOLE CLASS

Do a special art project which the class chooses.

Have 10 minutes of free time.

Watch a TV show or film.

Take a hike around the school.

Choose their favorite song or story.

INDIVIDUAL

Be an assistant teacher: dismiss class, call roll, pass out papers, etc.

Keep score during a game.

Change a bulletin board.

Take attendance for the day.

Check out a classroom game to take home.

Forming Groups

Working in groups can be very productive, but forming the groups is sometimes a hassle. The kids usually want to be with their friends, or don't want to be with certain others. Here are a variety of ways groups can be formed—all different, and fun too!

1. Mount Jewish symbols on different-colored tagboards and cut them into puzzles. Cut enough pieces of the same color so that each child in the group receives one. For example: If you want three groups of four, you will need three different colors and four puzzle pieces in each of the same colors. Pass out puzzle pieces, one to a child. Instruct them to find the corresponding pieces and put their puzzles together. Those whose

pieces fit together constitute a working group for the time being.

2. One or more of the following criteria can be used both for selecting partners and for forming groups. Instruct the children to join with others who—

are the same height as you.

have the same color clothing on as you.

were born in the same month as you.

have the same size thumb as you.

have the same color hair as you.

have the same number of letters in their first names.

have a belt on.

3. Another puzzle. Find a large magazine picture for each group based on your unit of study. Laminate so that you can use it more than once. Cut into the same number of pieces as the number of members you want in the group. Hand out the puzzle pieces as the kids enter the room. On your signal, they are to reassemble the pictures by locating the other pieces. Those whose pieces make up a picture become a working group.

Closures

When planning a lesson, don't forget the closure—the part of the lesson that ties all its components together to help the class focus on what has just been taught. Even closures that take only a few minutes are valuable parts of the teaching process. Closures can take many forms. Here are a few examples:

REVIEWING THE MATERIAL

The conventional way to review is to ask the students what they have learned.

Tell me three facts that you learned about Purim today.

What connection is there between the two stories of Creation?

Today we studied the Holiness Code; who can tell me what it means to be holy?

KEY WORDS

Ask the students to write a list of the key words or concepts they have learned and share their lists.

SUMMARIZING

Summarize what was done in class. For example, you might say: "We began today's lesson with a discussion of the items on the seder plate; what are they? And then we spoke about how these items were symbols; what are they symbols of?"

QUICK QUIZ

Keep quizzes short, no more than five minutes, and correct them right away. You can even have the class make up the quiz—each student contributing one question.

EXTENSIONS

Provide additional information on the topic. Or, extend the lesson. For example, after studying trees mentioned in the Bible in relation to a unit on Tu Bishvat, have the class identify the trees in the yard of the synagogue and label them according to their biblical names.

APPLICATIONS

This approach helps the students apply what they have learned to new situations. For example: You have been discussing tzedakah. Have the students choose one specific charity to which they will donate money or time. Or, move on from a unit on the Bible and its laws to identify biblical laws that correspond to contemporary secular legislation.

DEBRIEFING

In debriefing, the students take the raw materials and process them. One method is to have them write summaries in which they identify the gist of an experience or a reading. Answering "What did the reading assignment remind you of?" helps them to find common elements in what they have learned. Drawing pictures of important points in a reading assignment provides an alternative to writing. "How can you put this to use?" helps students to apply what they have learned today.

Closures for Use with Cooperative Learning Groups

TEN QUESTIONS

Prepare ten questions on your unit of study—questions which review the major points of the recently covered material. Ask a question. The students, working in groups, are to consider their answers. When the members of a group have decided on an answer, they choose one person to give it. If the answer is correct, make sure the whole class understands it. Continue until all the questions have been answered correctly.

CREATE A SYMBOL

Working in their groups, the students review the facts and concepts learned. They can use their textbooks and any class notes for review as they translate what they have just learned into pictures, then a symbol that represents their pictures. The completed design must reflect the whole group's understanding and interpretation of the material covered.

I Learned Today

Prepare a sheet that looks something like this:

I Learned Today!

Talk with the other members of your group about what you have learned today. The recorder in your group is to record the following information:

Today our group learned:

1. _____
2. _____
3. _____

   (List at least three things.)

Our group has these questions:

_____

_____

   (List any questions.)

Group member signatures:

_____

_____

Before the students can leave for the day they must complete this sheet. Collect the sheets as they leave. You will see what they have learned and what they still need to learn. The questions they ask will help you to plan the next lesson.

PARENTAL INVOLVEMENT

Keeping Parents Informed

Decide at the beginning of the year how you will keep the parents informed about what is taking place in the class. Here are a few suggestions:

BOOKLETS FOR PARENTS

Allow time at the end of class for the children to write letters to their parents about what took place that day. Provide folders in which they can place these writings. At the end of the study unit, or each month, have them put these writings together into a booklet, illustrating the pages and making covers. The children take their booklets home to share with their parents.

COLLEGE BOWL QUIZ

Invite the parents to a College Bowl Quiz at the end of the study unit. Put in all kinds of trivia questions that the children, but probably not the parents, will be able to answer.

LETTERS HOME

Have the children write letters to their parents, grandparents, etc., telling them about they have learned or what has happened in class. Ask the recipients to write letters back telling what they did, or remember they did, in the same grade when they went to religious school. The children can share the answers.

NEWSLETTERS

Newsletters are still a creative way to keep parents informed. The children design and write the paper, and you can make it the closure for a unit of study. Let the children design the newsletter's format. They can create a decorative logo, name, and portions of the newsletter. The newsletter format could be prepared in advance and enough copies made for the entire year.

GOOD NEWS

Be sure to share good news with parents as often as possible. Have some pre-printed certificates or cards, on which you can quickly fill in the child's name and the exciting thing that happened that day. Or, if you wish, design your own stationery to use for writing notes to parents. Parents will quickly spot your notes when the children bring them home. Be prepared in advance with envelopes already addressed to each child's parents, so as to be sure that each child receives, during the school year, at least one positive note from you.

WHAT'S HAPPENING?

Keep parents informed about important events that will take place in the school and how their children will be involved. You could even prepare a calendar for the year so that parents can help their children organize their time. If the parents know in advance what's happening, they too can become involved.

BRACELET MESSAGES

Notes sent home often get lost. Try putting notes on strips of colored paper. Photocopy several on a sheet of paper and then cut them into strips. Before dismissal, place a strip around each child's wrist and fasten it together with a colorful sticker. To make your own stickers, cut out Jewish symbol shapes from colorful contact paper. The kids will love their "bracelets," and the message is more likely to get home.

ASK ME ABOUT...

Make up enough small shapes (e.g., Jewish stars, shofars, dreidels) to take you through the year, one of each per child. Before class, place a message on the shape you will use that day. For example:

Ask me about Shabbat.

Ask me about Moses.

Ask me to say the *Shema*.

Tape or pin the message to each child right before dismissal time. These messages eliminate the possibility of the child answering "Nothing!" when the parent asks, "What did you do in religious school today?"

Ask Me About ... Newsletter

For older students, take the "ask me about" a step further. Have the students, once a month, create a handwritten one-page newsletter. Instead of articles, head the newsletter with "Ask Me About . . ." and follow it with a list of some of the topics covered during the preceding month. By providing the parents with this information, you are making it possible for them to ask *specific* questions of their children, thus becoming partners in the learning process.

Not-So-Trivial Pursuits

Each week give out a series of five to ten questions to take home. The questions can be serious ones relating to the lesson or trivia questions dealing with fun things to discover about Jews and Judaism. The students and their families see how many of the questions they can answer, and the students bring the responses back the following week.

Attention: Volunteer Help Needed!

Sometimes extra hands are needed, but if you ask people to help, be sure you have something specific for them to do. Here is a sample of the kind of letter you can send to parents and even to members of the congregation:

Dear _____,

During the year our learning activities call for additional help in the classroom. It also helps the children to have good role models and loving adults around them as they work. I know everyone is busy, but if you have a little extra time to help out, it would be greatly appreciated.

Please check off the areas in which you can be of assistance: (Here list all the activities where you will need some assistance, e.g., sewing, music, art work, photography, video, field trips.)

Below are listed the days and times when I can really use your assistance. Please check off the times which are best for you: (List the dates and times when help will be needed.)

Thank you for being willing to assist me.

Sincerely,
Your signature

When responses are returned, make up a schedule of when and how you will be able to make use of the volunteers. Send postcards to the volunteers thanking them for their willingness to participate, and including the date or dates when they will be needed. Send reminders, as needed, during the year, or if there is a change in schedule.

Be sure to write personal thank-you notes to parents or anyone who helps you in the classroom. A word of caution: Make use of everyone who volunteers. If you don't, they just might never volunteer again!

ARTS AND CRAFTS IDEAS

Clean Up the Mess: Our Environment

Talk to the class about littering, or read Shel Silverstein's poem "Sarah Cynthia Sylvia Street Would Not Take the Garbage Out," found in his *Where the Sidewalk Ends*. Take the class for a walk around the synagogue to pick up any trash found on the grounds. Using a large piece of butcher paper, have the class make a trash mural. To do this the children glue the trash they found onto the butcher paper, then decorate it and label it with a title, something like "Keep Our Synagogue Environment Clean." When the glue is dry, hang the mural in the hallway for everyone to see.

Paper Bag Balloons

Paper lunch bags make an inexpensive decoration for your room or for a special event. The bags can be decorated first or painted after they have been stuffed with newspaper. After stuffing with newspaper, tie the open end with colored yarn, leaving one end of the yarn hanging down. If painting, wait till the paint dries completely before hanging up in the room.

Making Candles

Let the children make some special Yom Tov or Shabbat candles. The only danger is the possibility of hot wax dripping on their fingers. Have some bowls of cold water ready for the victims to dip their hands into when this happens, but be sure to caution the kids about the hot wax. You will need:

> four coffee cans
>
> four jars
>
> old candle wax
>
> crayons—all colors, paper wrappers removed
>
> two wicks for each child
>
> a hot plate

Heat the candle wax on the hot plate, using the coffee cans. Add a crayon to each coffee can for color. Place the coffee cans of wax on each corner of a square table. Next to each coffee can place a jar of cold water. Give one wick to each child. Have the children walk around the table dipping their wicks alternately into the wax, then the water. They continue dipping the wick until the candle is the desired size. Repeat the process for the second candle. Each finished candle should be hung from a cord you have strung across the room until it is thoroughly set.

Expressing Ideas through Art

This activity can be used for all ages and for any Jewish subject. Whatever the subject, have the students paint or color a large piece of drawing paper with bright colors and no particular design, just bright colors for a background. Then, provide them with pencils and blank paper, scissors, glue, and colored construction paper. On the blank paper, with a pencil, they draw outlines of what they want to cut out from the construction paper to make their "pictures." Once they have decided what images they wish to place on their brightly colored backgrounds, they can proceed to cut them out and glue them to the background. Then, share with the class.

Some examples of subject matter include:

Ideas about God.

The meaning of Shabbat.

Feelings about the Holocaust.

Accepting responsibility.

The meaning of any holiday.

Holiness.

Roller Printing

Here are some simple and effective ways to create a unique design for greeting cards, class scrapbooks, or just border designs. This can be done with any cylinder that has been inked, painted, or pressed on a wet stamp pad and rolled out on paper.

Glass jar: wind string around it, criss-cross and tape ends.

Rolling pin: glue thin cardboard shapes onto the roller.

Empty thread spools (the old-fashioned wooden ones): cut notches in the edges of each spool so it will make a continuous design.

A pencil or pen: roll string around the pencil at an angle, tape ends.

Glitter Litter

Children love glitter, but it sure is messy. Of course, there are glitter glue pens and crayons, but plain old glitter is cheaper. So try this to save on your wear and tear: Place a box lid underneath the art. The lid catches the loose glitter. When finished, simply pick up the lid, tap the glitter into a corner of the lid, and pour it back into the original containers.

Using Cameras in the Classroom

With a camera, whether Polaroid or regular, you can do any of the following:

1. Take pictures of each child for use in making holiday or Mother's/Father's Day cards.

2. Take close-up pictures of each child to be used in making paper dolls. The children can trace the doll pattern, then glue the faces on. They also can make clothes to fit the lesson or a period of history.

3. Take slides of classroom activities all year long and use them as the basis for a media program for parents and students at the end of the year.

4. Polaroid pictures of each child on the first day of school can become "getting to know you" pictures, then can be used for roll call during the year. Each class morning, place the pictures on your desk. The children pick theirs up when they arrive and either put it on the bulletin board or clip it to a string you have hung for this purpose. Saves you the time of taking attendance; just look to see whose pictures are left on your desk and you'll know who is absent.

Hebrew Dictionary

Prepare enough pages for each letter of the Hebrew alphabet—one letter per page and one set per child. Each new word the child learns is to be written in the dictionary along with what it means and how it is pronounced. This way the children develop a handy, ready resource that can be referred to throughout the year.

Puppets Are Fun!

And they don't have to be difficult to make. Stick puppets are easy, just use popsicle sticks. Using magazines, children find pictures of faces. Cut out the number of faces they need; glue a face to one end of a popsicle stick—and presto, a puppet has been made! Working in groups, the children can improvise puppet plays based on your unit of study and present them to the whole class. To make it even more realistic, have a group prepare a big box to be the "stage." Cut out the bottom, hang "curtains," at either end, and decorate so it doesn't look like a box.

Color Your Windows

Your class can turn the windows of your room into colorful designs or murals. Just add two squirts of clear liquid detergent to a pint of tempera paint. This soaped-up paint sticks well and comes off easily.

Laminating without a Machine

No laminating machine! Don't fret, there is another solution. This is a little trick that Joel Lurie Grishaver taught me too many years ago to mention. Clear contact paper is available in rolls in the shelf-lining sections of most housewares stores. A tip: refrigerate the contact paper for a few hours before using; it will be less sticky and much easier to use.

When covering small items like index cards, cut off a piece of clear contact paper. Take off the paper liner; lay the contact paper on a smooth surface, sticky side *up*, of course; place the cards to be covered on the sticky side. Cover the other side in the same manner. Then, cut out your "laminated" pieces.

To laminate larger pieces, such as a folder, game board, or poster, cut the clear contact paper with at least a half-inch margin around all the edges. Place the item to be covered on a table or the floor. Peel the paper covering from the back about 3 inches at one edge. Lay that edge over one end of the item. Slowly pull the covering from the back of the contact paper with one hand, and use the other hand to smooth it over the item. Do this slowly so that no wrinkles appear.

If you want to cover a piece on which you have placed library pockets—which are excellent for holding cards for games, folders, etc.—just cover the whole item, pocket and all. Use an Exacto knife or a razor to carefully slit the opening of the pocket. When covering something in which you wish to place holes, just punch the holes, cover the item, and repunch the holes.

Big Pictures Made Easy

Want to make a big picture or a big map on a posterboard or a wall, yet you can't draw well? If you have access to an overhead projector, project the picture or map you want on the wall where you have placed your large posterboard or white butcher paper. Move the projector until the picture is the desired size, then just trace away!

Some Other Uses for Crayons

SCRATCHBOARDS

Scratchboards are good for Jewish holiday designs. Cover a piece of paper with strong crayon colors. Color over the colors with solid black crayon, india ink, or black tempera paint mixed with detergent to make it stick—1 teaspoon tempera to 4 teaspoons detergent. Let dry. Children then scratch the desired design with a paperclip, nail, or ballpoint pen, exposing the subsurface colors.

STAINED GLASS

Stained glass can be used for classroom decorations or Jewish holiday designs. Paint a picture, design, or symbol on paper with black india ink. Color the picture with crayons. Turn the picture over. Take a rag, dip it in vegetable oil, rub it over the back of the picture to make it transparent. Use a paper towel to wipe off excess oil. Let dry, then tape the "stained glass" transparencies on the windows.

CRAYON RUBBINGS

Crayon rubbing is an old technique, but it is included because we often forget the easy ones. Remove paper from the crayon. Place a thin sheet of paper over the object. Rub side of crayon over the surface. You can use any object that has raised patterns so that a design shows through the crayon rubbing. Coins are good for this purpose. Unusual ones from different countries can often be obtained from parents who travel a lot. The children can identify where Jewish communities live in the different places indicated on the coins.

WINDSOCKS

To make windsocks, use old posters, or let the children create new ones based on a Jewish concept from your unit of study.

Take a poster and laminate, especially if it is going to be hung outside. Roll the poster up and staple it in the shape of a tube. At one end, punch three holes spaced evenly apart. Thread yarn or string through the holes to hang the windsock. At the other end, glue or staple streamers made from crepe paper, ribbon, yarn, or scraps of material cut into strips with pinking shears so they won't unravel. Hang the windsocks around your room or outside your classroom window.

NEW USES FOR OLD "JUNK": RECYCLE

Old Workbooks

Don't throw old workbooks out! They are great sources for pictures and drawings. Turn them into activities, or have the children use them in their work.

Swap Box

Find space in your classroom for several boxes which the children can decorate. Label the boxes *Clothes, Toys, Books,* etc. Have the children bring in unwanted but usable items and place them in the boxes. This is a good way to recycle and collect things for the less fortunate.

More Uses for Contact Paper

Children gravitate to items that are brightly colored and in attractive containers. You can obtain contact paper in all colors and designs in most housewares stores. Use it to cover shoeboxes, fast-food containers, milk cartons, etc. Construction-paper titles can be fastened to the box with clear contact paper.

Free Storage Files

When you have finished with that very large box of soap flakes, wipe the inside clean. Using a heavy sharp scissors, cut the side on an angle and one-third of the way down. Cut both sides in this manner and cover the box with colorful contact paper. You now have what librarians call a Princeton file. It can be used to store periodicals, file folders, brochures, and worksheets.

No Space? Try This

No room to set up a learning center, or you are not in your own building so you can't leave things set up? Well, make a portable learning center that is easily folded to be taken from place to place. Most school supply dealers, and even grocery stores, have folding fiberboards. These are generally used for displaying student projects, but they also make great "learning centers."

Old Plastic and Oilcloth

Make use of that old plastic tablecloth or oilcloth. Use a sewing machine or sew the cloth by hand to a clothes hanger. Add pockets in the sizes you need, also made out of the tablecloth. Change the contents as needed for your classroom. Old plastic tablecloths can also be used to make game boards! Use permanent markers to draw the design on the tablecloth, for a durable, basic game board. Or use an overhead projector to transfer the desired design onto the tablecloth. It is easily rolled up for storage and wipes clean with a damp cloth.

Old shoe bags can also be put to good use to hold all kinds of goodies. Use them for storage of supplies, as portable learning centers, and for holding periodicals. Change the contents as needed.

Cardboard Soda Cartons

Recycle those cardboard soda cartons by covering them with contact paper. Then make some "bottles" out of tagboard and use them for mix-and-match games with the children. For example: Once the carton has been covered, label each section with the name of a Jewish holiday. Label the "bottles" with the names of rituals and symbols. For younger children, use pictures instead of words.

Classroom Uses for "Junk"

Lots of things that might otherwise be trashed can be used in the classroom. Ask parents for help. Send them a list of items you need and ask that they save some and bring them in. Set up a recycle box in your classroom ready to receive what the parents send. Among other things you might request:

CARDBOARD TUBES

Tubes from paper towels or wrapping paper can be used to send home papers the kids don't want to fold. The tubes will protect them. Also use for storage of posters, labeling the tube so you know what is inside.

To make napkin rings, cut the tubes into 2-inch lengths. Cover with wallpaper, contact paper, fabric, or felt. Decorate with beads, sequins, and the like to make napkin rings which can be used at your school's Shabbat dinner table or taken home.

Have the children paint the tubes in various bright colors. Cover with a nontoxic clear finish. When dry, they can be used to create artistic designs, for counting, to build a city/kibbutz, etc.

PIZZA BOXES

Pizza boxes make good displays for reports. As a display for reports, place the written pages on the inside of the upright top and use the bottom for an accompanying exhibit or decoration.

OATMEAL BOXES

Cylindrical oatmeal boxes, filled with sand and decorated on the outside, make great bookends.

SPRAY CAN AND DETERGENT BOTTLE CAPS

Caps from spray cans and detergent bottles can be used in several ways.

To make a planter, punch holes in the cap, place several pebbles in the bottom over the holes, and add earth. Place a plastic margarine lid under each to catch excess water, and plant seeds. Or get some narcissus bulbs and instead of earth use pebbles, with no holes in the top. Put bulb on top of rocks and water so that the base of the bulb is in the water. Place in the sun and soon you will have a bit of spring in the winter.

To make a candleholder, fill the cap with plaster of paris, place a candle in the center, and decorate as desired.

Spray can and detergent bottle caps are also good for individual paint containers.

FILM CANISTERS AND SMALL PLASTIC BOTTLES

Film canisters and small plastic bottles (e.g., aspirin or pill bottles) have many uses.

To make a spice box for Shabbat, decorate the outside of the canister. Punch a few holes in the lid and fill with spices.

To make a gragger for Purim, drill or melt a hole in the bottom so that a popsicle stick will fit through. Glue securely. Fill with beans and glue top on securely. Decorate and the kids have a small gragger.

These items also make great jars for paste or paint. All the children in the class can have their own individual paste or paint jars, and you save some money by being able to buy larger containers of these materials.

FROZEN JUICE CAN LIDS

Lids from frozen juice cans can make badges or buttons. Attach a safety pin to the back of the lid with a strip of strapping tape. Design the cover, cover with clear contact paper, glue to the front. Badges can be used as award pins or as a "selling" technique; a pin reading *recycle*, for instance, tells everyone to reuse materials, just as you are doing.

For a gift item, juice can lids can also be made into coasters. Cut felt circles for the inside of the lid; decorate the other side with felt, fabric, and colored markers.

For a decorative magnet, glue 2-inch strips of magnetic tape to the back of a lid and decorate the front.

NEWSPAPERS

The comics from the Sunday papers make great wrapping paper for gifts.

For placemats, cut several layers of newspaper into long strips. Weave together until you have a placemat in the desired size. Decorate, then laminate or cover with clear contact paper.

Another use would be to have the class decorate a large cardboard box with scraps of newspaper cut into tree and leaf shapes. Discuss trees with the class, referring to Deuteronomy 20:19–20. Help the children to understand that wasted paper is wasted trees. Encourage them to put paper that is no longer needed in their "tree box."

EGG CARTONS

Eggs cartons have many uses, especially those made from pulp. Use them for planting seeds; when the seedlings are the right size, they can be planted outside right in the container. To make flowers, cut slits in each cup to form petals, attach to pipe cleaners, and color. Styrofoam cartons make great paint trays, and the paint can be mixed right in the container.

MILK CARTONS

Milk cartons can be made into bird feeders. Cut round holes and add popsicle sticks for perches. For a desk organizer, just cut off the tops and staple several cartons together side by side. Small cartons make good graggers. Just fill with dried beans, cover the outside with decorated construction paper, and glue the top closed. Since milk cartons come in all sizes, they can also be used to build cities, towns, and villages.

CANS

Cans come in all sizes, and what you make from them depends on the size. Among other things, you can use cans to make hanging planters, pencil/pen holders, kitchen containers, tzedakah boxes, and graggers. Coffee cans with the plastic lids make great holders for all the crayons that lose their boxes. Pen/pencil holders can be made by gluing three cans together or sticking them together with double-sided tape and then covering with colorful contact paper. You now have a holder for pens, pencils, scissors, etc.

BEVERAGE CONTAINERS

Beverage containers with built-in holes in the lids can become neat, clean paint containers. Even if the brush bends when it is pushed through the hole, it comes out smooth and neat with just enough paint for the child to use.

SIX-PACK CARTONS; JUICE CANS

Six-pack cartons and empty, clean juice cans make good organizers for art supplies. The children can paint and decorate the six-pack containers and, when they are dry, place juice cans in each compartment.

GIFT BOXES

Gift boxes come in all sizes and make great frames for art work. The best for this purpose are the ones that collapse and fold down. Just center the art work within the sides, fold down, and glue or staple.

PLASTIC TRASH BAGS

The 30-gallon-size plastic trash bags make great smocks for your potential artists. Cut a hole for the head, a hole on each side for the arms, and the bag is ready to protect a child's clothes. For safety, remind the children to put the bags on only if they have holes for the head and arms and only when painting. You might also require that an adult be present when the bags are in use.

MARGARINE AND BUTTER TUBS

Plastic margarine and butter tubs are good for keeping paste or clay soft and are easy to store since they will stack.

CRAFT-TIME PLACEMATS

To make placemats, the children can glue pictures (either cut from magazines or drawn as part of the activity) on large sheets of construction paper. After they put their names on their works of art, laminate or cover with clear contact paper. The placemats are easy to clean and always ready— not only for art projects, but for snacks as well.

APPLIANCE CARTONS

Cartons from refrigerators, TVs, and other large appliances can be obtained from most appliance dealers. They can be used for additional wall space and are great for storage. They can also be made into learning centers.

OLD WINDOW SHADES

Don't throw out old window shades. Use them in your classroom. Attach the holding fixtures to the wall so the shades can be easily changed. Or tie a pretty ribbon from one end of the window shade roller to the other, then just hang it up on existing nails or hooks. Take it home if there is no storage room in the school. Use shades for maps, displaying creative art work, bulletin boards, and bulletin board games; also, for creating a generic learning center that can easily be changed from one subject to another.

PLASTIC MILK BOTTLES

Plastic milk bottles with handles are very useful. Cut off the bottom at an angle. Keep the lid on for it to be a scoop. With the lid off it becomes a funnel.

SHOWER CURTAINS

Plastic shower curtains make great bib aprons for crafts. Use another bib apron as a pattern, or measure children for correct dimensions. Cut strips from the reinforced border for the ties. Pin, sew, or staple the ties at the waist. If you use pinking shears to cut, the aprons are even easier to make.

NAIL BRUSHES

Don't throw away old brushes from fingernail polish. Clean them in nail polish remover and use as paint brushes for small and hard-to-reach places.

FREEBIE PAPER

Check out your local printing shop for leftover scrap paper. You will probably find pieces in all colors, sizes, and weights. Stock up for all your paper needs in the classroom.

CRAYON BOXES

Since crayon boxes fall apart quickly, try keeping them in plastic food-storage bags, or save metal band-aid boxes to keep sets of crayons in.

PUSH-UP PLASTIC DEODORANT CONTAINERS

Clean the container thoroughly and spray with cooking spray. Melt old crayons and pour the wax into the opening. When wax is hardened, push up to get out, or use as is in the container.

PAWN PIECES FOR GAMES

Save the caps from used-up felt-tip markers. They come in all colors and can be used as game pieces. Discarded keys can also be used for this purpose.

MAKING SLIDES WITHOUT A CAMERA

Ask parents for any old slides they may have. Take these and, using straight bleach, bleach the color out. Rinse them in clear water and let them dry overnight. You now have blank slides which the children can use to make their own slide show. One tip: when they draw on the slides, have them use fine-tipped felt markers and press hard to make the colors more brilliant.

IDEAS TO HELP IN THE CLASSROOM

Getting Ready for the First Day of School

The ideas in this section are intended to encourage you to get ready before the beginning of the new school year, which always seems to come up before you know it.

REVIEW THE SCHOOL YEAR

Take a few weeks off after school is out just to relax. Then spend a few hours every week going over your lesson plans. What was successful? What was a flop? Look at those plans you really didn't have time to prepare properly. Now you can revise, improve, and update them. Please do not wait till school is about to start to go over lesson plans. Plan at least the first month's lessons before school begins. Prepare a list of the supplies you will need and give it to your principal. The beginning of school will be much easier if you plan ahead.

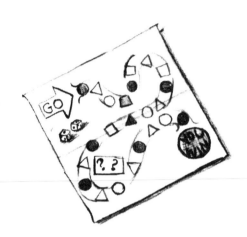

CLASS LISTS; IDENTIFYING YOUR ROOM

Class lists are usually ready well in advance of school. Obtain your list. Write letters to all the children, welcoming them to the class. Include a list of who is in the class. Give an overview of the subject matter so they will know what to expect. If you want them to bring something special to school the first day, mention that in your letter. Even tell a little bit about yourself. Finally, tell the children where your classroom is located and how it can be identified, other than the room number. How can the room be identified? Try something unique and different, like a huge eye-catching toy, a huge cutout of a Jewish symbol, or a huge cutout symbol which represents your unit of study. How about a huge cutout of the State of Israel?

NAME TAGS

Let's be different. Notepads of different shapes and sizes are available in stationery and office supply stores. Choose one. Label and laminate a page for each child.

Make name tags fun! For young kids, cut out Jewish symbols. For older ones, design a name tag with Jewish symbols around the border, leaving space for the name. Run the tags off on brightly colored paper. The "tacky-back sheets" in bright fluorescent colors available from teacher's supply stores make good name tags.

Make name tags that can be used over and over again. From brightly colored construction paper or tagboard, cut out Jewish symbols. If you wish, stamp the top with the name of your synagogue, which comes in handy if you are planning any field trips. Laminate the cutout symbols. Make enough for each child plus a few extra. Cut off strips of masking tape and place one on each laminated symbol. Write the child's name on the masking tape. Remove the tape at the end of the school year and you will have name tags ready for next year.

HELLO BINGO

This game is a fun way to get the children acquainted with one another. Duplicate a blank Bingo grid or cut 1-inch graph paper to size. When the children arrive, give each of them a sheet. They are to gather signatures from their classmates until the grids are full. Have Bingo markers available and play Bingo with the names. When a name is called, the players cover it with a marker. A player who covers a row vertically, horizontally, or diagonally is to call out, "Hello!"

BULLETIN BOARDS

Many classrooms serve double duty, but even if you do not have sole use of your room, you can still plan a unique bulletin board. If you share the room with others, make your bulletin board portable. There is foam board which comes in all sizes, some with three folding sections. These make good portable bulletin boards.

Make your first bulletin board special! Make it attractive! Choose a positive theme, e.g., First Class of Jewish Students, Amazing Jewish Students, Pick of the Crop, The IN Crowd, This Is Our Great Class, etc. If you wish, have the bulletin board ready for the children to decorate, using colored paper balloons with a child's name on each one. Give the children their balloons to decorate when they arrive, then place them on the bulletin board.

An exciting and decorative door displaying the names of all the children makes everyone feel welcome. Choose a theme for your decorations and carry it over onto the bulletin board.

INVOLVE THE PARENTS

Once you get your ideas set for creating an attractive opening-day classroom, begin to consider ways to involve the parents. Here are a few suggestions:

Prepare a volunteer sign-up sheet to send with your letter to the students. Ask the parents to return the sheet the first day of school or mail it to you. When designing your sign-up sheet, consider the needs you will have during the year and make a list of them, leaving room for the parents to check off and sign. Your list might look something like this:

Tell a story ____

Teach a song or some kind of music activity ____

Play a musical instrument ____

Work puzzles or play games ____

Create puzzles and games ____

Share hobby with class ____ What is your hobby? ____

Teach how to use simple carpentry tools ____

Tell about your occupation ____

Baking/cooking ____

Teach a specific subject ____ Which subject? ____

Help out as room mother/father ____

Telephone committee ____

Organizing field trips/driving on field trips ____

Organizing special events ____

Helping with drama activities ____

Photography ____

Arts and crafts specialty ____

When you receive the sheets back, make up an index card file to record who is willing to do what, then call on people when their help is needed.

POSTCARDS

Postcards are a wonderful means of communication: Why wait till the report cards come out to communicate with parents? Each semester, send two or three postcards to parents that make positive statements about their child's efforts in class. Design your postcards *now* to make sure they are ready to use throughout the year. Using 8.5 x 11 oaktag you can place six postcards on one sheet and copy them. Make them positive, decorative, and have space for the child's name, a short message, and your signature.

Planning Lessons

It is easy to reach the young children in grades Pre-K to 3, but after that problems begin to develop. Research has some answers for us, but it's up to you, the teacher, to accept the challenge.

When students reach fourth grade, frontal teaching no longer really works. Active teaching and learning, with the focus on actively involving the students, goes much further. Youngsters at this grade level will not easily be sustained by educational approaches that lack creativity. They will simply tune out.

Planning a creative lesson begins with having a clear understanding of the subject matter to be taught. The teacher must know the subject matter. Our kids are much too smart, and you cannot bluff your way through. Your lessons must be well planned as well as creative. Students know when the teacher has made no effort to plan the lesson, and they will respond by expending no more energy and effort than the teacher did.

Plan your lesson to actively involve the class. Participatory activities ensure that there is a sharing of ideas between kids and teachers. An ancient Chinese proverb says:

I hear and I forget.
I see and I remember.
I do and I understand.

Contemporary research tells us that we remember 90% of what is said as we do something!

Finding Out What Students Know or Don't Know

Students often complain, "We study the same thing year after year!" This can be avoided with a very simple activity to find out just what the kids know about a subject *before* you begin. List topics pertaining to your unit of study on 3 x 5 index cards. Each student selects a card and adds at least five topics to the list on the card. Collect the cards; when you see what is missing, you will know what you have to cover on that subject matter.

Teacher Resource Centers

Resource centers are a very valuable tool for teachers. Set aside a place in the synagogue to be made into a teacher resource center. An unused classroom, a corner of the library, even a storeroom can be used for this purpose. You will need shelving, a few plastic crates which can be used for hanging files, a good number of cardboard magazine holders of the type that can be obtained at any office supply store. Bring several teachers and parents together to help organize the mass of teaching materials that are probably already to be found, scattered helter-skelter, throughout the school. Use the magazine holders to separate the subject areas, and the file folders to hold teaching tips written on single sheets of papers. Categorize the subject matter under appropriate headings (e.g., historical periods, prayer, Israel, holidays, Bible, Jewish ethics). Continually add to your collection of teaching ideas.

You can also have game-making parties. Bring together a group of teachers and parents, even some of the kids. Have the games already identified and materials available for each game. The participants can socialize and make games at the same time. Before you know it you will have a well-organized teacher resource center where teachers know they can find new ideas.

Adding Machine Tape

A roll of 3-inch adding machine tape will go a long way. And look at the different things you can do with it:

1. Making film strips. On long strips of tape, students can draw a series of pictures for a story based on your unit of study.
2. Writing a long letter to a special friend.
3. Creating comic strips.
4. Drawing mini-murals.
5. Writing tall tales, or "long" tales.
6. Special greetings for special events.
7. Time-lines on life-cycle events or Jewish history.

Post-It Notes

Post-It notes are good for more than just notes.

HEBREW

Putting one letter on each note, write out several Hebrew words. Mix up the notes and have the students put them in the correct order.

PRAYER

Write out a prayer or prayer phrase, putting one word on each note. Post the notes on the board in the wrong order. Have the students put them in the correct sequence.

TIME-LINE

Write a series of events on separate notes. Put them on the board in the wrong order. Have the students arrange them in the proper order.

A Generic Game Board

Games can be valuable reviewing and learning experiences, and children love them. Take a posterboard and make an interesting trail with colored round stickers. Mark a place on the board for question cards. Be sure there is a beginning and an end to the game board trail. Laminate or cover with clear contact paper to make it more durable. Collect buttons of different colors or the tops of used-up felt-tip pens to be used as markers and several pairs of dice.

Prepare a set of index cards with a question on each card based on your unit of study. Put the answers in a pocket attached to the back of the board or let the students find the answers on their own if they do not know them.

Students play the game by rolling the dice, answering the questions, and moving their markers around the game board. Make new questions whenever you want the class to study or review another subject. The game board is always ready, you just have to change the questions.

Be Prepared

What do you do when you sense that the lesson you planned isn't working? The kids are not responding, and soon there will be mass chaos, or something close to it. Let's face it, this does happen. My experience has taught me to (1) stop in midstream and change the approach, and (2) always have alternative activities prepared and ready to do.

Become a "bag lady/man"! Carry with you a bag, box, file folder, or whatever, full of different ideas, backups for lessons, supplies, handout papers, etc. Even an index card file on your desk with different teaching ideas and approaches will help you to be prepared for any eventuality. Make the following activities part of your "bag of tricks," ready to use whenever your lesson needs to be livened up, and add to the list as you find new and unique activities.

Describe an object without naming it (Jewish symbol, ritual object, etc.).

Describe a day in the life of _____ (name a Jewish person).

Describe what you would put in a time capsule to tell about Jewish life, and give your reasons for including it.

Describe the holiday of _____ and how you will celebrate it when you are an adult (or 10 years from now).

Design and write an ad for a Jewish symbol, artifact, holiday, etc.

You find a Jewish artifact in a junk pile. Imagine its history and describe it.

List the qualities that comprise Jewish heroism.

Describe a meeting between _____ and your teacher (Moses, Ben-Gurion, etc.).

Role-play a meeting and discussion between your rabbi and _____ (Isaiah, King David, etc., or between any two persons; or even between Jewish artifacts and ritual objects).

Describe what Jewish life will be like 25 years from now.

Describe the difference between the Torah and the Talmud.

Role-play a meeting between the president of your congregation and Rabbi Akiba (or Hillel, or any other historical figure).

Debate the pros and cons of keeping kosher and not keeping kosher (or any other topic where choices are made).

Pretend you are Shabbat candlesticks. Describe your feelings on Erev Shabbat.

List all the Jewish items that would be found by _____ when visiting your home (Abraham, Sarah, Jacob, etc.).

Processing Classroom Experiences

We often use experiential learning to teach Jewish concepts. Processing the experience is as important as the experience itself. The following are the different stages of processing, adapted from the *1979 Annual Handbook for Group Facilitators*, published by University Associates:

EXPERIENCING

These are the key questions that aid the group in moving more deeply into the stage at hand or on to another stage: What is going on? How do you feel about it? What do you need to know to _____? Could you offer a suggestion? What would you prefer? If you could guess at the answer, what would it be? What is the worst/best that could happen? What are your suspicions? What are your objections? What else?

SHARING

Questions are directed toward generating data: Who would volunteer to share? Who else? What went on/happened? How did you feel about it?

Who else had the same experience? Who reacted differently? How many felt the same? Differently? What did you observe? What were you aware of?

INTERPRETING

Questions are directed toward making sense of data for the individual and the group: How do you account for that? What does it mean to you? How was it significant? How was it good/bad? How do these fit together? How might it have been different? Do you see something operating there? What does that suggest to you about yourself/your group? What do you understand better about yourself/your group?

GENERALIZING

Directed toward promoting generalizations: What might we draw/pull from that? Is that plugging into anything? What? What did you learn/relearn? Does it remind you of anything? What principle/law do you see operating? What does it help explain? How does this relate to other experiences? What do you associate with it?

APPLYING

Directed toward applying the knowledge gained to one's personal life: How could you apply/transfer that? What would you like to do with it? How could you repeat this again? What could you do to hold on to this? What are the options? What might you do to help/hinder yourself? How could you make it better? What would be the consequences of doing/not doing that? What modifications can you make work for you? What could you imagine/fantasize about that?

PROCESSING

The entire experience as a learning experience. Aimed at soliciting feedback: How was this for you? What were the pluses/minuses? How might it have been more meaningful? What's the good/bad news? What changes would you make? What would you continue? What are the costs/benefits? If you had to do it over again, what would you do? What additions/deletions would help? Any suggestions?

END OF YEAR ACTIVITIES

The activities in this section lend themselves well to reviewing materials that have already been covered. They provide an alternative to tests.

Puppet Shows

Show the children some examples of puppets they can make from paper bags, socks, paper plates on sticks, and old gloves or mittens (finger puppets). Divide the class into small groups. The members of each group decide what kind of puppets to make. Then they write a play using their puppets. The play will be based on one of the subjects they studied during the year, or you can assign a different subject to each group. Give the children time to make their puppets and rehearse their shows. Invite parents to the performance.

Design a Game

Divide the class into small groups. Give each a posterboard or large piece of construction paper, game cards cut from construction paper or 3 x 5 index cards, 20 to 30 colored sticky circles, a library pocket, a spinner or pair of dice, and some scrap paper.

Assign a different subject to each group based on what the class has studied during the year. Have available, to be used as needed, colored markers, crayons, picture magazines, and old workbooks. Pictures of ritual objects and Jewish symbols can be cut out of the magazines and workbooks or copied with markers and crayons, and then used to decorate the game boards. Tell the children to use the scrap paper to write out what they want to place on the game cards. After the members of a group finish this, they place the items on the individual game cards. On the game board, they make a trail with the colored dots. Attach a library pocket to the board and put the game cards inside. Finally, on the back of the board, the group writes out the instructions on how to play the game. The groups then exchange games and play.

Farewell and So Long!

On the last day of school, take a group picture of your class. During the summer have copies of the picture made. Write letters to the children telling them how much you enjoyed having them in your class and include copies of the class picture. (Just another example to the kids that the synagogue is really a happy place to be!)

Student Creativity

This is a good review. Divide the class into small groups and assign each a chapter of the textbook. You don't have to use every chapter in the book, just those the kids found the most interesting. Have each group create a worksheet, puzzle page, or series of questions based on the assigned chapter. Duplicate these and have the whole class do the activities created by the groups. (And keep the activities for future use by other classes.)

Thank You!

There are people in the synagogue who work in the school behind the scenes. Have your class make a list of who they are, including the principal, secretary, custodian, etc. Then have the class write each of them a note of thanks for all they have done during the year. Consider this an example of gemilut chasadim—a deed of loving-kindness.